FEELING GOOD ABOUT YOURSELF

IN THE STRUGGLE OF LIFE

FEELING GO⊗D ABOUT YOURSELF
IN THE STRUGGLE OF LIFE

Donald W. Weaver, M.D.

ELYSIAN
DETROIT

Table of Contents

Preface

LIFE IS A STRUGGLE. Life is complicated. Life is like a wrestling match, with its contested attempt to remain standing while life is trying to put you down. While this is true of life in general and the secular life in particular, it is often the inner life, the life of the soul, the things of the spirit, that we find most challenging, and most likely to stifle us.

It is most perplexing precisely at the moments when we need most clarity, most simplicity, and most reassurance of God's presence. At times like these, we seek answers; often to life's most difficult questions. We turn to our faith communities, to prayer, and to direct intervention by God to aid us in the battle.

The questions to which we seek answers are not such simple questions as how to find the local library, or whether we should go out to dinner tonight. The questions that concern us are existential questions of depth and discovery, questions that challenge our thinking and even call for creative new ideas. Questions such as: Is it OK to feel good about myself, even when I feel no goodness in me? And can my spiritual background really help me answer the questions of life?

For nearly forty years I have taught a Bible class centered around the asking of questions. The only criterion for attendance is a willingness to listen to other viewpoints and to share ideas. More than a few have found the questions too unsettling to make the class their Bible study home. Readers looking for neatly formed questions with "key text" answers should probably close this book now and return it for a refund. I would direct them to a faith community that has all the answers, which they simply need to memorize.

This book is for you if: (a) You were raised with a religious background but have found that the answers of your childhood no longer work for you; (b) You have long since dismissed religion as irrelevant and corrupt, but still feel connected with God; (c) You still attend church, but have doubts about what you read and what you hear when you're there; (d) You are a seeker after God but do not share the Christian concept of a triune God—you are a sheep "not of this fold"; (e) The stories and parables from the Bible provide an expansive new insight into the many attributes of the God you serve.

Or maybe: (f) You were just born curious about things of the spirit. In every age, God has created people who cannot accept the *status quo*. They are driven to examine, question, and reformulate traditional and conventional thinking about God. These seekers push back the boundaries and open new avenues in our thinking about God. While often declared heretics—and, in the past, burned at the stake—they are true messengers of God and keepers of the flame.

The irony is that the Bible is not a place where pat answers are easily found. Despite the objective of most religions to satisfy our need for answers by supplying them, the Bible is remarkable less for the answers it gives and more for the questions it asks. The God of the Old Testament, Jesus the Savior of the New Testament, and the apostles share a narrative replete with questions.

Jesus usually gave one of three responses to questions. The first was to ignore them entirely, as though they had not been asked. The second was to ask a question in return. The third was to tell a story or parable challenging the listener to find the answer within it. The straight answer was not His way.

I believe Jesus used the Socratic method of "teaching by asking questions" because He knew that the alternative—the straight answer, the short declarative statement, the delivery of data—only allows for memorization and indoctrination. The questions of Jesus reach beyond the intellect and beyond science and its data. They reach to the soul. They establish spiritual dialog. They are open-ended and creative.

Job found himself in despair, full of unanswered questions about why his life was in ruins. He even threatened to take God to court to sue for answers. God responded with questions that transcended Job's mundane questions and stretched his mind to the heavens. In the end, Job's questions remained unanswered, yet he was left nonetheless deeply satisfied with his encounter with God and now knew his error. He exchanged data for divinity, curiosity for communion, and the need to know for the need to be known by God.

Through science, knowledge is expanding at an ever accelerating pace, so we have little time to re-align our relationship with God on the basis of new knowledge. But if our relationship with God is based on conversation, then time and data are irrelevant.

Religion centered upon present knowledge, data, and information will inevitably obsolesce, but religion based on conversations with God will remain relevant for all time. A thousand years from now, we will know so much more about how the universe works. How much more will we know about God? What will God look like to us in a thousand years? Or a hundred, or maybe even just ten?

The story of Jacob and his struggle with God provides an important framework or template for a fresh look at the conflict which we call life. We find ourselves afraid, lonely, uncertain of the future, and end up bargaining with God. What happened to Jacob provides some insight into how God works. All of us—you, me—are Jacob, being ground down by life; but we shall see, as Jacob finally saw, that wresting with God is the solution, not the problem. That we would unexpectedly meet God, in the darkness, in our times of greatest distress, and that He would engage us in contest turns out to be The Gospel—the good news that blessing is at hand.

As you struggle with the questions presented in this book I hope your heart and soul will be stretched, like Jacob's, to a place where you will find the God of all mankind; a God who, instead of simple answers, provides Himself as the fulfillment of all the questions of life.

Donald W. Weaver

P.S. (1) The book assumes very little familiarity with the Bible. I have quoted from it where necessary (unless otherwise noted, quotes are from the *New American Standard Bible)*. (2) In hopes the book will stimulate your own thoughts and questions, empty pages have been left between chapters and at the end of the book for your notes.

Preface

Donald W. Weaver

Introduction

OUR DEEPEST existential questions—such as "Am I of any value? Should I be feeling good about myself? Do I ever have a chance to understand the meaning of life?"—are answered through Four Great Mysteries whose meanings are revealed—as far as I believe they can be revealed to the non-divine—through the messages and mission of Jesus. The mysteries are: Where does Goodness come from? What about Evil? Whose God is God? And: Is there life after death?

The Bible presents far more questions than answers, yet is clear on these mysteries; none more so than the mystery of whose God He is—which is to say, who His people are. The answer is that God is the God of all people, but there is a catch: It seems to exclude anyone who is not Christian, because the Bible says that Jesus Christ is the only way to God. The truth is, you do not have to accept Jesus as your God, but you do need to live by the principles He expounded, which include living more the life of a communal sheep and less that of the individualistic goat, doing more for your fellow wo/man instead of sitting back and feeling good about yourself. This is not to say that you have no value as an individual. Individuals are so important to Him that God will go to any lengths to save one. The problem is not the individual, it is individual*ism*. Jesus made the point unceasingly, yet churches today tend to teach personal, individualistic piety over communal caring.

It was not always so: The early Christian church was a true community, in all but one respect. It was a community only of Jews, who took some persuading that Gentiles should be welcomed as full members into what those early Jewish Christians mistook for *their* God, *their* church, and *their* Messiah.

It takes a transition to a higher level of faith to throw open the doors of one's exclusive club to absolutely anyone off the street, free of charge. The difficult transition is not made any easier by churches—clubs—that would rather not do so, and which therefore try to discourage those who would try by binding them with dictated and not infrequently dubious catechisms.

But those who express doubts about the catechism are then inevitably perceived as subversives who need to be brought back in line or else blackballed, shunned, excommunicated, or disfellowshipped, before they infect the whole flock. With this axe hanging over their lifeline to the community, can we wonder that those experiencing doubt and undergoing a crisis of faith feel empty and afraid? But through His teaching and His own example in the wilderness and indeed throughout His ministry, Jesus showed how to conquer emptiness and fear through faith and love, and emerge from the crisis stronger in both.

A person who has transitioned through doubt to a higher stage of faith might well have started the transition as a devout churchgoer, with the catechism engraved on his or her forehead. But s/he might end the transition still as a devout churchgoer, but with a blank slate of a forehead and a view of the catechism different from, but not inimical to, the one promoted from the pulpit and piously intoned by the spiritually secure neighbor sharing the pew.

Churches would have their members focus on personal piety and avoid sin at all costs. But very clearly, that was not the message of Jesus. He would rather we focus on forgiveness than on piety. If you want to know why the Bible is still relevant in the 21st Century, consider what a kinder, gentler world this would be if only we could manage this one thing alone. Jesus's parable of the Prodigal Son established without a doubt that it is God's grace that leads to forgiveness, not a tithed church membership, not immersion in Bible study, not the pious repetition of some catechism. God does not care nearly so much about our infidelity to Him as He does about our return and reconciliation to oneness with Him through fidelity to one another. He cares more than anything about the reconnection of the relationship severed when we fell from the garden of Eden as a result of our willfulness.

There is one thing and one thing alone that God cannot forgive, and that is our failure to forgive others, because in so failing we hoard the grace He gives so lovingly. We extinguish the inner light, God's grace and spirit within us that acts as a pilot light for the true fire of Enlightenment. When we extinguish the pilot light, then Enlightenment, reconciliation, and reconnection—oneness with God—are unattainable.

Individualism, tribalism, clubbiness, and general goatish behavior are not the way to oneness with God. They are not the way into the fold of the shepherd Jesus. God wants above all else for the individual to join His fold, to dwell in His kingdom; but His kingdom is not an exclusive club: It is a community open to everyone.

Forgiveness and reconciliation are the vital concern of communities, not just of individuals. Internal conflict destroys community, therefore there can be no kingdom of heaven community on earth unless and until we all learn to forgive and actively intercede to resolve conflict. For religious communities, excommunication, shunning, disfellowshipping, and other forms of blackballing are the antithesis of forgiveness, and are a sign of clubbiness rather than the true community Jesus taught. Sadly, all religions and nearly all churches practice some form of communal intolerance and unforgiveness—especially when it comes to doubters.

The blackball stick is often accompanied by the carrot of benefits. The Bible seems to say that God will give you anything you want if you ask for it in the right way. "Prosperity gospel" preachers promote and perpetuate this supposition and indeed, for them personally, it seems to work—they usually do indeed grow quite rich. But what the gospel seems to promise and what it actually says are often diametrically different. Scripture says, and it means, that we *should* pray. It says, and it means, that prayer *will* be answered. But it does not say that you should pray in ostentatious megachurch meetings (it says quite the contrary) and it does not say that prayer will be answered in the way you want it answered, or that you will necessarily recognize the answer when it comes. God answers in His own way and in His own time, and His way seldom involves lottery tickets, a new Mercedes in the driveway, or a cure for your child's cancer. If we pray for justice, we will get it; but we might not recognize it: It will be God's perfect interpretation of justice, not ours.

Disillusionment from seemingly unanswered prayer is a major source of doubt about God and a leading cause of lost or shaken faith. The less we feel our prayers are answered, the less sure we are that God is listening, or is even there. We begin to doubt His power, His nature, His word, and even His existence. Those fortunate to lead happy and uneventful lives may be inclined to think, *because* they are so fortunate, that God must be answering their prayers, that they are literally blessed. They may indeed be blessed, insofar as they are spared the agony of doubt.

But doubt is not necessarily all bad. If one can get through it, one may emerge at a higher level of faith based on a deeper, more enlightened understanding of God. Job, Jonah, and Jacob all went through periods of doubt and all emerged, in one way or another, more enlightened.

Doubt can be constructive and lead to spiritual growth, or it can be destructive and lead to spiritual stagnation. Churches could do more to help their members turn any doubts away from the destructive kind and toward the constructive kind. To do so, they need first to accept that doubt is not bad. Then, they need a philosophy and supports to guide doubters in the constructive exploration of their doubts. If God loves the opportunity to argue with His doubters—as Job, Jonah, and Jacob discovered, to their ultimate benefit, that He does—why shouldn't we? Why not at least forgive them? Why shun them?

Jesus spoke of forgiveness as one of the pillars that support true community. There could not be a kingdom of heaven, itself a community, if God did not forgive us our doubts and our sins; and there will not be a kingdom of heaven if we do not forgive one another. No wonder, then, that it is an unpardonable sin not to forgive others. God forgives us for *our* sake, but we must forgive others for *God's* sake. And, please note, it is no half-hearted "Let's forgive but not forget." God does not just forgive our sins. He *forgets* them.

In the Judaeo–Christian world, at least, doubt is fueled by the growing encroachment of physics into metaphysics. Science turns the marvelous and metaphysical into the mundane and mechanical. But it also uncovers new metaphysical mysteries. Secular science asks: What preceded the Big Bang? What are dark matter and dark energy? These are questions almost as big as "Where does Goodness come from?" "What about Evil?" "Whose God is He anyway?" and "Is there life after death?" In the end, science and religion seek the same thing: Ultimate Truth. Unfortunately, the devil is in the definition of it.

To science, truth emerges only by collecting data through observation, experimentation, and other tools of scientific method, and analyzing the data to produce new or revised information and knowledge about some aspect of our world. Yet science has the humility to recognize that today's truths might not hold true tomorrow. It therefore prefers the word "theory" to the word "truth," leaving open the possibility of change.

That does not preclude using science to study God's Creation: the Nature that surrounds, bears, and nurtures us. The key is not to substitute scientific understanding of Nature (which is not that hard to get) with spiritual understanding of the nature of God (which *is* difficult to get); not to confuse theory with truth. To many churches and religionists, truth is plainly written in the Bible. But it seems to me the Bible gently dismisses our efforts to know the ultimate truth—the truth about God. If study we must, then study the mystery of God; not to uncover it, but to wonder at its glory. To the extent we can know the mystery that is God, we can do so only *by liv-*

ing life—and the Bible helps by providing, first, questions that serve to guide us in living a life that will lead to some degree of Enlightenment, and, second, the exemplary life of Jesus—the ultimate example of how to live life. He told us He is the Way, the Truth, and the Life, but such declarative statements were rare. He generally resorted to questions and left it to our own hearts and souls to find Enlightenment. Following His Way, believing His Truth, and living His Life are hard; but to the extent we can manage even a part of it, to that extent we may understand something about God.

It is so hard to follow Jesus that we may feel a sense of frustration. How can anyone except God be *that* perfect? We know we cannot, so what are we supposed to do? What should we try to do? In my devotional prayer life—in my uncertainty about God—in my role as a peacemaker within my community, what matters most? What was it we wanted so desperately that we gave up Paradise for it? *It* is knowledge of good and evil. So what did we get out of our deal with the devil? What have we learned? Do we understand what we know about good and evil yet? We should not be surprised, as a rich young aristocrat was after he asked Jesus how to earn eternal life, to learn that obeying the Ten Commandments is not good enough, and that we must follow the Way, believe the Truth, and live the Life (crucifixion and all) of Jesus. The young man was sorry he asked. Are we, too?

Evil is the absence of good. Evil is going the wrong Way, believing in Falsehood, and (in contrast to community-loving sheep) living a selfish, goatish, individualistic Life. Unfortunately, like the rich young aristocrat, that's just what human beings tend to prefer. It seems less painful, and that's because it *is* less painful. Lucifer would not attract much of a following with an ad showing unhappy followers roasting on a spit over an eternal grill. Such blatant evil would be easy to resist, to say No to. Real evil is soft, luxurious, exhilarating, and fun. Pain is not a product of evil; it is a product of good that puts evil into stark relief. Pain is the antidote to evil. As a product of good, pain is always dispensed along with its own antidote: Grace, a remedy unerringly efficacious to those who don't reject it.

If there is only one Way, Truth, and Life, then why are there so many religions, each with its god(s) and different definitions of them? Surely, only one (or none) can be true. Or could there be some divine purpose behind the proliferation of religions? No mortal can hope to see and understand an eternal, infinite, divine God. Does it help to have a multitude of religions each acting as one of the six blind Indostani men of the poem[1], so that we end up with a composite picture which resembles the real thing at some gross level?[2] Or are all religions exercises in futility? If God is indescribable from

the outside (we are told His light is too bright to look upon) should we not rather look inwards, towards the inner light that is His spirit? In other words, why not seek to understand ourselves first? Enlightenment through self-awareness was the message of the Prodigal Son, and of the humbler of the two convicts crucified next to Jesus. The convict was saved for the kingdom of heaven by acknowledging his sin.

It is only through self-examination and self-awareness that we can begin to find the Way to Enlightenment and the Truth, and to lead a life starting to resemble that of Jesus. Before the Fall, when Man was one with God and the will of Man was aligned with the will of God, awareness neither of God nor self was at issue. But the oneness was severed during the Fall and can only be re-connected through awareness of ourselves and our sins. This awareness is not a superficial, cosmetic self-assessment but a deeply humble recognition of our fallen nature, of how far we have wandered from our Father's house, which leads to the startling reality that we need God's grace.

Could and should churches and religions do more to help humanity reconnect with God? This book will assert that they should, and presents the Christian principles underlying that normative assertion. It begins with a fresh look at the story of Jacob wresting with God. Jacob represents you and me. More than almost any other story in Scripture, we find ourselves beset with the travails of life, trying our best to "work things out," when out of the blue—or, more accurately, out of the darkness—God emerges to focus our attention on Him. This is not just some take-it-or-leave-it encounter with God, but an up-close, in your face, *mano-a-mano* struggle remarkably complex in meaning and remarkably simple in outcome.

The struggles of our individual spiritual lives are seen metaphorically in this story. We struggle with who we are as individuals, how we fit into community, and we strive to pray, to forgive, and to develop our own personal piety. We clash with doubt, we combat faith, we skirmish with grace. In all of these endeavors, we seek clarity, not confusion. We want answers, not questions. We'd like to pray but we're not sure how to do so "effectively." Above all, we wish to understand God and to be able to discriminate between right and wrong. We will look at all of these as embodied in the struggle that Jacob had with God.

This book is about the relationships between the individual and himself or herself, the individual and his or her community, and the individual and God. Both God and community demand a denial of individualism in deference to themselves. The book unfolds as a series of conflicts that face us in life. The first is *You vs. God* (Chapter 1), about our doubts about the existence and attributes of God. Chapter 2—*Faith vs. Doubt*—asks if faith is the antidote to doubt and investigates the ideal dosage—"stage"—of faith for the doubter. The differences between people of faith and of no faith are examined in Chapter 3—*Sheep vs. Goats*—using the common Biblical metaphor, and finds that the community—the fold—of faith is global and non-denominational.

The individualism of goats vs. the communalism of sheep, and the consequences for faith, is examined in Chapter 4: *Me vs. We*, while Chapter 5: *Father vs. Son*, shows how goatishness—individual self-centeredness—inhibited the humble self-awareness that was eventually to lead to the Prodigal Son's reunion with his father. It examines the grace that our Father extends to every one of His children, regardless of their behavior. Chapter 6, *Me vs. You,* asserts that this does not mean He approves of our goatish head-butting behavior toward one another; and reasserts the key principle that such self-centered individualism is a stumbling block to a true community of faith.

As self-centered individuals, we look—nay, we *pray*—to God for magical solutions to our problems and magical interventions to improve our mortal lives and those of our friends and family. In our desire for self-aggrandizement we also seek to understand God and His magical powers better, in order to use them for our own benefit. Chapter 7, *Grace vs. Magic*, examines our great consternation in finding that God intervenes only when we are at the end of our spiritual tether—and only when we humbly acknowledge that we are in His hands. Praying for a miracle won't cut it. Chapter 8, *Prayer vs. Free Will*, shows that true prayer, as demonstrated in the great prayers recorded in Scripture, is not centered upon one's own wishes but, rather, upon God's wishes—upon God's will. Jesus taught us to pray: "Thy will be done." He did not teach us to pray: "Give me this day my daily bread, and forgive me my trespasses." Rather, he taught: "Give us this day our daily bread, and forgive us our trespasses." And when He does forgive us our trespasses (as indeed He does) we in our self-centered arrogance wonder where's the justice in that, when some of us don't deserve it? Chapter 9, *Forgiveness vs. Justice*, examines that question.

Such apparent irrationality drives many away from religion and towards science. But many people and communities of faith, including entire religions, fail to see that both Scripture and science recognize that we cannot know ultimate Truth. As I try to show in Chapter 10, *Science vs. Religion*, we can only approximate it. The result of our failure to reconcile religion with science is two contradictory ultimate Truths about

God and the origin of everything, which Chapter 11, *Truth vs. Truth*, discusses.

Chapter 12, *Seed vs. Soil*, proposes that God does not expect His children to know the Truth about Him, not even the approximate Truth, equally well; while Chapter 13, *Knowledge vs. Mystery*, asserts that the Truth about God can only ever be guessed at because it is fundamentally a Mystery; yet misunderstanding the Mystery of God and His ways is what drives doubt and division among us, while accepting the Mystery *as* mystery is the key driver of faith. To put it another way, the acceptance of Truth as a Mystery *is* faith, yet most religions seem to view their role as to demystify Truth for us. Chapter 14, *Religious-awareness vs. Self-awareness*, examines the relationship between the Truth into which we are indoctrinated by religion and the Truth with which we were all born.

The difference between indoctrinated and inborn Truth is the difference between our lives before and after the Fall in the garden of Eden. It is the difference in the Prodigal Son before and after his travel. It is the difference between arrogant self-centeredness and humble self-awareness. It is the difference between eternal life and death. It is the difference discussed in Chapter 15, *United against Death*.

These, then, are the conflicts and the antagonists in the wrestling match we call life. The conflicts define us but, with God's grace, they refine us as well. This book seeks to provide the Scriptural foundation and spiritual argument for the need for personal and communal spiritual renaissance through just such struggle with God. It does so by reexamining the teachings of Jesus concerning the kingdom of heaven—teachings that emphasize not only the importance of the individual, amplified by innocence and emptiness, but also the primacy of *true* community, which is rooted in principles of forgiveness and conflict resolution. After all, if the kingdom of heaven is within us here and now, then (as Jesus said) it ought to be visible in how we treat both friend and foe.

The book is written unapologetically from a Christian perspective. That is, after all, who and what I am. It is my hope, however, that the book might have broader appeal to those who seek God, albeit not in my tradition. A devout Moslem friend who read the manuscript wrote:

> *When I read this book, I realized more than ever meanings from the Koran that I wasn't aware of from study of my own religion.*

My friend's statement speaks to the expansiveness of God and the power of God's questions to provoke spiritual insight.

In the pages that follow, I hope to convince you that the religion of Jesus, created more than 2,000 years ago on the dusty hills of Judea and rooted in the principles of the kingdom of heaven, is as relevant today as it was then, and will still be relevant a thousand years from now. The kingdom principles are relevant because they arise out of the great, the infinite, the timeless, and the eternal questions of life. They are not to be found in simple answers, bound by our knowledge of data available to us at some finite moment in history.

This is why I believe that faith is relevant in the modern, scientific world.

Notes to the Introduction

[1] The complete poem is reproduced on p. 186.

[2] Image credit: The image of the elephant once appeared on a defunct website (www.godloveseveryone.org) now mirrored at http://www.cs.toronto.edu/~yuana/blindmenelephant/modelingparable.html. The mirrored page credits Kaiser Aluminum News with the artwork, but we were unable to find any such publication and no reference to the image within the Kaiser Aluminum corporate website.

1

You versus God

THE BIBLE IS FULL of stories about doubt. We see it in some of the great prayers of the Bible as well as in the lives of Scriptural giants such as Moses, Abraham, Sarah, and "Doubting" Thomas, the disciple who refused to believe that the other disciples had seen the resurrected Jesus until he could see for himself.[1] Even Jesus, in the final hours of His freedom, seemed to doubt whether His impending crucifixion was really necessary, whether it was really God's will. And on the cross He expressed the most dolorous of doubts: "My God, my God, why have you forsaken me?"[2]

Doubt is not a tool of the devil. Quite the contrary: Constructive or "holy" doubt, which spurs action and continues the quest for Truth, is a Christian virtue. Jesus talked about the simplicity of faith of children, but children never stop asking questions. God seems to anticipate and desire this childlike degree of questioning in those who seek Him. He might not answer in a way that we would recognize as an answer, but the important thing is to ask the questions.

As a Christian virtue and a powerful component of faith, constructive doubt ought to be encouraged. But to many, it seems to run counter to faith. People then tend to think—and the following Scripture seems to imply—that doubt is to be discouraged:

> *But if any of you lacks wisdom, let him ask of God, who gives to all generously and without reproach, and it will be given to him. But he must ask in faith without any doubting, for the one who doubts is like the surf of the sea, driven and tossed by the wind.*[3]

It would seem that if doubt raises its ugly head it should be smothered under a thick blanket of faith. Yet Bible story after story is about men doubting and questioning God, His goodness, and His plan. The very first story, in the garden of Eden, has the serpent introducing doubt into Adam's and Eve's minds. Moses doubted his ability to lead the Israelites out of Egypt even with God's help. Elijah doubted whether God could protect him from a Jezebel out for his blood. Gideon needed three miracles to allay his doubts about God. Job, Jonah, and Doubting Thomas all had their doubts at some point. John the Baptist had to ask if Jesus was *really* the Messiah, and even Jesus Himself doubted the necessity of His impending crucifixion and doubted God's loyalty during it. What *should* we doubt? What is doubtable? What makes *this* doubt poisonous but *that* one medicinal?

Jacob's physical struggle with God serves as a metaphor for humankind's mental wrestling with God and might give us some insight into doubt and a number of other important issues. Jacob's name is associated in Hebrew with deceit and duplicity and such was indeed his character. He ended up facing retribution for usurping the birthright of his first-born elder brother, Esau. In a cowardly act during the night before what he supposed would be a violent confrontation with Esau and an avenging army, Jacob sent his family ahead of him as a human shield. It was at this, his lowest, point that God engaged Jacob in that most intimate of sports, wrestling, which has a degree of physical contact normally reserved for very close relatives. Although God was able to dislocate Jacob's hip with a single touch, he seemed unable to overpower him completely. Perhaps he did not want to.

There has to be some meaning in such a bizarre story. Perhaps the meaning was in the struggle, not in the outcome. In other words, perhaps God engaged Jacob (metaphorically, all of us) in a wrestling match not to overpower him (or us), not to conquer, but because of the intimate encounter in and of itself. To be sure, He wants us to know that He is all-powerful and could easily defeat us, but He also wants us to know that it is not His plan to do so. Perhaps too, He did not overpower Jacob completely because it would have been pointless: Jacob had to come to grips with himself—he needed to recognize his need to submit his nature to the transforming power of God's grace.

God's plan is to force us to struggle through our doubts and fears to reach a place beyond them. It is not a curse but a blessing. In Jacob's case, it resulted in a complete change of character. The change was reflected in the change of name God gave him. Instead of Jacob the deceiver and supplanter, he became *Israel*, one who (in its Hebrew connotation) struggles intimately with God and the ideas that God wants us to understand.

Intimate conflict with God serves to allay our fears about what is happening to us, and it confirms that God answers—

even though He refuses to answer direct questions—with His blessing, with His removal of our fear, and with His willingness to wrestle with us for as long as we are willing to wrestle with him.

Is doubt the opposite of faith? Jacob's misplaced faith in a compliant God who would overlook or even condone and support his deceitfulness changed when he was renamed as Israel. It became instead faith in a God with whom one must struggle. His faith was juxtaposed with fear. So it was, too, when Jesus calmed a stormy Sea of Galilee to allay the fear and doubt of the disciples in the boat. Jesus asked them: "Why are you afraid? Why have you no faith?"[4] So perhaps fear, not doubt, is the opposite of faith. President Franklin D. Roosevelt would seem to have agreed, when he told the nation in his 1933 inaugural address:

> *...let me assert my firm belief that the only thing we have to fear is fear itself—nameless, unreasoning, unjustified terror which paralyzes needed efforts to convert retreat into advance.*

Some say that certainty is the opposite of faith. Some say it is unbelief. But fear seems to be the strongest contender. Fear of things spiritual is a matter of the heart, whereas doubt is a matter of the mind, the brain, the intellect. Do we approach God, do we relate to him, more through thought, or more through feeling? Is it more a matter of the brain, of intellect; or more a matter of heart, emotion, or spirit?

Doubt is a double-edged sword. It can drive one to seek deeper spiritual understanding, to open one's mind to God; or it can lead to spiritual disillusionment, fear, and eventual paralysis. Jacob's story provides a window on the struggles we have with our faith, and what God does about it—for us, and with us.

Some people struggle with God because He seems so remote, so unapproachable, so disinterested in their needs and their points of view. Some struggle because they see the relationship with Him as a contract—a conditional promise—rather than as a covenant—an unconditional pledge. They feel aggrieved when God (apparently) fails to uphold His part of the contract by (apparently) not answering their prayers.

Some people struggle because they just don't like the way God runs the universe—He allows little children to suffer and lets bad things happen to good people. And some people struggle with the very concept of God, though many more question the way God operates than question His existence.

Jacob's story shows us that God seems to want to meet us in our darkest hour, when we are at our wits' end. God does not shy away from darkness. He will struggle with us there and, ultimately, enlighten the darkness with His blessing.

There is a hint, in both the intimacy of the struggle (as suggested by the wrestling metaphor) and in God's apparent inability or unwillingness to win the match, that there is something deeply important about the struggle itself. In a wrestling match, the legs are perhaps the most vital limbs. They have the strongest muscles in the body. God chose to inflict a disability to Jacob's legs by dislocating his hip. It was as bad a break as any wrestler could fear, yet still Jacob struggled until he was assured of God's blessing.

What exactly was the blessing he wanted and prayed for? And what was the blessing he got? He had emerged from his mother's womb grasping the heel of his twin brother Esau, who emerged first and was thus the eldest, the firstborn, entitled to inherit everything from their father.

The twins grew up to be very different characters in terms of physique, interests, abilities, ethics, and parental relationship, in all of which Esau was the better man. This evidently irked Jacob so much that he deceived his dying father, Isaac, disguising himself as Esau in order to receive Isaac's deathbed blessing and the birthright that properly belonged to his elder brother. Though frail and blind, Isaac sensed that the person asking for his blessing did not quite sound, feel, and smell like Esau, so he asked for his name. Jacob replied "Esau," and the deception worked.

When Esau found out, he vowed to kill Jacob. Coward as he was, Jacob took to his heels and went to hide out with his uncle for a number of years, during which the uncle deceived Jacob over a number of things, so for a while Jacob found himself at the receiving end of deceit. But eventually he succeeded in life and grew rich. After a number of years Jacob agreed to meet with Esau, but with great reluctance. What the meeting would hold for him was uncertain: War or peace? Conflict or reconciliation? This was the setting for Jacob's wrestling match with God.

As mentioned, Jacob's name is associated in Hebrew with the sense of grasping, holding onto things, as well as with deceit and duplicity. He *grasped* for his brother's heel, for his brother's birthright, for a beautiful wife, and for riches. And in wrestling with God, he was grasping for God's blessing— as are we. Just as Isaac asked Jacob his name before blessing him, God likewise asked Jacob his name before blessing him.

Jacob seemed to know that it was God with whom he was wrestling, yet he was prepared to continue wrestling for the blessing even at risk of death, which would occur if he were to see God in the light of day. What was the blessing this cowardly man risked so much for? The answer lies in Jacob's answer to God's question: "Who are you?" which was: "I am Jacob."

To admit that he was who he was, was a momentous confession, both to God and to himself, that he was a deceiver, a supplanter, a grabber, and a sinner. He was finally facing up to his faults and admitting: "I feel bad about myself." He needed God's grace, and was ready to relinquish his old ways. And God's grace, and a new name—a new identity, is exactly what he then got from his intimate struggle, his wrestle, with God about himself.

We all seek physical comfort, an easy life, and solace from God. Jacob's story shows the priority God places on the spirit compared to the body. The blessing that comes from God is a spiritual blessing, not a physical one. That God's interest is your immortal existence, not your mortal body, is good news. Jacob exchanged physical health for spiritual wealth. Fear, uncertainty, and inner turmoil was replaced with peace for his soul. A dislocated hip and a walking stick is a small price to pay for God's abundant grace. How poorly we understand God's ways.

In wrestling with God, Jacob not only learned something about God but more importantly he learned something about himself, and that is perhaps the message for all of us. If we open ourselves truthfully to God, He will forgive us, and He will not take us to task for our sins. But Jacob paid a price, in the form of a physical disability. This disabling perhaps signifies the result of relinquishing one's will to God: One is no longer free to act contrary to the will of God.

The blessing of forgiveness and grace that Jacob received demonstrates that God's grace and forgiveness are infinite and so is the distance He will put between us and our sins. Psalm 103 states unequivocally that God forgets our sins,[5] He doesn't just forgive them. But if we don't say the same things about ourselves that God says about us, we exclude ourselves from grace and forgiveness.

It seems to be an element of the Unpardonable Sin: If God says He has forgiven His prodigal children but we do not forgive others—and even more importantly, if we do not confess our sins and forgive ourselves—then we become disconnected. We "log out" from what would otherwise be a permanent connection with God. When we willfully disconnect in this way, we put ourselves beyond the reach of forgiveness.

The mercies described in Psalm 103 are the mercies Jacob received—not as Jacob, but as Israel. His identity, his character, his very being was transformed. So we might say that the underlying blessing for Jacob, and for us all, is genuine self-realization through the recognition of our character defects, imperfections, weaknesses, and of our need and desire for a more gracious relationship with a forgiving God. Like Jacob, we tend to try to disguise our wickedness, to pretend that we are not the sinful person we really are (or sometimes the opposite: Thinking that we are more sinful than we really are.) More so than our new awareness of God, it is this self-recognition that opens the door to the blessing of God's grace and forgiveness.

In Shakespeare's *Measure for Measure,* the saintly Isabella reminded Angelo, the "self-righteous Pillar of Society," of the divine scheme of redemption when she said:

> *How would you be,*
> *If He, which is the top of judgement, should*
> *But judge you as you are? O, think on that;*
> *And mercy then will breathe within your lips,*
> *Like man new-made.* [6]

Robert Burns also reminded us of this when he wrote:

> *O wad some Power the giftie gie us*
> *To see oursels as ithers see us!*
> *It wad frae mony a blunder free us,* ...[7]

While Jacob went to great lengths to hide his true self in his struggle with God, God was even more relentless in struggling to save him, even though God had the power so easily to force him to change. This is the lesson for all of us. It is that God does not judge us in our mortal lives; but He helps us to judge ourselves.

Doubt in its destructive form can damage or even destroy our faith in God and our relationship with Him. How, then, can we hope to judge the state of someone *else*'s relationship with God? Yet this is what we do every time we refuse to forgive and forget the behavior of people who hurt us.

Notes to Chapter 1

---

[1] John 20:24-25

[2] Matthew 27:46

[3] James 1:5-6

[4] Mark 4:40

[5] Psalms 103:1-10

[6] The quotes are from Aldous Huxley (who wrote the classic and still chillingly relevant science fiction book *Brave New World*, about a false, technology-driven, Utopia) In a deathbed essay published posthumously in *Show Magazine* in 1964 and reprinted in Huxley, Aldous (1992): *Huxley and God: Essays on Religious Experience*. San Francisco: Harper Collins.

[7] From "To A Louse, On Seeing One on a Lady's Bonnet at Church," a 1786 Scots language poem by Robert Burns.

2

Faith versus Doubt

FAITH HARDWIRES MAN TO GOD. It is God's way of maintaining communications with us since our Fall from the garden of Eden.[1] It goes by other names, such as an "eternity in the heart,"[2] the Holy Spirit, the holy ghost, and the inner "light that lighteth every man."[3] It is seen most clearly in children and even babies. Indeed, Jesus told us our faith must become like that of a child, innocent of worldly knowledge, in order to be effective.[4] Faith not only does not require, but indeed is impeded by, accumulated worldly wisdom and intelligence. Adult maturity is a millstone. Jesus went so far as to say that unless we become like children, we will not enter the kingdom of heaven.[5]

In that kingdom—in the garden of Eden—before the Fall, there was neither faith nor doubt. Adam and Eve "walked by sight and not by faith." There was no ambiguity about who owned and ran the garden: It was God.

The tree of life and the tree of knowledge of good and evil that stood in the garden have been taken as metaphors respectively for obedience and disobedience, dependence and independence, and creator and creature. Perhaps they can also be considered respectively as "the way of grace" (the gift of God) and "the way of works" (Man trying to discriminate moral authority). One might say the tree of life represents certainty and the tree of knowledge uncertainty.

For a while following the Fall, God communicated with humans directly. He took Abraham to a hillside to see the stars, and told him he would rule a nation as plentiful as they were. He spoke to Moses at the Burning Bush, telling him to take off his shoes and giving him a direct message. He led the children of Israel through the wilderness, in the form of a cloud by day and a pillar of fire at night. He communicated His will to the people of Israel through stones embedded in the breastplate of the high priest of the Sanctuary.[6]

But after the Israelites demanded a king and a secular government to replace the sacred priestly government, God seemed progressively to withdraw from direct intercourse with them. He continued to send messages through the prophets, but they were less specific and more general than before; messages such as to turn from evil ways. This left a clouded Scriptural picture of God until Jesus came to re-introduce God to Man—but in a form (his human form) radically different to the one generally accepted at the time.[7]

Like Jacob, how we define ourselves in relation to God—that is to say, how strong (or weak) is our faith and how we behave accordingly—very much influences our devotional life and specifically how we pray. Indeed, it influences our very concept of prayer. There has to be a direct link between prayer and faith. But faith can be elusive, changing from moment to moment and subject, we know, to growth or regression.

Piaget and other social psychologists have posited a progression of stages in social development as we age. James W. Fowler, former Professor of Theology and Human Development at Emory University, thought spiritual growth to be similarly analyzable, definable, and organizable, as "Stages of Faith."[8] M. Scott Peck simplified and consolidated some of Fowler's stages, resulting in the smaller set[9] which forms the basis for the interpretation presented below. These stages of faith are critical to understanding the journey through doubt.

I feel compelled to stress that the stages of faith apply to all religions, not just Christianity; and that God loves everyone equally and provides salvation to all, no matter their stage of faith. The stages are a description, not a judgment.

Stage 1 faith is a chaotic, antisocial, pretending kind of faith. Stage 1 people are what Peck called "people of the lie" who only *pretend* to love and care for others; they only *pretend* to be good. In reality they lack moral principle and their relations with others are manipulative and self-serving. Their relationships tend not to last, and quite a few end up in jail. But some remain functional and can even rise to leadership positions. Jonah, a preacher, was an example.

Stage 2 faith, said Peck, is formal, institutional, and "fundamental." Its members commit themselves to the principle of law, which they view as a way out of the chaos and gross selfishness of stage 1. They tend to be legalistic, dogmatic, and parochial people who do not understand the *spirit* of law —they do not see that law is a means to an end and not an end in itself; that law has an underlying spirit and meaning and is not to be taken always at face value.

Stage 2 people see things in black and white. There is only Truth (which they alone possess) and Untruth (which others —unbelievers—possess) and which threatens them and their Truth. It is therefore their logical responsibility to convert unbelievers to their beliefs, infidels to their faith. They expect clear-cut answers from religion, and religion—whether it be based on Biblical, Koranic, Buddhist, Hindu or other Scripture or prophetic writing or authority—is only too happy to their expectations. The methods and doctrines prescribed in their liturgies specify the constraints and boundaries of the lives of stage 2 people and relieve them from fear of the unknown. Having a sense of certainty and an unwavering commitment to a way of thinking is central to stage 2 faith.

Stage 2 people consider stage 1 people to be sinners in need of conversion and ripe for redemption, but tend not to grasp even the potential for levels of faith and spirituality higher than their own. They don't understand people in stage 3 and even less do they understand people in stage 4. Most people who attend religious services on a regular basis are in stage 2. Their belief in cause and effect has a strong bearing on their prayer life.

Stage 2 faith might usefully be further refined along two sub-dimensions:

1. **Experience-based Stage 2 faith** is an introductory or elementary type of faith, typically developed in young children. It is stimulated by participation, by learning the liturgy, doing the rituals, following the traditions of the church, lighting the candles, singing the songs, saying the prayers, and so on. It is a sensory faith, being highly de-

pendent on the sights and sounds and smells of church. It is a meaningful and final faith to many.

2. **Affiliation-based Stage 2 faith** is a faith strengthened by joining an organized faith group—a church or a study group and so on. It might entail going through some induction ritual such as baptism or affirmation of faith. It seems especially attractive to adolescents, who join church youth groups, Pathfinders, Boy and Girl Scouts, and so on.

Stage 3 faith is the faith of the skeptic, the individual, the questioner. It is the stage of doubt. Stage 3 people include agnostics and atheists. But they also tend to be scientifically minded "seekers" who demand reasoned, logical explanation of phenomena. Stage 2 answers do not satisfy stage 3 people. They may themselves have been at stage 2 for many years, having perhaps been raised in a religious family or society. As time passed, the answers at church were no longer answers to the questions they were asking, and the simple explanation no longer satisfied their longing.

Thus they came to be despised as unbelievers, infidels, and sinners by their former stage 2 brethren. Stage 3 people nevertheless are often more highly developed spiritually than them. And despite being individualistic, they tend to be unselfish people committed to social justice who stay in their communities. They tend to make loving and devoted parents, to be good neighbors, to be compassionate towards the poor, and to be concerned for the environment and animal welfare. People at an advanced level of stage 3 also tend to be active seekers of Truth—to be curious about things of the spirit, often seeking unconventional approaches.

People who have entered stage 3 are seldom to be found in church, mosque, or temple, because it no longer meets their needs and cannot answer their questions. It is the wrong context for them. The greatest dilemma facing established religions is how to understand and deal with people who are transitioning from stage 2 to stage 3 and are therefore in the process of being lost to the religious establishment. Despite being agnostic or even atheist, their advanced spiritual nature has them on a path that may eventually lead them to stage 4. Stage 4 is less inimical to stage 2 than stage 3 is.

Another name for stage 3 might be "the Searching stage," since the certainties of affiliative faith begin to seem less certain. Standard catechisms and nearly everything else that was taught by indoctrination are questioned. It is a faith that seeks answers, and is often seen in late adolescence when young people enter college or the workplace and begin to be exposed to ideas and worldviews different from the closeted ideas and worldviews from which they are emerging. The primary attribute of "Searching faith" is fear of the unknown; yet, at the same time, they are drawn to it, and that leads many to retreat back to an earlier stage of faith in order to recover their sense of certainty and lose their fear.

But it is only through this doubting, searching, fearful stage 3 of faith that one can advance to the next stage, by sheer manifestation of God's grace. Defined and expressed as a willingness to ask questions that may be disturbing, doubt is in fact a *responsibility* of the individual seeker of Truth, whether the Truth sought be spiritual or scientific. The Scriptural record is full of encounters in which doubting Man asks God questions. Doubt is not a faith-breaker: It is a key element of faith growth itself. In the absence of doubt, there is no need for faith. Certainty renders faith irrelevant.

Organized religion, it seems to me, has not thought nearly enough about doubt and questioning and skepticism, and about how to provide a safe haven within its community of faith for people transitioning to and through the highly vulnerable stage 3.

Stage 4 faith, said Peck, is the mystical or communal faith of people who have actively sought Truth and who, out of love and commitment to something bigger than themselves and bigger than what they have been part of before, have developed the ability to transcend the constraints of their religious and social backgrounds and their upbringing, acculturation, and indoctrination, and have turned instead to a more global view of who God is and what He is interested in.

They no longer see themselves as the center of the universe but as a participant in a larger community of faith consisting of all people who see a transcendent God. They do not seek clear-cut answers, but find questions far more interesting and compelling and rewarding than answers. They are the opposite of people in stage 2. They enjoy meditation, contemplation, study of things of the spirit, and prayer. They achieve communion with their Inner Light.

The ironic thing about this internal reconnection with God is that it often leads stage 4 people back to the stage 2 establishments they once felt compelled to leave. Back at church, they come to view God, church, holy books, liturgy, and ritual as the language of faith but they do not accredit to these concepts and artifacts the importance and necessity stage 2 people do. Even so, they often find comfort in their old community of faith, and thus find themselves seeking freedom and mystical transcendence and enlightenment about the greatness and universality of God in the very same pew as the stage 2 person seeking certainty and clarity and sectarian rules, dogma, and doctrine by which to govern their lives. This creates tensions in church, as stage 2 people cling ferociously to minute points of liturgy and doctrine, what hymns to sing, and so on, fearful of contamination and ultimate destruction. Stage 2 people feel under threat from stage 4 people who just don't care about these things.

To stage 2 people God is so great and distant as to be almost unapproachable. He is a God who measures us carefully by our behavior. Stage 4 people see the opposite: A God who is immanent, in-dwelling, the God of the Holy Spirit, of the Inner Light. Indeed, stage 4 might well be called the stage of Enlightenment achieved through the individual's analysis of his or her personal experiences and exposure to ideas during the phase 3 "Searching" stage. The Searching phase is pre-requisite to the Enlightenment stage. There may be some residual doubts, but they are not spiritually disabling.

The best Biblical example of the transitions from stage 2 through stage 3 to stage 4 is seen in the life of Job. Job was a wealthy but pious and good (stage 2) man. Satan argued with God that Job was good only because of his wealth; that if he lost his wealth, he would curse God. God allowed Satan to destroy Job's livestock, kill his children, and inflict a terrible illness on him. Job cursed his life and had doubts about God (stage 3), but his doubts led him to a higher (stage 4) faith.

This passage describes his enlightenment at the moment of his final transition:

> *"I know that you can do all things; no purpose of yours can be thwarted. You asked, 'Who is this that obscures my plans without knowledge?' Surely I spoke of things I did not understand, things too wonderful for me to know.*

> *"You said, 'Listen now, and I will speak; I will question you, and you shall answer me.' My ears had heard of you but now my eyes have seen you."*[10]

Job had gone back and forth between his stage 2 friends' argument for the law of cause and effect, which meant in essence that God could be understood on human terms, where y always follows x, and his own uneasy feeling that they were missing something of fundamental importance. This was his period of doubt—his transition through stage 3—until at last he saw the spirit behind the law rather than just the words of the law; in other words, until he transitioned to stage 4.

At the other extreme, Jonah was a stage 1 individual who pretended to be loving and to be interested in the Ninevites he was sent to minister to as a prophet of God. But at heart he was antisocial, selfish to the core, and arrogant. He expected everyone—including God—to accept his views.

Gideon's famous doubts, expressed through prayer and accompanied by demands for physical proof of God's existence, show *him* to have been firmly in stage 2. The existence of God was black or white, for Gideon, with nothing in-between and nothing outside the box.

But God responded—and responds—to people in all stages of faith. He tried to move Jonah out of stage 1. The relinquishment of His will to God by Jesus, in a final prayer before His arrest in the garden of Gethsemane, showed His human incarnation to be in stage 4.

It is not a given that everybody goes, or needs to go, through every stage of faith. One can be arrested at any stage, and stay there. We all know people stuck forever in stages 1 or 2. Furthermore, one can revert to a previous stage. We all waver in our faith, and sometimes seek more certainty to avoid our fears.

People at lower stages are threatened by people at higher stages, but not *vice versa*. Stage 2 people view stage 1 people not as threats but as opportunities for conversion. But stage 3 people have rejected stage 2 people, and—maybe worse—stage 4 people have infiltrated their church and are undermining its very foundations right under their noses. And just to rub it in, stage 4 people seem to be more *joyful*, with no fear or concern about the tampering with the key elements that establish their stage 2 faith.

Stage 3 people are afraid of stage 4 people because the latter are just as skeptical as they are, yet have evidently found something that renders their own skepticism impotent yet enlightening. It is what stage 3 people lack and still must seek.

It is difficult to minister to people more than one stage below oneself. A stage 3 person, who has rejected the rule of law, can hardly make a difference to a stage 1 person who has little concept of law anyway.

After one understands the stages of faith it might be possible to recognize where one stands in one's own journey through them. Even so, the journey seems not to be under one's direct control. It has its own spiritual progression. It is the kindling of the inner light; it is the spirit working on the heart.

The primary ingredient of the transition from stage 2 to 3 is the questioning, doubt, uncertainty, ambiguity, and so on concerning stage 2 tenets and belief systems. Stage 2 people tend to regard *any* doubt about things of the spirit and about God Himself as heretical and to be avoided at all costs.

To eliminate doubt in one's life one must adopt one of two extremes on the continuum of belief. The first extreme is to believe everything. The second is to believe nothing—to doubt everything. There can be no other way to eliminate uncertainty. Either extreme requires no thought, no analysis, no weighing of evidence. One simply says: This is the way things are. Period. The first extreme might be called fundamentalist faith; the second, radical skepticism.

Many if not most of us are somewhere in between these extremes. We feel it is important to weigh, to analyze, the evidence. A person in stage 1, who by definition has no belief system, will tend to feel and respond to the attraction of the "static certainty" of a stage 2 belief system if s/he comes across one or is introduced to one. Static certainty makes sense of everything, provides answers to every question through key texts of Scripture, and there are no open, ambiguous, or unresolved issues. By definition, there can be no uncertainty in a world of static certainty.

That certainty starts to crumble in stage 3, both destructively and constructively. Stage 3 neophytes who continue to question and examine and analyze their doubts eventually regain a sense of certainty. But it is a flexible and dynamic certainty that retains an ability to absorb and accommodate new understanding, new data, fresh insights.

To some, it is normal and rational to be puzzled, intrigued, or sometimes even obsessed by the unknown. Curiosity is to a large extent governed by personality. Some people go through life without much curiosity, willing to do what they are told without needing to question or analyze. But most of us are not like that. Even atheists and agnostics are just as obsessed with the concept of God as believers are, though of course they reach a different (and perhaps ambiguous) conclusion.

Most of us sense that the universe has a grand dimension about which we know nothing; that there is something "out there"—some force, some energy, some ethic—that is bigger, better, and stronger than us by such orders of magnitude that it is outside the realm of scientific knowing. Unless one knows everything spiritual, physical, and metaphysical about the universe, then one has incomplete knowledge. If knowledge is limited, then knowledge and ideas and beliefs based on assumptions about the universe could very well be wrong. That's partly what drives our insatiable quest for new knowledge.

We are amassing new scientific knowledge at an exponentially accelerating rate, but neither we as individuals nor our churches and religions seem to have a framework and methodology, a dynamic spiritual or religious paradigm, to assimilate new ideas and knowledge at the spiritual and religious level. Many denominations and doctrines have not changed in centuries. and either simply ignore what might be unsettling new knowledge—which results in a great deal of cognitive dissonance in the members of those denominations —or dismiss and reject it as untrue.

But stage 3 faith provides a personal paradigm of sorts, allowing a person to continue to have a faith experience and grow in faith without having to completely reject old beliefs or to completely accept new ones. It enables one to work through one's doubt and uncertainty and either retreat back to the comforting certainty of stage 2 or transition into stage 4. In either case, one is still a member of a community of faith and still has a belief in the holiness of Scripture.

It seems clear that stage 1 people find neither historical validity nor moral authority in the Bible. It is to them just a book. Stage 2 Christians view it as the literal and veritable word of God. A stage 3 person would concede there are good things in the Bible, but also so many inconsistencies, ambiguities, and contradictions that it challenges reason and makes it difficult to understand. To the stage 4 Christian, the Bible is a book of great Truth, the historical and scientific validity of whose individual parts and stories is irrelevant: What is relevant is the underlying spiritual Truth in them, and the spiritual invigoration they bestow. Things in the Bible that don't make sense only add to the mystery, and make it that much more interesting and exciting.

No matter what its holy book, every religion is like a single language with dialects—rituals and liturgy—that differ among different groups, which express beliefs and faith in dialectically different ways. We may "speak" different liturgies, even in stage 3, but we share a common core faith—a common language. To make a virtue of doubt, we must be prepared to enter into an exhausting place of tension in our minds. We must not run from that place as though faith did not exist there. We must recognize that faith is just as active there as faith in either a static certainty phase or in a dynamic uncertainty phase. We must not fear the loss of faith. We must understand that God's help has to be put into the service of building faith, of making faith grow, of answering (or, better yet, asking) questions that allow us then to continue with an enriched spiritual life.

Churches, synagogues, temples, and mosques ought to be just as interested in nurturing the faith of the stage 3 doubter / seeker as they are in nurturing the faith of the stage 2 believer. Yet most are not. Instead, they strive to pressgang everyone into phase 2 static certainty and keep them there. They ought to be prepared not just to put up with doubters; they ought to be ready and willing to engage and even to encourage those entering the questioning phase and to impress upon them that they—the doubters—are embarking on a legitimate phase of spiritual growth which is necessary if they are to find a more living, vibrant, dynamic, and fulfilling faith.

Doubt can be a paralyzing poison that undermines faith and one's relationship with God. We fear that doubt puts the very soul in jeopardy. But it can also be a potent medicine that helps a person transition from static certainty to dynamic faith.

The primary task of the individual during this phase of doubt is to continue to seek. By God's grace, perseverance will lead to a state of more flexible certainty; a certainty not necessarily about doctrine but about God, an understanding that God wants to be an active and leading partner in one's life, that you figure in His plan.

While many factors can initiate and sustain skepticism, nothing throws the heavy veil of doubt over the believer more than unanswered prayer. To reach out to God—to call upon Him in our hour of greatest need—and to hear nothing but silence accelerates skepticism into doubt. Doubt grows when our entreaties are unrequited. We live our lives thinking that we must seek and find God. Failure to hear from God leaves us disconsolate.

As it did with Jacob, God's long arm finds us in our darkest, most fearful, despair. Ample evidence from the parables of Jesus speak to the commitment God has to finding us. In this regard, the old adage "Don't just do something—Stand there!" applies. The Shepherd is coming.

Faith versus Doubt

Notes to Chapter 2

---

[1] Romans 12:3

[2] Ecclesiastes 3:11

[3] John 1:9

[4] Luke 10:21

[5] Matthew 18:3

[6] The stones were called Urim and Thummim (Heb. אוּרִים וְתֻמִּים) and described by The Jewish Virtual Library as "a priestly device for obtaining oracles. On the high priest's ephod (an apron-like garment) lay a breastpiece (חֹשֶׁן) – a pouch inlaid with 12 precious stones engraved with the names of the 12 tribes of Israel – that held the Urim and Thummim (Ex. 28:15–30; Lev. 8:8)." https://www.jewishvirtuallibrary.org/jsource/Judaism/urimthummim.html

[7] John 14:9

[8] Fowler, James W. (1995). *Stages of Faith: The Psychology of Human Development and the Quest for Meaning*. New York: HarperOne.

[9] Peck, M. Scott (1998). *The Different Drum: Community Making and Peace*. New York: Touchstone.

[10] Job 42:2-5

3

Sheep versus Goats

"What do you think? If a man owns a hundred sheep, and one of them wanders away, will he not leave the ninety-nine on the hills and go to look for the one that wandered off?

"And if he finds it, truly I tell you, he is happier about that one sheep than about the ninety-nine that did not wander off." [1]

SHEEP AND SHEPHERDS appear throughout the Bible, all the way from Genesis to Revelation. Many of the heroes of the Bible—Abraham and Moses, for example—were involved in the business of herding sheep. Jesus used sheep as illustrations in his parables, to teach us much about God.

Sheep have strong flocking and herding instincts, a survival mechanism that may have spiritual implications. Flocking makes it harder for predators to destroy the group. Sheep follow their leader (occasionally, a ram) even to the point of death if the leader walks over a cliff. They are very social and they need to see each other. Their eyes can see a little bit to the rear, as well as to the front and sides, which helps alert them to predators and keeps them aware of the rest of the flock behind them.

The flocking instinct of sheep makes it easy for humans to control them. Sheep are so docile and domesticated that they probably could not survive in the wild. A sheep that becomes isolated from the flock is probably ill or lost. It would be against its nature to choose to leave the flock. Meanwhile, left to its own devices when the shepherd takes off after the stray, the inclination of the flock will be to stay together, and by doing so it will remain relatively safe.

The relationship between the shepherd and the flock is an intimate one. Jesus said the sheep know the shepherd by his voice, and the shepherd knows each of his sheep by name.[2] In situations of distress, hearing our name being called brings relief. It tells us somebody is looking out for us. When Adam hid in the garden of Eden, afraid for having eaten the forbidden fruit, God called out Adam's name in evident concern.

The Lost Sheep parable has three kinds of sheep: Those inside the fold ("Insiders"), those outside ("Outsiders,") and those that are missing ("Lost"). The Lost and the Outsiders seem to be the object of deliberate, intentional activity by the shepherd. Jesus said He *must* go get them and bring them into the fold. Are Jews the insider sheep, and Gentiles the outsiders? Paul seems to say that the Jews were "predestined" to be God's chosen people on the basis of following the religious law, but they ended up failing and the Gentiles became God's people instead, on the basis of their faith.[3]

As well as three kinds of sheep, there are also goats. Goats are a different—an *other*—species from sheep.[4] They are capricious, impulsive, unpredictable, devious, and contrary. They are never content with what they have. They hate to be confined. They are not good followers—each wants to be leader. Their herding instinct is weak.

In Scriptural metaphor, goats represent people destined to end up in an eternal fire prepared for the devil and his angels (along with anyone whose name is not written in the Book of Life[5]):

"But when the Son of Man comes in His glory, and all the angels with Him, then He will sit on His glorious throne. All the nations will be gathered before Him; and He will separate them from one another, as the shepherd separates the sheep from the goats; and He will put the sheep on His right, and the goats on the left.

"Then the King will say to those on His right, 'Come, you who are blessed of My Father, inherit the kingdom prepared for you from the foundation of the world. For I was hungry, and you gave Me something to eat; I was thirsty, and you gave Me something to drink; I was a stranger, and you invited Me in; naked, and you clothed Me; I was sick, and you visited Me; I was in prison, and you came to Me.' Then the righteous will answer Him, 'Lord, when did we see You hungry, and feed You, or thirsty, and give You something to drink? And when did we see You a stranger, and invite You in, or naked, and clothe You? When did we see You sick, or in prison, and come to You?' The King will answer and say to them, 'Truly I say to you, to the extent that you did it to one of these brothers of Mine, even the least of them, you did it to Me.'

"Then He will also say to those on His left, 'Depart from Me, accursed ones, into the eternal fire which has been prepared for the devil and his angels; for I was hungry, and you gave Me nothing

*to eat; I was thirsty, and you gave Me nothing to drink; I was a
stranger, and you did not invite Me in; naked, and you did not
clothe Me; sick, and in prison, and you did not visit Me.' Then
they themselves also will answer, 'Lord, when did we see You hungry, or thirsty, or a stranger, or naked, or sick, or in prison, and did
not take care of You?' Then He will answer them, 'Truly I say to
you, to the extent that you did not do it to one of the least of these,
you did not do it to Me.' These will go away into eternal punishment, but the righteous into eternal life.'* *

Why were the sheep and the goats surprised at the judgment
they received? Sheep are born sheep, and goats are born
goats, and goats just don't belong in the kingdom. But why?
Why should they be excluded from all hope of salvation?

In other references to goats in the Scriptures, one was used
as a sacrifice and another was made the "scapegoat"—loaded
with all the sins of Israel and taken to the desert and left to
die, taking the sins with it.[7] Biblical scholars differ about
whether the scapegoat is a metaphor for Jesus—bearer of the
sins of mankind—or for Satan. Regardless; sin seems to be
the hallmark of goats.

Ostensibly, the judgment passage is simple. Good people
end up in the kingdom, while bad people end up in a bad
place. We seem to know intuitively that we have in us a certain amount of both good and evil, but in this passage the distinction is absolute and binary: You are one or the other.

Everlasting punishment in a burning hell hardly seems
consistent with the loving God of Jesus, and out of all proportion to the crime of neglecting to visit one's criminal
neighbor in jail. The passage hints at a connection to something being judged at a far deeper level, at the very root of
evil. It hints that something is being finished here that was
begun at the foundation of the earth:

Now if any man builds on the foundation with gold, silver, precious stones, wood, hay, straw, each man's work will become evident; for the day will show it because it is to be revealed with fire, and the fire itself will test the quality of each man's work. If any man's work which he has built on it remains, he will receive a reward. If any man's work is burned up, he will suffer loss; but he himself will be saved, yet so as through fire.

Do you not know that you are a temple of God and that the Spirit of God dwells in you? [8]

The concept of "burning up" is used here in respect to "work," not to people. Fire is a way of testing the quality of people's work, and even if the work is of poor quality (and therefore succumbs to the flame) the person responsible for it will still be saved, the passage assures us. The passage also asserts the presence of the God element—the Spirit, inner light, or "eternity" inside each of us. That this would be subject to the flames is flatly rejected in that passage. Judgment is our salvation, not our destruction:

For God so loved the world, that He gave His only begotten Son, that whoever believes in Him shall not perish, but have eternal life. For God did not send the Son into the world to judge the world, but that the world might be saved through Him. He who believes in Him is not judged; he who does not believe has been judged already, because he has not believed in the name of the only begotten Son of God. This is the judgment, that the Light has come into the world, and men loved the darkness rather than the Light, for their deeds were evil. For everyone who does evil hates the Light, and does not come to the Light for fear that his deeds will be exposed. But he who practices the truth comes to the Light, so that his deeds may be manifested as having been wrought in God. [9]

Might the Judgment passage refer not to individual judgment but to the judgment of Evil itself? If so, then this metaphor is not about you or me, but about Ultimate Good and Ultimate Evil. We think of God primarily as being in the business of uniting and the devil as being in the business of dividing. Jesus gathered the sheep into a unity but individual goats were not necessarily excluded from that unity. What *was* excluded was Evil itself.

Jesus said He would bring sheep "not of this fold" into it.[10] Clearly, God is in the business of gathering, of bringing together, of forming a community—the community known as the kingdom of heaven. Adam and Eve were part of that community, that fold, that flock, with God and with other creatures in the garden of Eden. Yet they were driven out, secluded, separated from it. Community, then is identified with Good, in contrast to separation, individualization, and isolation, which are identified as Evil.

Is goodness, then, inherent in community, or is a community dependent on its individuals for its goodness? Can a community be morally evil, or is immorality only a function of individuals? Radical individuals, like Jesus, reach out and help others. They form community through their own individualism and leadership. Yet most of us don't do that very well; and when people reach out to us, it seems we don't know how to respond very well either. Part of being a community involves not only reaching out to others, but also allowing them to reach out to us.

It seems as if those of us in Western civilization live (or aspire to live) as a society of individuals. Arguably, modern capitalism could not function without its own radical individuals. Inability or unwillingness to form community may be why Christianity is not flourishing as well in developed

countries as it is in some developing countries. The only
sense of community in Westminster Abbey on a Sunday
morning is that of a voyeuristic tour group, there to gawk at
the tombs of Livingstone and the poets and nobles. The
Christian gospel is assumed to be a gospel of individual salvation and piety and the acquisition of personal holiness, so
we expect people in our churches to have individual gifts.
But when those gifts clash, we have discord.

Of all the themes that Jesus included in His preaching and
teaching, the importance of the community of the kingdom of
heaven—and in particular its importance in the here and now,
in the kingdom of heaven on earth—is not just paramount: It
is antithetical to the individualistic, pious, personal, salvific
message we call gospel today.

The kingdom of heaven is not a group of like-minded people working to a common goal. It has an individual leader —
a shepherd—and the flock of sheep he leads. It is a central
element of the gospel message that the sheep, the kingdom
people, are all things to all people. They become servants to
others, as the apostle Paul put it. They are less concerned
about their own personal relationship with God, of what God
thinks of them, of their standing before God, than they are
concerned about what is going on in the world and what is
happening in the lives of those who do not see themselves as
being part of the kingdom—those "others."

In fact, *everyone* must come through the Door of the fold.
Does that mean that everyone must become a Christian to get
through it? It might seem so, given that Jesus Himself said:

"I am the way, and the truth, and the life."[11]

But this statement is not about His person or His name. The
concepts it embodies are descriptive more than prescriptive:

The *way* to the kingdom is *via* the message of Jesus, but even if you don't know that Jesus was the messenger, His way to the kingdom of heaven is still open to you, His *truth* that He is your God is true for you, and His *life* of teaching, humility, love, and sacrifice is livable—to some extent—by you. The way is through Him because He is the dispenser of grace.

The parable of the Lost Sheep not only accurately describes the relationship between God and His people, the intimacy of that relationship, the nature of the voice of God, and God's persistence in communicating with us, but also the relationship between God and "other" people. But then how, if at all, does the relationship between God and those "others" differ from that between God and His "own" people?

Christians believe (because of the statement just discussed) that only through Jesus can anyone join the fold; only through Jesus can the process of oneness, of reconciliation, of joining the flocks, occur. Then what about all the people who lived before Jesus, or who even today live and die without ever hearing the name Jesus? The gate, the door, is the only way into the sheep pen—into the kingdom of heaven. If you climb through a window, you are just a fraud or a thief. Jesus said He was the Door and that anyone could go in and out.[12] Why in and out? How does this relate to "others"—to non-Christians? Jesus said:

> *"You have scattered the flock all over the world and I will gather the remnants and bring them back to the fold."*[13]

What about those other, lost, outsider, isolated sheep? How are they faring, and what needs to be done to bring them into the fold? Kingdom people don't seek conflict, not even with enemies, whom Jesus said to love. They do not set themselves apart on the basis of theology, liturgy, practice, or ritual. Rather, their kingdom principles reflect the life, the work, and the teaching of Jesus, who stood accused and convicted of spending time with sinners, with the poor and sick and oppressed, with those outside the mainstream.

Jesus steadfastly pleaded guilty as charged. He welcomed and reached out to all, in everyday life and not just in sermons on the Sabbath, with His core values of love, forgiveness, patience, and unselfishness. In the Lord's Prayer, He taught us to pray that the kingdom of heaven should be manifested here and now, on earth:

Thy kingdom come, thy will be done, on earth as it is in heaven.

Most Christian churches today teach that sanctification and salvation are achieved through personal holiness, which is actively to be sought, they say. The emphasis is on one's personal standing before God. This was not always the case. Centuries ago (and still more recently in other cultures) personal and religious identity was not individualistic. Until the Reformation, the mindset of Christendom was bound up with community, not with the individual. One belonged to a family, a class, a guild, a manorial estate, a government, a church. Such was the nature of society. There was "community belonging" at many levels, and it underwrote a person's identity. The substance of *being* was found in the social order of things.

But the Reformation changed the order of things. It not only changed a religious idea but the Western mindset as well. Martin Luther's idea of a priesthood of believers justified by faith and dependent only on the Scriptures inspired a movement that led away from a sense of belonging to a church that held the keys to salvation. Instead, it led toward a sense that personal salvation was a contract between oneself and God: God wants me to do certain things, I will respond,

God will correct me, refine me, educate me…. This is just between me and God.

This Reformatory mindset has so eroded community in the West that the most strongly held community we have left is the family, and even that is weak, compared to the extended family of early America. In Asia and other parts of the world, this is not yet so despite pressure from Western culture, and much of the structure of community remains intact there.

The gradual erosion of the concept of *belonging* in the West has brought us the emptiness we find in too many great cathedrals. There was a time when being excommunicated from the church was tantamount to a loss of salvation, of life, of personhood as one knew it. The church held the keys to heaven. That notion is lost today. Nobody fears the church any more. Excommunication is not the eternal death sentence, the loss of salvation, the consignment to the everlasting fires of hell, it once seemed to be.

Even in our evangelism, as we "share" the gospel with others, there seems to be little emphasis on community, on a requirement to extend ourselves on behalf of others. The idea is not to win others to a community or some kind of special status within the community; rather, it is about getting them to ditch the bad in their lives, to be baptized, to give their hearts to God, to learn how to pray more effectively, to learn to study the Bible. Jesus enjoined us to take the gospel of the kingdom of heaven to all the world, and then the End would come. It is specific about what should be taken: It is the gospel of the kingdom—*a community*—that should be taken to all the world.[14]

Sheep versus Goats

Notes to Chapter 3

[1] Matthew 18:10-13

[2] John 10:3-4

[3] Romans 9

[4] While both hail from the subfamily Caprinae, sheep and goats diverge at the genus level and arrive as distinct species. Sheep (*Ovis aries*) have 54 chromosomes; goats (*Capra aegagrus hircus*) have 60. Source: http://www.treehugger.com/natural-sciences/difference-between-sheep-and-goats.html

[5] Revelation 20:15

[6] Matthew 25:31-46

[7] Leviticus 16

[8] 1 Corinthians 3:12-16

[9] John 3:16-21

[10] The Book of John.

[11] John 14:6

[12] John 10

[13] Jeremiah 23:2

[14] Matthew 24

4

Me versus We

W HEN A RICH YOUNG ARISTOCRAT asked Jesus what must he do to achieve eternal life, Jesus left him no wiggle room. It was all or nothing. It was either "Serve yourself, or serve the community of the kingdom of heaven":

As He was setting out on a journey, a man ran up to Him and knelt before Him, and asked Him, "Good Teacher, what shall I do to inherit eternal life?" And Jesus said to him, "Why do you call Me good? No one is good except God alone. You know the commandments, 'Do not murder, Do not commit adultery, Do not steal, Do not bear false witness, Do not defraud, Honor your father and mother.'" And he said to Him, "Teacher, I have kept all these things from my youth up." Looking at him, Jesus felt a love for him and said to him, "One thing you lack: go and sell all you possess and give to the poor, and you will have treasure in heaven; and come, follow Me."

At this point, Jesus went from individualism to community, from a smaller to a larger perspective. This is the essence of the difference. But it was too much for the rich young man:

But at these words he was saddened, and he went away grieving, for he was one who owned much property.

And Jesus, looking around, said to His disciples, "How hard it will be for those who are wealthy to enter the kingdom of God!" The disciples were amazed at His words. But Jesus answered again and said to them, "Children, how hard it is to enter the kingdom of God! It is easier for a camel to go through the eye of a needle than for a rich man to enter the kingdom of God." They were even more astonished and said to Him, "Then who can be saved?"[1]

The rich young man chose his own individual interest over that of the community. Jesus invariably came down strongly in favor of community over individualism. Furthermore, He warned against ostentatious displays of one's individual service to community.

In the very center of the Sermon on the Mount He addressed the three central pillars common to all the major religions: Prayer, fasting, and the giving of alms. He pointed out that if you feel compelled to give alms you should do it in such a way that your left hand doesn't know what your right hand is doing. *Ditto* with prayer and fasting: Don't make a big deal of them. Yet all religions do precisely the opposite. Jesus scaled their importance way back:

"Beware of practicing your righteousness before men to be noticed by them; otherwise you have no reward with your Father who is in heaven.

"So when you give to the poor, do not sound a trumpet before you, as the hypocrites do in the synagogues and in the streets, so that they may be honored by men. Truly I say to you, they have their reward in full. But when you give to the poor, do not let your left hand know what your right hand is doing, so that your giving will be in secret; and your Father who sees what is done in secret will reward you.

"When you pray, you are not to be like the hypocrites; for they love to stand and pray in the synagogues and on the street corners so that they may be seen by men. Truly I say to you, they have their reward in full. But you, when you pray, go into your inner room, close your door and pray to your Father who is in secret, and your Father who sees what is done in secret will reward you.

"And when you are praying, do not use meaningless repetition as the Gentiles do, for they suppose that they will be heard for their many words. So do not be like them; for your Father knows what you need before you ask Him.[2]

By all means act with pious intent, but don't seek public recognition for it. In the kingdom of heaven salvation is a communal effort. It is not, as the core teaching of modern organized Christianity would have it, that we are judged on the basis of how pious we were in life. The Judgment scene is explicitly about what we did for our neighbors in the community of the kingdom of heaven on earth, not what we did to inflate our piety.

Jesus knew that in the process of doing things for others, we become better people, not obsessed over personal religious piety. When we unselfishly worry about our fellow human beings we subconsciously become better persons. Community and love transform not only the person helped but also the helper. In the community of the kingdom of heaven, the answer to the question Cain asked God of his brother Abel: "Am I my brother's keeper?"[3] is a resounding: "Yes!"

To Jesus, individualism was clearly a state of incompleteness. The idea that any one of us individually can represent any sort of self-contained, self-sufficient whole seems manifestly impossible. Each of us has different strengths, weaknesses, skills, and so on. Qualities such as creativity depend upon some sort of communal wholeness; they cannot exist in the vacuum of individualism. The central theme of the message and the ministry of Jesus is that community—the kingdom of heaven—is the body that brings the greatest wholeness and strength to the individual.

As we know from personality development and as we have seen with faith progression, communities have a sequence of maturation as well. M. Scott Peck described four stages of community development:[4]

1. *Pseudo community*, where everybody "plays nice." There are no major issues or strife, at least not openly. From the outside, it looks great, but it's a surface community only.

2. *Chaos*. To become a true community, a pseudo community must go through a period of major difficulty, of crisis. Crisis accelerates the process; otherwise, chaos can hang around for a while. Crisis cannot be overcome by action, by organization. It can only be overcome by passing through stage 3.

3. *Emptiness*, in which people empty themselves of their preconceptions, prejudices, needs, and desire for control. This leads to:

4. *True community*.

Much of the teaching of Jesus exemplifies these stages. Even His own closest community—the disciples—started as a pseudo community. It went through a leadership crisis when Jesus induced chaos by telling the disciples to reverse their preconceived notions—to hate their mother and brother, to disengage from community, to become vulnerable to their enemies, to turn the other cheek.

The community Jesus built was a true community of caring misfits, dissidents, ne'er-do-wells, and outcasts; of "other" sheep too different—too lost—to be normal members of the fold. In contrast, man-made communities are pseudo communities of like-minded people. Most religions consist of people who share common beliefs, understanding, rituals, liturgies, expectations, and so on. In contrast, Jesus' ministry was a priest's or a social worker's nightmare: A community of people from every different strain and background.

Religious communities have developed ways of dealing with what they perceive as threats from contrarian points of view and behaviors and from people who get out of line. Those methods are known variously as disfellowship, isolation, excommunication, shunning, etc. All churches have something like it. Excommunication in the Middle Ages was practically a death sentence. Some Amish communities still "shun" members who transgress the requirement to conform, as do the Jehovah's Witnesses (who refer to it as "disfellowshipping").

Jesus was negative about the idea of a kingdom of heaven based on like-mindedness, belief, and behavior:

"Not everyone who says to Me, 'Lord, Lord,' will enter the kingdom of heaven, but he who does the will of My Father who is in heaven will enter."[5]

There is apparently something more than belief and even action; something utterly *unlike* that is characteristic of the kingdom:

> *"Many will say to Me on that day, 'Lord, Lord, did we not prophesy in Your name, and in Your name cast out demons, and in Your name perform many miracles?' And then I will declare to them, 'I never knew you; depart from Me, you who practice lawlessness.'"*

You would think that those who prophesy, cast out demons, and perform many miracles all in God's name could be forgiven for thinking that the statement: "[H]e who does the will of My Father who is in heaven will enter" would apply very much to them. Yet there seems to be a contradiction between this passage and that below, taken from a chapter that talks about the richness and grace of God's mercy as a primary qualification for entry into the kingdom of heaven:

> *But now in Christ Jesus you who formerly were far off have been brought near by the blood of Christ.*[6]

Community building and peace are the work of Jesus.

In the Sermon on the Mount and particularly in the Lord's Prayer we find another characteristic of the kingdom of heaven seemingly antithetical to the kind of thinking we generally associate with commonality of belief in a religious community: In teaching the disciples how to pray, Jesus made the provocative statement that we should pray that...

> *Thy kingdom come, thy will be done, on earth as it is in Heaven.*

In other words, the kingdom of God on earth is run according to the will of God, not the will of Man. The will of God is community; the will of Man is self-centered individualism.

The parable of the Lost Sheep makes clear that isolation from community is a threat to eternal life. The dogged determination in the shepherd's pursuit to bring the errant individual back to the fold, back to the community, gives one a sense of how much is at stake; of how great is the need to protect the isolated individual.

Individualism was sharpened by the Reformation. Martin Luther was the champion of "righteousness by faith," making it our personal responsibility to approach God and contract with Him in order to be saved. This concept competed against Calvin's deterministic notion, voiced in vigorous debates (which precipitated the Renaissance), that God foreordains all things. Most Renaissance men would agree that virtually 100 percent of what happens to you in life is determined by your own choices, volition, and will; as opposed to being predetermined.

That thinking spilled over especially strongly into the New World. Today, the concept of individualism is more strongly held by Americans than any other nation. A majority (64 percent) of Americans believe in the notion of free will; that it is they themselves who determine their success in life. In contrast, a majority (72 percent) of Germans think it is determined by external forces. At the same time, the data show overwhelmingly that Germans have amongst the best opportunities for success in life and that the most important determinant is the education of the parents—it's not by exercising good judgment, etc.[7] A study by the Institute of Medicine reported that young Americans die at a higher rate and live in a poorer condition than their peers in other developed countries.[8]

The choices that young Americans make in terms of guns, motorcycle helmets, and seatbelt wearing put them at higher risk than their peers in other countries, because they are given the right of choice in such matters and Americans tend to believe there is something sacred about that right. Although one not infrequently hears an American give a nod to fatalism in saying such things as "Well, it wasn't meant to be" or "It wasn't in the cards," the ideology of individualism deeply affects their theological understandings. The inevitable, emerging, uncomfortable question for Americans is: Is individualism antithetical to the teaching of Jesus?

Many eastern cultures have a much stronger belief in determinism. The Turks have *kismet*. Their fate has been predetermined; they have no control over it. Something else is doing the control. Individual free will is subservient to the community's will, and what happens to the community strongly influences what happens to the individual.

In the garden of Eden, God was in control. Adam could not bargain with God. He had no choice about being brought into existence, or in whose image he was made, or in what he might or might not eat. He *had* to name the animals, he *had* to have a wife (he didn't ask for one), he was put to sleep and had a rib removed without informed consent. He had to *be*. God laid down the rules. When, through the serpent, Adam and Eve finally *did* discover that they had a will of their own and exercised it, God threw them out.

The core of the Lord's Prayer, *Thy will be done*, justifies the judgment passed on Adam and Eve. Subjection and submission to God's will also appeared in the garden of Gethsemane, when Jesus accepted God's will that He must suffer. But comfort will come:

Come to Me, all who are weary and heavy-laden, and I will give you rest.[9]

Jesus took responsibility for us, so we don't need to go it alone in life—Jesus is there to shoulder our burden, which is our individual self, and carry it back to the fold.

Members of the early Christian church were Jews. It was thus a community of members of like mind and culture, and it was wonderful:

> So then, those who had received his word were baptized; and that day there were added about three thousand souls. They were continually devoting themselves to the apostles' teaching and to fellowship, to the breaking of bread and to prayer.
>
> Everyone kept feeling a sense of awe; and many wonders and signs were taking place through the apostles. And all those who had believed were together and had all things in common; and they began selling their property and possessions and were sharing them with all, as anyone might have need. Day by day continuing with one mind in the temple, and breaking bread from house to house, they were taking their meals together with gladness and sincerity of heart, praising God and having favor with all the people. And the Lord was adding to their number day by day those who were being saved. [10]

This heartwarming picture of the early church reflects what M. Scott Peck would identify as pseudo community of people who shared a common background, heritage, way of life, set of beliefs, goals, and even possessions. They were of one mind. They loved it. And why not? There is nothing wrong with pseudo community in itself; the problem (if that is what it is) lies in what it leads to, which is: Chaos, the second stage of community-building.

Inevitably, non-Jews started to want to join a church so enticing. But the recruitment of people who were not like the Jewish members—especially, a hated Roman centurion[11]—

introduced discord. The Christian Jewish community in general (including even the apostle Peter) was aghast at its contamination by outsiders. Paul and Peter argued about whether Gentiles (non-Jews) should be allowed in. Paul was for, Peter was not, on the grounds that Gentiles did not observe the Jewish law.[12]

But Peter was given a lesson in what God thought of the law through a dream in which a basketful of strange creatures was lowered to earth from heaven. Some were creatures that the law forbade Jews from eating. But a voice told Peter to kill and eat them.[13] He refused at first, because in Jewish belief and law it would have made him unclean.

The dream was God's way of telling Peter that He wanted the community of faith to be inclusive, and Peter did then accept the Roman centurion and indeed baptized him. However, others continued to challenge Peter for accepting sheep who were not of the fold. Some brought the issue to a head by arguing that non-Jewish males should be required to undergo circumcision. Paul argued against that, too.[14]

So there was chaos in the early Church community; the chaos of ideas that drive people apart. This was quite unlike the chaos that follows a natural calamity, which tends to bring people together. A chaos of conflicting ideas and beliefs is destructive of pseudo community, yet it is only through the crucible of chaos that true community can be attained. The test of true community is whether the like-mindedness of pseudo community is exchanged for love, open acceptance of people and new ideas, and suspension of judgment.

Following chaos, the next phase in the transition to community is emptiness, which produces, and is revealed by, silence, the criterion for emptiness; or at least, one of the criteria. Some lines from T.S. Eliot's *Choruses* from his play *The*

Rock (which is itself grounded in Scripture) reflect this need for quiet, for contemplation, in our chaotic lifestyle:

> *The endless cycle of idea and action,*
> *Endless invention, endless experiment,*
> *Brings knowledge of motion, but not of stillness;*
> *Knowledge of speech, but not of silence;*
> *Knowledge of words, and ignorance of the Word.*
> *All our knowledge brings us nearer to death,*
> *But nearness to death no nearer to God.*
> *Where is the Life we have lost in living?*
> *Where is the wisdom we have lost in knowledge?*
> *Where is the knowledge we have lost in information?*[15]

All churches have people who do not think in quite the same way as the majority. The tendency is to ostracize them, to shun and disfellowship them in order to prevent them from contaminating the bigger community. How can churches overcome this so that new community can be born? Silence seems to be the answer. The ability to keep silent and *listen* in the midst of chaos may be the key to transitioning to true community. But it goes against our instinct, which is to speak up, to defend, to push back. Could churches initiate a process of emptiness intentionally, by designing silence/listening into their liturgy? A branch of the Quakers has done just that for a long time.[16]

The pseudo community thinks it needs to defend against sheep not of its fold. Churches fear that new ideas or new people will undermine their solidarity, unity, thinking, and sense of rightness. The group thinks it has a moral obligation to protect these things. But a condition for entry to true community is not the elimination of different ideas; rather, it is a recognition by the group of the existence of some under-lying unifying principle that overrides differences and makes them irrelevant. To Christians, the unifying principle should be that everyone is saved by the grace of God.

Is there some deliberate intervention that could drive a pseudo community into emptiness, the precursor of true community? If true community could be achieved through intentionality and deliberation, it would clearly be highly desirable. But is it even possible?

The way to true community for the early Christian church involved that period of silence among the people having just witnessed the arguments and the chaos among their leaders.[17] But God was the author of the chaos. It was He who allowed and even enforced the idea that outside influences were to be brought in to the church. He promised a specific intervention —bringing in the Gentiles—to do this.[18] God introduced chaos in order to get to true community.

We ought to be aware of what is going on with those different "others" trying to enter our own church communities. The principle (enshrined in Scripture[19]) seems to be that those who are in the process of turning to God (and for that reason alone want to be brought into our church) should not be given any trouble and should not be required to conform to our ways.

But Scripture also makes clear that those responsible for dealing with the chaos must be credentialed in some way.[20] In the early church, the credential was that they must have risked their life for the sake of Jesus. So this is not a task for just anybody; it is only for people who have some very special relationship with God.

The leaders of the early church concluded that the rules of a Christian community should be few and general.[21] This didn't make all of the trouble and chaos go away; it persists today in our churches, where outsiders are seldom welcomed with no strings attached.

The Western mind shuns emptiness, which it equates with an undesirable, unnatural state of boredom, alienation, and isolation. But the Eastern mind equates emptiness with opportunity, so embraces it. To the Eastern mind, emptiness is a void to be filled, by means of meditation, with something better than what was there before.

But emptiness could open the door to something worse than was there before, as it did for Jesus when He emptied Himself in the empty desert and Satan tried to fill the void, tempting Him with power and material rewards.[22]

It seems that the great temptation that arises during emptiness is to fill it with material "stuff" such as bread and protective measures. But Jesus wanted only to fill Himself with spiritual things. In the desert, He sought to replenish the Divinity He had become emptied of in order to be human— though an humble and obedient one.[23] Humility in servitude is a key element of the emptiness that leads to that true community, the kingdom of heaven.

The desert is a common Scriptural metaphor for emptiness. Perhaps Scripture can help illumine whether we should all seek the desert experience, whether it is vital to us personally and/or on a community level, and how it is possible to enter into that experience.

Moses, who was sent into the desert for 40 years to find God, found Him in the form of a burning bush. Moses experienced the desert again during the Exodus of the Israelites from Egypt, where they had been slaves. The journey through the desert, back to the Promised Land, gave the Israelites plenty of experience of emptiness. But so great was the disunity and chaos in their community that they needed even more emptiness, so God sent them back into the desert until true community re-emerged among them, before He let them enter the Promised Land.

After his successful invocation of God's power on Mount Carmel, Elijah fled into the desert to escape the wrath of Jezebel, the pagan foreign queen of the Hebrew king, who wanted to kill Elijah for thwarting her efforts to suborn her husband. He encountered God there in the desert again, but this time God did not manifest in grand style—not as a whirlwind or thunder or storm—but instead as a still small voice, which said to Elijah essentially: "What are you doing here in the desert? I don't want you here—I want you some-where else."

The prospective king David also retreated to the desert to hide from the reigning king Saul. John the Baptist proclaimed a ministry in the desert and fulfilled Isaiah's prophecy of a voice crying in the wilderness: "Prepare ye the way of the Lord." We are given a picture of his privations there—a camelhair coat, a minimal diet. Paul the Apostle passed through the desert on the road to Damascus, and met God in the form of a blinding light. Soon thereafter he retreated to the Arabian desert for a three-year period of introspection.

In reminding us that we are familiar with knowledge but not with stillness, with speech but not with silence, T.S. Eliot also reminded us that all of us are influenced by relationships and stimuli antithetical to emptiness. To avoid such influences, many early Christian fathers isolated themselves in the desert. Perhaps the most notable of these was Simeon Stylites, who sat on a pillar outside the town of Aleppo for 37 years. The pillar was heavily damaged in a rocket attack in 2016.[24]

An organization in New Jersey called the *Hermits of Bethlehem in the Heart of Jesus* offers a five-day "silent retreat"—a hermit-like solitude, in which the guest is alone and must remain silent. Its literature calls it "a desert-like experience" aimed at a "deeper conversion." Do we all need something like this, as individuals and as communities, in order to reach true community?

Pseudo communities are closed to outsiders. Closed systems in physics are subject to entropy, chaos, and breakdown assured by the Second Law of Thermodynamics.[25] In contrast, true communities are open systems, not subject to the Second Law. (One wonders if physics could shed light on the notion of emptiness, and especially on how to engineer it, if engineering it is desirable. After all, a barren, empty, arid, lifeless environment is easy to replicate in the laboratory.)

The fear that can drive us to seek refuge in the desert is related to the loss of something important, something critical to our security and self-esteem. It also seems to be responsible for the chaos we experience individually and communally. At the same time, the desert itself can be a fearsome place, a veritable "valley of the shadow of death."

Fear is one of the strongest motivators and a powerful emotion. Our fight or flight response to it shows its importance to survival. Fear is a critical component in Maslow's famous hierarchy of human physiological, security, social, self-esteem, self-actualization needs. Successful living requires a progressive freedom from fear through this hierarchy in order to reach self-actualization.

The key to the desert—to emptiness—is not to fear it. How hard can that be? A National Institute of Mental Health survey[26] reported that 60 percent of the things we fear never actually happen, 30 percent have already happened, 90 percent are insignificant, and 88 percent of things we fear about our health will never happen. Seven million people have been diagnosed with a phobia, of which the most common is fear of public speaking (74 percent), followed by fear of death (68 percent), followed by fear of spiders, darkness, heights, people/social situation, flying, confined spaces, open spaces, and thunder and lightning. One is struck by the triviality of many of these fears. It reminds one of Roosevelt's dictum that "the only thing we have to fear is fear itself."

There are at least 200 references to fear and its antidotes in Scripture. The most famous is the 23rd Psalm, which describes the orator's lack of fear in the desert—"the valley of the shadow of death." His confidence is supreme and absolute:

The Lord is my shepherd; I shall not want.
He maketh me to lie down in green pastures: he leadeth me beside the still waters.
He restoreth my soul: he leadeth me in the paths of righteousness for his name's sake.
Yea, though I walk through the valley of the shadow of death, I will fear no evil: for thou art with me; thy rod and thy staff they comfort me.
Thou preparest a table before me in the presence of mine enemies: thou anointest my head with oil; my cup runneth over.
Surely goodness and mercy shall follow me all the days of my life: and I will dwell in the house of the Lord for ever. [27]

Some of the disciples were experienced sailors, yet even they were afraid when a storm beset their boat on the Sea of Galilee. Their cries woke the sleeping Jesus, who proceeded literally to calm the storm,[28] which frightened the disciples even more. It's not the only instance of God's causing fear, and of the chaos that can ensue.

Metaphorically, we are all floundering on the sea of life; yet, like Jesus in the boat, God seems to be asleep when we need Him. We tend to need Him when we are afraid. It seems as if one of our great needs is to empty ourselves of fear that may be real, or imagined, or even unspoken.

When Jesus said there were others who must be brought into His fold He was talking about introducing something new, something unknown, into the community. We tend to find the new, the unknown, to be disturbing, even horrifying. Pseudo communities fear disruption of their *status quo*. New ideas are particularly troubling, especially to a church community. People grow distressed merely at the introduction of a new hymnal, or the modernizing of archaic but comfortingly familiar liturgy.

New relationships also bring challenges. We are discomfited by people who don't look, think, and act like us. They seem to threaten our community, our faith, the way things are. To enter into true community, we must empty ourselves of this fear. Family seems to be closer to true community than, say, church. Fear is less easily provoked in a family than it is in a church. The challenge for pseudo communities is to eliminate, accommodate, or set aside fear. How? Is faith the antidote to fear? In the storm, Jesus asked the disciples why they were afraid and why they had so little faith. When Peter tried to walk on the water and—terrified—began to sink, Jesus again responded: "Why are you afraid, you men of little faith?" [29]

But faith is not the only antidote to fear. Paul said that love is an antidote, too.[30] He was speaking not about everyday love in a general sense, but about love for one's brother, a perfect love that does not allow fear to get in its way.[31] This love is beautiful, but it is demanding and radical as well. It is patient, kind, modest, and includes everyone. It is not jealous, boastful, or arrogant, is not provoked, does not hold a grudge, In Paul's almost poignant yet inspiring words, it is a love that "bears all things, believes all things, hopes all things, endures all things."[32] It demands a release of our ideas and prejudices, of supposed truths and knowledge and expectations, and it never fails.[33]

Paul contrasted love with knowledge. Are they the opposite ends of a spectrum? Must we sacrifice, on the altar of love, ideas and "truths" we have long held to be self-evident, in order to establish true community? M. Scott Peck wrote with respect to theological truth (and this probably applies to political belief also) that we feel uncomfortable with people who do not share our beliefs because it calls our beliefs into question. To resolve the discomfort, we would rather convert the other to our beliefs which, if successful, then serves to reinforce the rightness of our beliefs.[34]

Must we pursue truth to a fault, in order to arrive at the necessary stage of emptiness on the road to true community? Not necessarily. Theologist Gordon Smith warned that zealotry and a "passion for truth"—even a real truth—"blinds us to other perspectives and prevents us from disagreeing graciously and from learning from others—that is, others who see differently than we do." He added: "A genuine love of truth is always complemented by humility, evident in a gracious and teachable spirit."[35]

How humble? The apostle Paul made himself "a slave to all." When with Jews, he behaved like a Jew; with Gentiles, like a Gentile. With the weak, he behaved like one of them. He became "all things to all men," in order to save some.[36]

If beliefs, ideas, and notions are the pillars of community, is it possible to hold onto them and at the same empty oneself of them, in order to come to true community? What is at risk in the emptiness of true community?

Jesus made the pillars of community come alive through parable and declarative statements. When the disciples asked him: "Who is the greatest in the kingdom of heaven?" Jesus answered that unless people became like children, they would not even get in. The primary attribute we ascribe to children is innocence. It seems therefore that innocence is one of the pillars of community. The question the disciples were really asking was: "Who is in charge in the kingdom of heaven?" The response—that innocence, a state of being childlike, empty, and un-self-aware is in charge—is puzzling.

Taken together with the pillar of the authority of innocence, Jesus' statement that "unless one is born again he cannot see the kingdom of God"[37] seems to imply that a transformation must take place; a transformation that reverses all our acquired knowledge, experience, sophistication, and worldliness.

In the beginning, Adam and Eve were naked and unashamed, just like newborn babies—until they ate of the fruit of the tree of knowledge. How could one become like a baby again, feeling not the least bit of embarrassment about running around naked? A reversal to this degree of child-likeness is essential to entry to the kingdom of heaven.

Jesus was specific about the necessary degree of childlikeness when He said we must be born again. One might conclude that He was talking about a newborn rather than about a child, because we think of a "child" as having attained some years of age and an accompanying level of development, whereas a newborn has none. It is utterly innocent, dependent, guileless, and perhaps fearless. All this soon begins to disintegrate, however. Indeed, one of the natural processes in bringing up children is to *teach* them knowledge and lead them toward independence, and to teach them fear to help them survive as their independence grows: "You will get hurt or even die if you run into the road, or talk to a stranger, or touch the fire," etc.

The story of the birth of Jesus Christ might offer insights into the meaning of being born again. As a story, it is compelling and full of enchantment for young and old, with its shepherds and wise men, cattle, donkeys, manger, inn, star of Bethlehem, angels singing, intrigue, suspense, and even sex and violence.

But as Protestants in particular tell it, the key player—the leading actress—in the Christmas story does not figure much in it. The Virgin Mary appears only three times in the top ten Christmas carols.[38] If there were no manger, no donkeys, and no stars, there would still be a Christmas story. But if there were no Mary, there would not.

Mary was a child of only 12–13 years of age when the angel Gabriel came to tell her she was chosen to bear the Son of the Most High. Though already betrothed to Joseph, she was still a virgin, and "very perplexed."[39] She was probably old enough to know how babies were made and to know that she could not be both a virgin *and* a mother.

In the end, Mary responded with humility and acquiescence, but she did not seem fully to fathom the magnitude of what was happening (which was surely unfathomable, after all). Like Mary, we too are but innocent tools in the hands of God. We are to receive God's grace without expecting it, without asking for it, and without understanding it.

The last verse of the carol *O Little Child of Bethlehem* goes:

> *O holy Child of Bethlehem*
> *Descend to us, we pray*
> *Cast out our sin and enter in*
> *Be born in us today*
> *We hear the Christmas angels*
> *The great glad tidings tell*

O come to us, abide with us
Our Lord Emmanuel

This is the essence of the Christmas story. Through re-birth, each of us becomes brother or sister to one another and with Jesus and God. This is not the work of ovary and sperm; it is an act of grace. It is a new divine light implanted in us by the Holy Spirit.

Just as He chose Mary, God chooses us. We don't choose Him. Like Mary, we are His tool, He is not our tool. Like Mary, we must allow the Holy Spirit to enter in—we must bear and give birth to the God within us. It will fill us with grace and produce a new life within us, making us be born again into the kingdom of heaven, into the community of brotherhood and sisterhood. Woe betide anyone who tries to thwart the entry of the Holy Spirit into others: "it would be better for him to have a heavy millstone hung around his neck, and to be drowned in the depth of the sea."[40]

This shocking language is *meant* to shock, in order to emphasize that we are personally responsible for the spiritual well being of others. In a community, we have a responsibility for each other's spiritual development and spiritual life and are expected to be tolerant towards others and accommodate their spiritual needs. When we abrogate that responsibility, we become "stumbling blocks," a phrase used more than a dozen times in Scripture in referring to the relationship between someone who is spiritually mature and someone who is not. Paul elaborated this vital principle at length, saying that since God accepts the meat-eater and vegetarian alike, so should we. Food and drink matter not to God. The important things are: "Righteousness and peace and joy in the Holy Spirit"; that whatever we do, we do it for God; and that, above all, we do not judge others.[41] We should put love before knowledge and God before idols.[42]

Scripture gives guidance on what may be eaten and drunk, what days are sacred, etc., but we should be careful not to let such details become bones of contention, Instead, we should focus on the key instruction of Jesus: "Don't be a stumbling block to each other."

In the kingdom of heaven—indeed, in any true spiritual community—we are not alone. I am responsible for you, and you are responsible for me. We are each responsible for one another. We stand before God to be judged on how we treated one another. We must show that we have done our part to have served as God's eyes, ears, hands, and feet in caring for each other.

This is really quite a different understanding of judgment from the common understanding of it today, because the context is clearly not judgment of you as an individual but judgment of your relationship with others. The context in which you stand before God on the day of judgment is your having been a stumbling block, or not, to somebody else; an enabler or disabler of spiritual growth in others. Whether or not you believe that eating pork is clean or right, I have a duty to respect your belief and refrain from doing things I know will offend you (such as eating, or refusing to eat, pork).[43]

All of us have different ideas about what is right and wrong in terms of superficial behaviors such as eating pork. But we have responsibility for others in this regard. To those others, eating pork might not be considered superficial. We "shall not curse a deaf man, nor place a stumbling block before the blind.[44] The verse is meant metaphorically; clearly, it would be cruel and inhumane to put obstacles in front of blind people. What is it that is blinding you and me, and how may we not offend or disable one another by putting some sort of stumbling block before one another?

Paul talked a lot about freedom and liberty in Jesus.[45] You are free to do whatever you want, eat whatever you want, go wherever you want; there is no such thing as pollution. But if your brother thinks that there is, you must respect his belief and not be a stumbling block to him.

You and I are linked in our relationship with God. Ours is not just an individual, one-on-one, relationship with God. In the end, judgment is not about your personal piety, purity, and righteousness, but about your relationship with others.[46] And in that context, Jesus stated that what you do for the least of his brothers, you do for him.

Jesus was not in the fire and brimstone business, yet He described stumbling blocks in language so graphic and so horrific as to sound almost un-Jesus-like:

> *If your hand or your foot causes you to stumble, cut it off and throw it from you; it is better for you to enter life crippled or lame, than to have two hands or two feet and be cast into the eternal fire. If your eye causes you to stumble, pluck it out and throw it from you. It is better for you to enter life with one eye, than to have two eyes and be cast into the fiery hell.[47]*

What did He mean? It sounds like the sternest of commands to shun evil and do good; but unlike the community-oriented command to take responsibility for the spiritual development and spiritual life and accommodate the spiritual needs of others, this command seems to be a call for *self*-responsibility, *self*-control, and *self*-judgment.

The lesson Jesus taught to the rich young aristocrat and all of us who—like him—see ourselves as self-reliant and law-abiding, is that we are incapable of keeping the law, therefore we *must* rely on God's grace. The Pharisees tried to overcome this obstacle by dumbing down the law so they could comfortably live within its bounds. But it was not real law.

The real law, as the apostle Paul told us, is a good and pro-ductive thing. It serves as a mirror showing us our clinical condition of being fallen. But if you want to try to live by it, if you look in the mirror hoping to see a righteous reflection, then you must be perfect—which is impossible.

Individualism, it seems, is fine provided it is used in the ser-vice of others. It seems also that the sheep of Jesus's fold are indeed successful community builders insofar as they do not have socioeconomic classes and they share a sort of owner-ship of the ultimate means of production: The grace of God.

Communism has become a dirty word, mostly because of monstrosities perpetrated in its name by the likes of Stalin and Mao. This is not a political book, but Scripture is quite clear that the society—the kingdom of heaven on earth—ad-vocated by Jesus is closer to the Maoist philosophy: "From each according to his ability; to each according to his needs" than to the capitalism that produces rich young aristocrats unwilling to share their wealth in any but a token way.

The point is important because it is true according to Scrip-ture *and* because it provides guidance as we face the fact of a large and growing disparity between rich and poor in modern society. The disparity will grow as increasingly intelligent and autonomous machines put more and more people out of work, and it could be calamitous in a global civilization that has permitted the proliferation of weapons of terrible destruc-tive power. To the extent the proliferation of such weapons is managed without regard to principles of love and care for others, catastrophe is inevitable. Scripture is a divine legacy of these timeless principles to future generations. It is so be-cause the kingdom of heaven is built on the eternal bedrock of God's grace.

Me versus We

Notes to Chapter 4

[1] Mark 10:17-26

[2] Matthew 6:1-8

[3] Genesis 4:9. Cain, who had just killed his brother Abel, asked this disingenuous rhetorical question when God asked him where Abel was.

[4] Peck, M. Scott (1987). *The Different Drum: Community-Making and Peace.* New York: Touchstone.

[5] Matthew 7:21-23

[6] Ephesians 2:13

[7] Pew Research Center, 2011. "The American-Western European Values Gap." Published online, November 17, at http://www.pewglobal.org/files/2011/11/Pew-Global-Attitudes-Values-Report-FINAL-November-17-2011-10AM-EST1.pdf

[8] Institute of Medicine, 2013. "U.S. Health in International Perspective: Shorter Lives, Poorer Health" Published online September 1 at https://iom.nationalacademies.org/Reports/2013/US-Health-in-International-Perspective-Shorter-Lives-Poorer-Health/Report-Brief010913.aspx

[9] Matthew 11:28

[10] Acts 2:41

[11] Acts 10

[12] Galatians 2:11-21

[13] Acts 10:9-16

[14] Acts 15:1-11

[15] Available at http://www.westminster.edu/staff/brennie/wisdoms/eliot1.htm among many other links.

[16] Their worship consists primarily of "expectant waiting," reflecting the Psalmist's call: "Be still and know that I am God" (Psalm 46:10). Marsha D. Holliday wrote:

> We meet in plain, unadorned rooms because we have found that, in such places, we are less distracted from hearing that still small voice. There are no pulpits in our meeting rooms because we minister to each other. Our benches or chairs face each other because we are all equal before God. We have no prearranged prayers, readings, sermons, hymns, or musical orchestrations because we wait for God's leadings (guidance and direction) and power in our lives.
>
> During worship, a message may come to us. Friends have found that messages may be for our personal reflection or for sharing on another occasion. Or they may be a leading to stand and speak. Friends value spoken messages that come from the heart and are prompted by the Spirit, and we also value the silence we share together. Following a spoken message, we return to the silence to examine ourselves in the Light of that message." (https://www.fgc-quaker.org/resources/silent-worship-and-quaker-values)

[17] Acts 15:12

[18] John 10:16

[19] Specifically, in Acts 15.

[20] Ephesians 6:1-9

[21] 2 Corinthians 3:1-3

[22] Matthew 4:1-11

[23] Philippians 2:5-8

[24] http://www.telegraph.co.uk/news/2016/05/13/syrian-monastery-where-st-simeon-sat-on-a-pillar-for-four-decade/

[25] The second law of thermodynamics states that the total entropy of an isolated system never decreases, because isolated systems always evolve toward thermodynamic equilibrium, the state with maximum entropy. *Source:* Wikipedia)

[26] National Institute of Mental Health study report dated April 27, 2015 cited at http://www.statisticbrain.com/fear-phobia-statistics/.

[27] The 23rd psalm is perhaps most impactful when read in the majestic prose of the King James Version of the Bible, as shown here. Psalm 27 offers sentiments similar to Psalm 23.

[28] Mark 4:35-41

[29] Matthew 8:26

[30] 1 John 4:18

[31] 2 Timothy 1:7

[32] 1 Corinthians 13:4-7

[33] 1 Corinthians 13:8

---

[34] Peck, M. Scott. 1987. *The Different Drum: Community Making and Peace.* New York: Touchstone. p. 97.

[35] Smith, Gordon T. 2011. *Courage and Calling: Embracing Your God-Given Potential.* Downers Grove IL: InterVarsity Press. p. 88.

[36] 1 Corinthians 9:19-22

[37] Spoken to Nicodemus; John 3:3.

[38] The ten are:
    i.   *It Came Upon a Midnight Clear*
    ii.   *Silent Night*
    iii.   *Angels We Have Heard On High*
    iv.   *Joy To the World*
    v.   *Hark the Herald Angels Sing*
    vi.   *O Come All Ye Faithful*
    vii.   *Away In a Manger*
    viii.   *The Little Town of Bethlehem*
    ix.   *The First Noël*
    x.   *Angels From the Realm Of Glory*

[39] Luke 1:26-38

[40] Matthew 18:4-6

[41] Romans 14

[42] 1 Corinthians 8

[43] Romans 14:19-21

[44] Leviticus 19:14

[45] 1 Corinthians 8

[46] This is clear from Matthew 25.

[47] Matthew 18:7-11

5

Father versus Son

GRACE IS THE MEANS by which God shows His love for fallen mankind. So in essence grace is a product of God's love, or is perhaps simply synonymous with it.

The angel who showed up at the birth of Jesus said:

Fear not, for I bring you good news of great joy.[1]

The "good news" was that God loved us enough to send His son to us. This was, and is, news that should bring us a great deal of joy. Religion brings with it a certain baggage, a sort of yoke, but joy can bear and lift that burden. Surely we should rejoice in a God who loves us so much that He gives His grace to us for free, even if we don't deserve it. This is difficult for us to understand. It sounds like the proverbial free lunch, something for nothing. We distrust such promises.

Yet it is precisely what the gospel of grace, the gospel of good news, brings.

All the great religions emphasize the importance of doing something to make ourselves pleasing and acceptable to God. In the Sermon on the Mount, Jesus talked about three things we do to please God, three elements of religious ritual and piety: Prayer, alms-giving, and fasting. Christians often feel they should be fasting more, praying more, and giving more; for God, with God, and to God.

Grace makes this effort irrelevant, in the end, to salvation, but don't we have a duty to try to deserve grace by overcoming our weaknesses, our tendencies to sinfulness, and our natural inclination to selfishness? Should we not use the power of our free will to make good choices, to allow God to work for us, and to follow other such common religious exhortations? If we do, does it make a difference? Has going to church, temple, or mosque made you a better person today than you were ten years ago; less prone to sin?

Many of us, I suspect, cannot answer an honest "Yes" to that question. Even if I were to see a little bit of progress in myself, I would still be a long way from the mark set by Jesus when He said: "...you must be perfect as your father in heaven is perfect."[2]

In so saying, Jesus shined a great light on the issue of law-keeping, especially for the self-righteous. But for those who feel they are sinners He preached a gospel of grace and freedom from guilt, and sought to dissuade the self-righteous that their way was a valid and viable route to salvation.

Grace is given freely and is all but impossible to escape. The Apostle Paul said that love bears, believes, hopes, and endures all things.[3] Grace is the side of God's love that we, in our state of having fallen from it, tend to see. This is the extent and the pervasiveness of grace: It is all embracing, it is all things to all people at all times, and—excepting only those guilty of the unpardonable sin—it cannot be escaped.

Having just delivered a schizophrenic talk about wanting and trying to do the right thing but being thwarted by his human nature,[4] Paul painted a moving portrayal of the grace of God, ending with some of the most encouraging words in the Bible, words that convey an unfathomable inclusiveness:

For I am convinced that neither death nor life nor angels... nor any other creative thing.... can separate us from the love of God.[5]

That God's ubiquitous love might be cheapened by our efforts—that our work could diminish God's grace—is a concept so startling that it took some convincing even for Paul, and it certainly does for us. Unearned grace seems, on the face of it, to be too cheap to be true. But the grace Jesus described is not.

He made this point in the parable of the Prodigal Son. We often think of grace as being about forgiveness, but in that parable, the father completely ignored his prodigal younger son's request for forgiveness and instead called for a celebration. The dutiful elder brother of the prodigal son complained of unequal treatment. Unlike his brother, *he* had worked hard to please his father, yet *he* was never given a fatted calf. His father completely ignored the point. The parable emphasizes the ubiquity of grace and exposes its extravagance.

Grace is a bit like oxygen: All around us, free, essential for life, and in unlimited supply. Its intake is as natural as breathing. Physical exertion requires more oxygen—but here the metaphor breaks down because grace requires no effort.

Is there a spiritual equivalent to putting a plastic bag over one's head to deprive oneself of God's oxygen—his grace? Is this the unpardonable sin? Three parables may help to answer these questions. The context for all three was that Jesus was attracting sinners to Him, and the Pharisees and the scribes didn't like that. He addressed their concerns through three parables: The Lost Sheep, in which He said there was more value to God in one repentant sinner than in ninety-nine righteous persons who need no repentance; the Lost Coin, which repeats the principle but with a different metaphor; and the Prodigal Son, which elaborated in depth on the principle. Here is the parable of the Prodigal Son:

A man had two sons. The younger of them said to his father, "Father, give me the share of the estate that falls to me." So he divided his wealth between them. And not many days later, the younger son gathered everything together and went on a journey into a distant country, and there he squandered his estate with loose living. Now when he had spent everything, a severe famine occurred in that country, and he began to be impoverished. So he went and hired himself out to one of the citizens of that country, and he sent him into his fields to feed swine. And he would have gladly filled his stomach with the pods that the swine were eating, and no one was giving anything to him. But when he came to his senses, he said, "How many of my father's hired men have more than enough bread, but I am dying here with hunger! I will get up and go to my father, and will say to him, 'Father, I have sinned against heaven, and in your sight; I am no longer worthy to be called your son; make me as one of your hired men.'" So he got up and came to his father. But while he was still a long way off, his father saw him and felt compassion for him, and ran and embraced him and kissed him. And the son said to him, "Father, I have sinned against heaven and in your sight; I am no longer worthy to be called your son." But the father said to his slaves, "Quickly bring out the best robe and put it on him, and put a ring on his hand and sandals on his feet; and bring the fattened calf, kill it, and let us eat and celebrate; for this son of mine was dead and has come to life again; he was lost and has been found." And they began to celebrate.

Now his older son was in the field, and when he came and approached the house, he heard music and dancing. And he summoned one of the servants and began inquiring what these things could be. And he said to him, "Your brother has come, and your father has killed the fattened calf because he has received him back safe and sound." But he became angry and was not willing to go in; and his father came out and began pleading with him. But he answered and said to his father, "Look! For so many years I have been serving you and I have never neglected a command of yours; and yet you have never given me a young goat, so that I might celebrate with my friends; but when this son of yours came, who has devoured your wealth with prostitutes, you killed the fattened calf for him." And he said to him, "Son, you have always been with me, and all that is mine is yours. But we had to celebrate and rejoice, for this brother of yours was dead and has begun to live, and was lost and has been found."

To put this parable in cultural and historical context:

- A younger son's request to be given his share of an estate while the father was still alive would have been seen, at that time and in that culture, to be highly disrespectful; yet *this* father granted the request.

- The son went a long way away from home, to a distant country. The distance is significant.

- Just when the prodigal had squandered all his money, famine struck the far country and he ended up on skid row, sharing a trough with pigs.

- When he came to his senses (or "returned to himself" in the Greek translation, which suggests that he had left not only his father but also left himself) he assessed only his own personal need, his desperate hunger, his privation. He seemed concerned about nothing and no-one else.

- His plea to his father was similar to that made by the Pharaoh to Moses after plagues struck Egypt:

"I have sinned this time; the Lord is the righteous one, and I and my people are the wicked ones. Make supplication to the Lord, for there has been enough of God's thunder and hail...." [6]

So the idea was not original to the prodigal son. Was it true repentance?—Not in the case of the Pharaoh. Was it a calculated approach by the prodigal, perhaps suggested to him by his reading of Pharaoh?

The key character in the parable is the father, who longed so much for his son's return that he *ran* to him—an undignified act for an elder. He ignored his son's attempted apology and called instead for a celebration. He ordered: A robe to cover his son's filthy rags, thereby visibly restoring his son's nobility; a ring to restore some sort of authority to him; and a pair of sandals, since only servants went barefoot. These are all evidence that he was being reinstated as a son and not merely as a servant.

The elder son's complaints are similar to the complaints of the scribes and Pharisees when they accused Jesus of consorting with sinners. Evidently, the elder son also had a less than perfect relationship with his father, since he became angry with his father and refused to participate in the celebration of his brother's return. Oh, the unfairness of forgiveness! The injustice of grace!

The elder son had a justification for his anger ready to give his father. He painted himself as having acted humbly, almost in the role of a servant (and recall that it was servitude that the prodigal son intended to ask his father for, but his father never gave him the chance). But he, the dutiful elder son, never once in his law-abiding life was feted with a fatted calf.

His father responded that there was no option but to rejoice. Joy was imperative and inevitable. He said in effect: "He was dead, he was lost, and now he is back and he lives again. So we must celebrate." It is a story of grace.

Throughout the ages, much discussion has taken place about the role of grace and works in our salvation. The Bible says:

> For by grace you have been saved through faith; and that not of yourselves, it is the gift of God; not as a result of works, so that no one may boast. (Ephesians 2:8-9)

But the Bible also says that we are judged by our works, for example:

> For we must all appear before the judgment seat of Christ, so that each one may be recompensed for his deeds in the body, according to what he has done, whether good or bad.[7]

So which is it? Grace or works? The prodigal's brother presented his efforts—his diligent work for his father—as the criterion for judgment. He believed *he* deserved the fatted calf, not his wayward brother, because of this. Similarly, in the parable of the laborers in the vineyard,[8] some laborers worked all day while others worked only an hour, yet all received the same pay at the end of the day. Those who worked all day expected, like the prodigal's elder brother, to be judged and rewarded on the basis of their work.

We seem thus to be faced with two choices: Either to put forward our own work and effort for evaluation into the judgment, or to accept the grace of God. If we deliver a fair day's work we will receive a fair day's pay for our effort, but

God will make up the difference for those who, for reasons we are in no position to judge, fail to put in a fair day's work. In other words, we are *both* judged by our works *and* saved by grace.

Our problem is that although we are all guilty of sin, we want to plead not guilty to it, citing our works as evidence. The Judge does not disregard such evidence and, indeed, is clearly pleased by it. But if, instead, we plead guilty and throw ourselves on the mercy of the court, He lets us off anyway.

Doctors are often accused (perhaps often rightly) of playing God in the sense of lording it over their domain, but in one sense the analogy holds true: A doctor seeks to restore *every* patient to good health, regardless of any abuse to which patients subject themselves. The doctor will work just as hard to treat the liver cancer of the hopeless alcoholic couch potato as that of the physically active teetotaler. A doctor's compassion is absolute and non-judgmental, not only as required by the profession but also, in most cases (I believe), as dictated by the doctor's heart.

In sum, we all avoid punishment for our sins—we are all saved—by virtue of God's grace. Those of us with fewer works need, and get, more grace than those with more works; but in the end, all of us are saved from the consequences of our sin.

But if grace is ubiquitous and all-encompassing, how can there be an unpardonable sin? Christians have always lived in fear of committing it. So what is it? Jesus explained that while any sin including blasphemy would be forgiven, one form of blasphemy—blasphemy against the Holy Spirit— would not. Say what you like about me in my human form, He said, but don't speak against the Holy Spirit.[9]

Blasphemy is contempt for God, a posture of hostility taken by a creature against its Creator. Blasphemy against the Holy Spirit is a denial of the power of the Holy Spirit within us. We sometimes hide that inner light under a bushel, or we put a plastic bag over it to deprive it of oxygen and the spark dies out. We find some way to switch it off.

This light of life and of Man began at the Creation.[10] The Book of Acts describes it as a "flame." It is a penetrating light that overcomes darkness. John called it "the true Light which, coming into the world, enlightens every man."[11] It is also called "the Spirit" [12, 13, 14] and an "eternity" set within Man's heart.[15] By whatever name, the Holy Spirit seems to function as a transceiver set to the frequency of God, establishing a connection and enabling communication with Him. Connectivity with God has important functions as a judge of sin, giving mankind a sense of his eternal need of grace, and as a guide to truth.[16]

Although grace needs this inner light—this sensor, this director and guide—to fulfill our connection with God, and although it is programmed into us, free will gives us the ability to switch it off, to disconnect from God. Our natural condition (which is also a supernatural condition) is to be connected to God, so choosing to disconnect from it is not a common act of wickedness but an unnatural act and a momentous commitment to self-righteousness and independence. It is a conviction of not needing God or His grace. It is the belief that *I know what is right*, which in turn leads me to think I am without sin, like the Pharisee who prayed, more to himself than to God: 'God, I thank You that I am not like other people: swindlers, unjust, adulterers, or even like this tax collector. I fast twice a week; I pay tithes of all that I get.'"[17] This is the condition of people who commit the Unpardonable Sin.[18] To claim that we have no sin is to deceive ourselves, to deny the truth, to call God a liar. To admit our sins is enough to merit redemption.[19]

Self-righteousness switches off our transceiver and masks our natural state of being a sinner in need of God's grace. In turning off the inner light, we also deprive others of the grace we are expected to pass on through serving them—through letting the light shine on them, too.[20] In effect, the grace of God is hoarded by the self-righteous individual, who confuses his own supposed goodness with God's grace, and is thereby prevented from sharing that grace with others, especially those whom he regards as sinners.

We not only need to receive God's grace, we have to transmit it, too. Manna, the bread God gave daily to the Israelites as they trudged through the desert during the Exodus from Egypt,[21] is a metaphor for grace. We get as much manna—as much grace—as we need. God's grace is sufficient for our needs but we have a responsibility to share it. The prodigal son's elder brother tried to hoard his father's grace and was jealous at having to share it with his younger brother. It seems that the hoarding of grace, self-righteousness, and independence conspire to switch off the God transceiver and snuff out (or at least dim) the inner light, the Holy Spirit. But it is important to note that God's grace continues to reach out to hoarders of grace, to get them to re-kindle their inner light.[22]

God works with mankind through the Holy Spirit to try to ensure that no-one is lost forever. He works persistently to overcome our resistance. The parable of the Prodigal Son shows that there can be a re-kindling of the fire, that the connection can be restored. Only our persistent disregard for God's efforts and our claims of self-righteousness stand in the way.

In the parable of the Marriage Feast,[23] a wedding guest declined to don the robe of righteousness—the wedding garment offered to all the guests. He was therefore thrown out on the street. Perhaps the wedding garment was like Hans Christian Andersen's "Emperor's New Cloak"—it did not, materially, exist. But unlike the fairy tale emperor, whose vanity led him to delude himself that the cloak was real and visible, the wedding guests knew perfectly well that their garments were invisible yet all but one took off their own clothes and enter the banquet hall careless of their nakedness.

Forgetting their nakedness signified that they had given up their free will and accepted God's, and had returned to the state of child-like ignorance and innocence—and the grace that goes with it—enjoyed by Adam and Eve before the Fall. The guest who refused to wear the wedding garment was trying to assert his self-righteousness essentially with a fig leaf. Like Adam and Eve, he was aware and ashamed of nakedness and declined to let go of the fig leaf, of his clothes.

Before the Fall, Adam and Eve were naked, clothed only in light. Perhaps such a garment of light is evidence that God's grace covers us. Being external, it is distinct from the inner light. Adam was created in the image of God. Taking that as a baseline premise, then looking at how God was clothed might give us an insight into how Adam was clothed. It is always referred to as supernatural clothing of light.[24, 25, 26.] To be clothed in this garment of light is to be clothed in righteousness and grace.[27, 28]

It seems that when Wo/Man made the willful choice in the garden, the clothing of light fell away and they found themselves—we found ourselves—in the darkness of unrighteousness.[29, 30] In the end, the wedding guest chose this outer darkness rather than the garment of righteousness.

God wants us to throw what we consider to be our spiritual clothing into the trash. What we consider to be a covering of "righteousness" is to God a filthy rag. Like the wedding guest, we must in a sense disrobe before donning the gorgeous clean robe of righteousness, and in so doing, we must be prepared to be spiritually naked in public, without the self-delusion and shame of Andersen's Emperor.

This is essentially what the prodigal son had to be prepared to do. On one level, the parable is about the relationship between God and Wo/Man, about God's graciousness, and about the open arms of God. Without undermining this face-value meaning, at a deeper level we may see it as a story about Wo/Man's relationship with herself and himself. It shows the turmoil that occurs within us as we live out our lives as sinful human beings. And yet, I think that we see our original and proper standing before God as His sons and daughters. We are created in His spiritual likeness, we are in His spiritual image. We have, as it were, God's spiritual DNA within us.

Several key themes emerge from the parable. First, by leaving home, the prodigal son was really making an unspoken but clear statement that he no longer wished to be his father's son. Strictly speaking, the inheritance should only have come to him upon the death of his father, so in demanding it while his father was still alive he was, in a way, saying to the father: "You are dead to me, and I do not desire any longer to be your son."

A second key theme is re-connection. The word *religion* means to reconnect, to re-establish a connection with the source of origin.[31] So the reconnection which occurs as the parable unfolds may be what religion is really all about (or should be.)

Third, there are correlations between this parable and the story of the Fall. Adam and Eve left the garden of Eden in a sense of their own accord, by willfully disobeying God. The prodigal son left *his* Paradise also of his own volition, after making the willful decision that he no longer wished to be his father's son. He left, furthermore, with his father's inheritance, which was not simply a monetary inheritance but a spiritual inheritance—a blessing —as well. His father gave him spiritual wealth, spiritual capital that seems to have served him well for a long time, but because he was disconnected from his father this capital could not be replenished and could not be expected to last forever. Similarly, God did not leave Adam and Eve entirely unprovided for: He gave them the ground to cultivate and live on, but it was cursed and would not support them forever. Both accounts teach us that there needs to be some connectedness to God in order for our spiritual capital to be replenished.

In the parable, the spiritual as well as the monetary capital is spent in "a far country," which emphasizes the extent of the prodigal son's alienation from his spiritual roots, his spiritual moorings. His spiritual identity was established at his father's house, but he became estranged, alienated, lost in the far country. He suffered spiritual loneliness and disconnection.

Nonetheless, as the story unfolds, it becomes clear that the father was closer to the son than the son was to the father. The kingdom of God, Jesus said, is within us. So despite the fact of being in a far country, despite having separated himself physically, his father's spirit—his spiritual DNA— remained within the prodigal son. It had never left him.

As he made his way home, his father saw him from "afar." It was as if the father was able to see his son all the way back to the "far" country to which the son had journeyed. It seems that no matter how far away he was, the son was still within the view of the father.

No matter how far we stray from God, the inner light, the Holy Spirit of our Father still flickers within us. Despite his geographic distance from home, the prodigal son was still functioning within the context of the spiritual mooring that his father had given him at home. In that sense, there was no distance between them. This leads me to conclude that this is as much a story about Wo/Man's struggle with her- and himself as it is about Wo/Man's struggle with God. From the father's point of view, his prodigal son had not really left him. The parental DNA was still within him. His father still loved him and reached out to him and indeed could still see him, no matter how far he journeyed.

In that same sense, although we left the garden of Eden, we never really left the Father's presence. The willful distancing of ourselves from God is an illusion, a self-delusion, self-deceit, an egocentric denial and betrayal of reality. What *we* think has happened—either that we have left God or that He has forsaken us—is just not true. We remain forever His sons and daughters, we are still made in His image, of His DNA. We are still one with Him, provided we do not commit the Unpardonable Sin.

The original sin therefore seems to be that we either forgot or suppressed who and what we were originally, though that is who we still are. The sin of the prodigal was not that he took his father's wealth, not that he left for a far country, but that he forsook, forgot, or suppressed who and what he was. He represents none other than the false self that causes us to feel alienated from God. We betray our own identity before God. We are His sons and daughters, but in our self-delusion we sever the filial bond and vital spiritual mooring, and leave. Deviating from the mark, straying from being what we should be, deluding ourselves that we are something we are not, is literally what sin means: It is a term from archery meaning "to miss the mark."[32]

So the paradox is that to God, there is no journey, no far-off destination, and no alienation; but to us there is, because *in our souls* we have put ourselves there. We have lost our core identity and fallen into the delusion that we have lost or squandered our spiritual heritage.

In the first part of the parable, the son received the inheritance from his father. In the second part, he journeyed into the far country and squandered the wealth. In the third part, he confronted his sense of want, or need, or lack. The context was the famine in the far country. It was more than just a physical famine. He was spiritually famished, spiritually devastated. He recognized, for the first time, what he had done: He had separated himself from his roots, from his father, and from his own true self. That is why the very next phrase about "coming to himself" is so significant: It signified a re-awakening, a recollection of who he was and what was his true source and his true nature. It was "the truth that set him free"[33] from a prison of self-delusion and doubt, of trying to satisfy his (spiritual) hunger by eating (spiritual) pig swill.

As he came to himself, he realized how far he had deviated from his roots and from himself. So in the fourth and final part of the parable, he came home to take his right and proper place in his father's home, the kingdom of heaven.

This is a parable about what true religion is all about: Re-connecting with God. It shows that God's grace is everlasting, ubiquitous, and free, and the authentic message is that we should forsake our self-delusions, our egocentric misperceptions of who we are, and sacrifice our egos so that we see

that the true recollection of self is a realistic return to wholeness because God is right here, within us, right now.

The parables of the Lost Sheep, Lost Coin, and Prodigal Son
are about the importance of the individual to God, who will
spare no resources to find the single lost sheep—no matter its
station in life, its history, its culture, its education, its gender
—and bring it back to the fold, to the community, to the
kingdom of heaven.

The notion that every person is vitally important is not en-
dorsed by all cultures. But in Western culture in general and
in America especially, it is. The psalmist found it rather perplexing, and questioned why one is important in the eye of a
God whose other works—the stars, the sky, etc.—seem so
much greater:

When I consider Your heavens, the work of Your fingers,
The moon and the stars, which You have ordained;
What is man that You take thought of him,
And the son of man that You care for him?[34]

Man was made in the spiritual image of God. God is invested
in every individual. Within each of us is something of the
spirit and the nature of God, the inner light, the Holy Spirit.
That investment continues to bring dividends in terms of
man's relationship to God.

Jesus told the disciples that they should all, like God, value
individual human beings, who are so much more than birds—
and yet God provides for *them*; or lilies that do no work, yet
are clothed in finery grander than Solomon's. Like the birds
and the lilies, we need not worry. God will provide.[35]

Peter's dramatic dream in which he was instructed to kill
and eat animals considered unclean to his religion[36] was
pointing out the importance of every woman and man. God

was making a statement of ethnicity. A trial in 2014 over the death of a young black man, Trayvon Martin,[37] at the hands of a white man, Mr. Zimmerman, was just one of sadly many examples of the deep distrust that continues to exist between ethnicities in our society. A woman visiting from Homs, in Syria, told me about the dreadful devastation resulting from ethnic and sectarian hatreds.

How did we come to this? How have the instructions of Jesus, which point to the importance of the individual to God and therefore of the importance of the other individual to ourselves, gotten so lost?

As a surgeon, nearly every day I open up the skin of patients and look inside. From the inside, I cannot tell the difference between any of them. We have a common identity at our core that is literally much more than skin deep, yet the hatred and vitriol between groups belies that vital fact. The woman from Homs believed there was no solution. Her son thought the only solution was to partition Syria, to separate the community into groups.

How have we come so far from the teaching of Jesus? The level of malevolence is shocking. Even more shocking is that the malevolence arises among and within religious groups—communities of faith—ostensibly committed to the cause of love and peace.

Jesus may have hinted at the importance of communities of faith when He said that "where two or three have gathered together in My name, I am there in their midst."[38] The Book of Hebrews also encourages "assembling together" for the purposes of faith enhancement and mutual encouragement, and "to stimulate one another to love and good deeds."[39]

How are we doing today, as far as "assembling together" goes? Western culture has begun pushing back against this time-honored concept. So many people now consider themselves "spiritual but not religious" that the acronym "SBNR" is becoming recognized as a formal religious classification. SBNRs are people who feel a closeness to God, a connection with the spirit, but not a connection to any religious group.

The rise of the SBNR notwithstanding, it is generally held that one cannot "do" religion on one's own; that to find religion, to approach God, to have a relationship of the spirit, it is necessary to join a community of faith.

While some mainstream faith communities are declining in membership, others are growing. The Mormons, who believe in such nonstandard concepts as baptism of the dead and polygamy (though they don't practice or condone polygamy any more) are said by some to be the fastest growing church. Or it might be the Jehovah's Witnesses, who believe in imminent Armageddon, or the Seventh Day Adventists, who keep the Sabbath and believe there should be no premarital sex.[40]

Why are these non-mainstream churches growing so fast, at the apparent expense of mainstream churches? The re-owned health and education programs of the Seventh Day Adventist church[41] might account for some of its growth, but do they amount to *the* compelling attraction?

What should a faith community bring to individual spiritual growth? Is a faith community even necessary for most people? No doubt there are the SBNRs who grow spiritually without a faith community, but Scriptural descriptions of the development of the early Christian church shows that communal activity was a key element of spiritual growth.[42]

But whose community is the Christian church really? Does Jesus' statement that He is present wherever two or three are gathered in His name mean that only Christians can have a relationship with God? Scripture gives hundreds of different names for God. One of them is "Love." Since love is com-

mon to all humankind it puts everyone—not just Christians
—in touch with God.

Nevertheless, several passages in Scripture seem, on their
face, to suggest that something Christian, something distinctly related to the theology, the understanding of, and particularly the belief in Jesus is important. Other passages seem to
have a much broader application. In the seminal verses that
make the case (accepted by many) that salvation as recorded
in the Scriptures is the private purview of Christians, it is the
name of Jesus rather than His *person* that is referred to:

> *For this reason also, God highly exalted Him, and bestowed on
> Him the name which is above every name, so that at the name of
> Jesus every knee will bow, of those who are in heaven and on
> earth and under the earth, and that every tongue will confess that
> Jesus Christ is Lord, to the glory of God the Father.*[43]

> *And there is salvation in no one else; for there is no other name
> under heaven that has been given among men by which we must be
> saved.*[44]

> *There is one body and one Spirit, just as also you were called in
> one hope of your calling; one Lord, one faith, one baptism, one
> God and Father of all who is over all and through all and in
> all.*[45]

This is a singular concept of God. But Paul immediately
qualified it:

> *But to each one of us grace was given according to the measure of
> Christ's gift.*[46]

Against those are such passages as the one we met earlier, in
which Jesus talked about sheep "not of this fold," implying
that God's net is much broader than Christendom;[47] another
stating that the propitiation for our sins, achieved through the

sacrifice of Jesus, was for everyone, not just Christians,[48] and yet another stating that Jesus is the savior of everyone, although believing in Him apparently confers some sort of special status because while He is the Savior of all men, He is "especially" the savior of believers.[49]

If we consider salvation as it is presented in the parables of the Lost Coin, the Lost Sheep, and the Lost (the Prodigal) Son, and do so from the perspective of the Lost rather than from that of the Seeker of the Lost, then we have to ask: Who or what was saved? The answer is: A coin, a sheep, and a son. Then we need to ask: Who do the coin, the sheep, and the son represent? There is a big difference between what is lost in the three parables, but there is no difference in the joy over the recovery, the salvation, of that which was lost.

Coin, sheep, and son each represent certain kinds of sinner. A coin cannot lose itself; it can only be lost through someone else's carelessness; it cannot help in the process of being found; and it has no knowledge or awareness of being lost. A sheep is a bit more complex. It probably knows it is lost when it becomes lost. Perhaps it can get lost on its own. Perhaps it can deliberately leave the flock, though it's hard to know what runs through a sheep's mind. But its departure would probably not be malicious or premeditated. In the case of the Lost (Prodigal) Son, however, his departure was voluntary, willful, and somewhat malicious.

So we go from absolutely no intentionality in the case of the coin to absolute intentionality on the part of the son, with the sheep somewhere in between. And yet, in all three cases, there seems to be equal and equivalent graciousness and industry of the seeker in seeking their return. Though individually different in kind, the Lost are all equally valued and actively sought.

This display of grace and effort to save the Lost—whoever they may be—epitomizes the life and work of Jesus. The coin, an inanimate object that can have no concept of being lost, reminds us that there are indeed also people who have no concept that they are lost, or that they are being sought, or that there is such a thing as the saving grace of God. This being so, could the statement: "I am the way, the truth, and the life; no one comes to the Father but through Me"[50] be simply a *de facto* description of something that just *is*, like gravity? Whereas gravity is a universal natural law, God's grace—which is extended to all mankind through the word, the ministry, the effort of Jesus—seems to be a supernatural, spiritual, law of salvation. Laws are laws, whether we understand, believe, or know them, or not.

That God is the savior of all mankind but "especially" of Christians[51] means perhaps that understanding this universal spiritual law confers upon Christians some special *insight* into God but not a special *relationship* with Him. God is just as interested in saving the coin as He is in saving the sheep and the prodigal son.

The process of salvation as given in Scripture is more descriptive than prescriptive. It describes how God's grace operates and is not restricted, in its application, only to those who understand it. It is also a strong statement that any religion centered around "me," my work, and my effort is really an idolatrous religion. In asserting that there is no other way to be saved than through Jesus, the statement removes the emphasis from "me" and places it where it belongs: On the grace of God.

This is the key lesson in the three parables. To be genuine and true, religion must center on what God is and does, not on what Wo/Man is and does. Yet we fall so easily into religions that require us to behave in a certain way, through piety and ritual and the "law" of Scripture, in order to put ourselves into a "right" contractual relationship with God.

The "Lost" parables show that God is interested in and extends His grace to every individual, every one of us, regardless of who and what we are, and of what we know or don't know. The responsibility for who and what we are, do, or know is assumed by God, through His grace.

But that's just the beginning of the matter, not the end of it. God doesn't just want to love us all individually. He wants us all to love one another individually. With all the conflict in the world today, how is that possible?

Father versus Son

Notes to Chapter 5

---

[1] Luke 2:10

[2] Matthew 5:48

[3] 1 Corinthians 13

[4] In Romans 7.

[5] Romans 8:37

[6] Exodus 9:27

[7] 2 Corinthians 5:10. See also:
Romans 2:6 ... who will render to each person according to his deeds....
1 Corinthians 4:5 Therefore do not go on passing judgment before the time, but wait until the Lord comes who will both bring to light the things hidden in the darkness and disclose the motives of men's hearts; and then each man's praise will come to him from God.
1 Peter 1:17 If you address as Father the One who impartially judges according to each one's work, conduct yourselves in fear during the time of your stay on earth;
Revelation 20:12 And I saw the dead, the great and the small, standing before the throne, and books were opened; and another book was opened, which is the book of life; and the dead were judged from the things which were written in the books, according to their deeds.
Psalm 62:12 And lovingkindness is Yours, O Lord, For You recompense a man according to his work.
Proverbs 24:12 If you say, "See, we did not know this," Does He not consider it who weighs the hearts? And does He not know it who keeps your soul? And will He not render to man according to his work?
Colossians 3:25 For he who does wrong will receive the consequences of the wrong which he has done, and that without partiality.
Proverbs 11:31 If the righteous will be rewarded in the earth, How much more the wicked and the sinner!
1 Corinthians 3:8 Now he who plants and he who waters are one; but each will receive his own reward according to his own labor.

[8] Matthew 20:1-16

[9] Matthew 12:30-32

[10] John 1:1-5

[11] John 1:6-10

[12] 1 John 3:24

[13] Ezekiel 36:26-7

[14] Ezekiel 37:14

[15] Ecclesiastes 3:11

[16] In contrast, M. Scott Peck describes people who have severed this connection—who have cut themselves off from God. Peck, M. Scott. *People of the Lie: The Hope for Healing Human Evil.* Touchstone, 1998.

[17] Luke 18:9-12

[18] M.Scott Peck calls them "People of the Lie," *ibid.*

19 1 John 1:8-10

20 1 Peter 4:10

21 Exodus 16

22 2 Peter 3:9

23 Matthew 22:1-14

24 Psalms 104:1-2

25 Matthew 17:1-2; Mark 9:3

26 Mark 9:3

27 Isaiah 60:19

28 Isaiah 61:10

29 1 John 1:5-7

30 Proverbs 13:9

31 The Wikipedia entry on Religion states (among other interpretations): "Modern scholars such as Tom Harpur and Joseph Campbell favor the derivation from ligare 'bind, connect', probably from a prefixed re-ligare, i.e. re (again) + ligare or 'to reconnect,' which was made prominent by St. Augustine, following the interpretation of Lactantius."

32 Wikipedia: "The Biblical terms translated from New Testament Greek (ἁμαρτία —amartia) and from Hebrew as 'sin' or 'syn' originate in archery and literally refer to missing the 'gold' at the centre of a target, but hitting the target, i.e. error.

33 John 8:31 *et seq.*

34 Psalms 8:3-4

35 Luke 12:22-32

36 Acts 10:9-16

37 A white man, claiming he felt threatened by the presence of a young black man, shot and killed him. He was acquitted of the sole charge of second-degree murder.

38 Matthew 18:20

39 Hebrews 10:24-25

40 Citations for the assertions made in this paragraph have regrettably been lost

41 The Seventh-day Adventist educational system is the second-largest Christian school system in the world, after the Roman Catholic system. It has a total of 7,598 educational institutions operating in over 100 countries around the world with over 1.5 million students world-wide. The non-profit Adventist Health System operates facilities within the Southern and Midwestern United States. It is the largest not-for-profit Protestant healthcare provider in the nation, with 45 hospital campuses with nearly 8,300 licensed beds in 10 states, as well as urgent care centers, home health and hospice agencies, and skilled nursing facilities. (Source: Wikipedia)

42 See Acts 2.

43 Philippians 2:9-11

---

[44] Acts 4:12

[45] Ephesians 4:4-6

[46] Ephesians 4:7

[47] John 10:16

[48] 1 John 2:2

[49] 1 Timothy 4:10

[50] John 14:6

[51] 1 Timothy 4:10

6

Me versus You

THERE WERE 1,335,963 active licensed attorneys in the United States in 2017.[1] The number suggests that *conflict resolution* —which is essentially what lawyers are all about —is in strong demand in this country, and that interpersonal and inter-institutional legal conflict must be a pretty significant problem, in the United States at least. But the impact of legal conflict in the United States pales in comparison with the impact of the socially, politically, and religiously inspired conflict and terrorism rampant in the world today.

By definition, conflict of any sort in a community of faith cannot be the will of a God of love, mercy, and grace. The fact that there always *is* conflict is a sign of humanity's selfish, sinful nature. There is a way to resolve it, Jesus said, significantly sandwiching His remarks on the issue between remarks on humility and remarks on forgiveness:

If your brother sins, go and show him his fault in private; if he listens to you, you have won your brother. But if he does not listen to you, take one or two more with you, so that by the mouth of two or three witnesses every fact may be confirmed.

If he refuses to listen to them, tell it to the church; and if he refuses to listen even to the church, let him be to you as a Gentile and a tax collector.[2]

The conflicts Jesus wants us to resolve are person-to-person disputes, not issues about community beliefs, opinions, or principles.

Some Bible translations say "If your brother sins," go and have it out with him; but the complete translation is to have it out with your brother only if he sins *against you*.[3] In other words, it is not a matter of dealing with every little sin, which would be a tough proposition, prolific sinners that we are. Rather, Jesus meant interpersonal sinning, such as personal animosity, inability to get along with someone, slandering others, and so on.

He underscored the importance of conflict resolution by elevating it above even worship:

Therefore if you are presenting your offering at the altar, and there remember that your brother has something against you, leave your offering there before the altar and go; first be reconciled to your brother, and then come and present your offering.[4]

It was a little out of character for Jesus to be blunt, but He could hardly have put His feelings on this matter more bluntly. If you are engaged in worship and remember an unresolved conflict with someone, then you should abandon your worship at once, and go talk to that person instead. You honor God more by being at peace with your brother than by worshiping Him. John made a similar point:

*If someone says, 'I love God,' and hates his brother, he is a liar;
for the one who does not love his brother whom he has seen, cannot
love God whom he has not seen.* [5]

John also espoused the important principle that reconciliation
and peace within the community of faith are an essential ex-
pression of true worship, of true love of God.

But some people are more gifted at reconciliation than others. Jesus reserved a Beatitude just for them:

Blessed are the peacemakers. [6]

The implication is that not everyone has the gift of making
peace, but there are some who do. Furthermore, not every
conflict, not every transgression, needs to be resolved. There
are some that discretion might overlook and let pass:

*A man's discretion makes him slow to anger, And it is his glory to
overlook a transgression.* [7]

Beyond saying that they are personal, Scripture does not give
us much guidance about the *kind* of transgression and conflict we have the discretion to overlook, but it does provide
three guiding principles: [8]

1. Conflict should be resolved *quickly*, even if it means in-
terrupting one's worship. Conflict should not be left to
smolder.

2. Conflict should initially be resolved *face-to-face* and *in
private*. Resolution cannot easily be achieved indirectly, it
cannot easily be mediated. Jesus seems to insist that initially at least, it needs to be one-on-one; that there is no obligation to drag everyone in the community of faith into the
conflict resolution process, unless...

3. If one-to-one resolution does not succeed, then one may
seek guidance from the wider community.

Are these principles relevant and practical today? For one thing, they involve direct confrontation, which discomforts those of us who prefer to avoid it. And for another, modern technology provides many more media and channels—from emails to video calls to text messages—for conflict resolution, than were available then. Are they good enough? Jesus was addressing a Skype-less generation. Would He consider Facebook-to-Facebook as good as face-to-face?

If he were still alive, M. Scott Peck might say that the remarks Jesus made on conflict resolution were really about the difference between true community and pseudo community. Peck noted that true community takes time and effort, whereas pseudo community tries to buy community through pretense, telling little white lies, and withholding the truth when it is discomforting. In essence, pseudo communities seek to avoid conflict, whereas true communities seek to resolve it.[9]

The etiquette of pseudo community requires that we do not upset other people, but if they upset us, we should act as if we are not bothered in the least. If disagreement looks set to break out or persist, then we should smoothly change the subject and talk about something else instead.

In this way, pseudo community can be very pleasant; and it would be wrong to condemn or try to change a pseudo community of faith. To do so would be tantamount to being a stumbling block. But the path to true community runs through conflict and chaos and emptiness. It seems that Jesus was telling us that there is power in the *process* of conflict resolution and forgiveness. Something happens inside the individual who goes through the process.

When conflict is serious enough to require resolution, just walking away does not produce a deep-seated true community. But not everything needs to be raised to this level of seriousness: As the Proverb said, transgressions can be overlooked, and as Jesus said (to the consternation of the Jewish religious establishment, the Pharisees) even sin can be forgiven:

Now one of the Pharisees was requesting Him to dine with him, and He entered the Pharisee's house and reclined at the table. And there was a woman in the city who was a sinner; and when she learned that He was reclining at the table in the Pharisee's house, she brought an alabaster vial of perfume, and standing behind Him at His feet, weeping, she began to wet His feet with her tears, and kept wiping them with the hair of her head, and kissing His feet and anointing them with the perfume. Now when the Pharisee who had invited Him saw this, he said to himself, "If this man were a prophet He would know who and what sort of person this woman is who is touching Him, that she is a sinner."

And Jesus answered him, "Simon, I have something to say to you." And he replied, "Say it, Teacher." "A moneylender had two debtors: one owed five hundred denarii, and the other fifty. When they were unable to repay, he graciously forgave them both. So which of them will love him more?" Simon answered and said, "I suppose the one whom he forgave more." And He said to him, "You have judged correctly." Turning toward the woman, He said to Simon, "Do you see this woman? I entered your house; you gave Me no water for My feet, but she has wet My feet with her tears and wiped them with her hair. You gave Me no kiss; but she, since the time I came in, has not ceased to kiss My feet. You did not anoint My head with oil, but she anointed My feet with perfume. For this reason I say to you, her sins, which are many, have been forgiven, for she loved much; but he who is forgiven little, loves little." Then He said to her, "Your sins have been forgiven." Those who were reclining at the table with Him began to say to themselves, "Who is this man who even forgives sins?" And He said to the woman, "Your faith has saved you; go in peace."[10]

Albert Einstein is said to have asked Mahatma Gandhi the meaning of the traditional Hindu greeting, *Namaste*. Gandhi is said to have replied that to him it meant: "When the God in me sees the God in you, then we are one." The story is probably apocryphal but adds poignancy to Gandhi's use of *Namaste* in the context of reconciliation and forgiveness over Britain's mistreatment of India and its people.

A number of peer-reviewed medical studies have found strong correlations between a forgiving nature, on the one hand, and psychological, emotional, and physical health, on the other. Two studies showed that patients who were assessed to have a forgiving disposition tended to sleep better and had healthier heart rates and blood pressure than those lacking a forgiving nature. One found stronger immune system function in forgiving HIV patients. And another found forgiving heart patients had lower stress and lower cholesterol.[11]

In light of all this, should we be more ready to intercede in conflicts?

If [someone in conflict with someone] *refuses to listen even to the church, let him be to you as a Gentile and a tax collector.*[12]

The common interpretation of this verse is that ultimately we should shun, excommunicate, or disfellowship people who will not reconcile with us or our church or congregation. We should treat them as we would treat gentiles and tax collectors. But gentiles and tax collectors were people of dearest concern to Jesus!

Have we then completely misunderstood the message of this verse? Might it not mean that an ultimate failure to resolve conflict should be responded to *via* forgiveness and grace—the ultimate expressions of love? This is the very opposite of the common interpretation.

The verse following has also perhaps been seriously misunderstood over the centuries:

> *Truly I say to you, whatever you bind* [prohibit] *on earth shall have been bound in heaven; and whatever you loose* [permit] *on earth shall have been loosed in heaven.*[13]

The passage has often been used by churches to justify the power they wield over their individual members. The context for it is this:

> *Now when Jesus came into the district of Caesarea Philippi, He was asking His disciples, "Who do people say that the Son of Man is?" And they said, "Some say John the Baptist; and others, Elijah; but still others, Jeremiah, or one of the prophets." He said to them, "But who do you say that I am?" Simon Peter answered, "You are the Christ, the Son of the living God." And Jesus said to him, "Blessed are you, Simon Barjona, because flesh and blood did not reveal this to you, but My Father who is in heaven. I also say to you that you are Peter, and upon this rock I will build My church; and the gates of Hades will not overpower it. I will give you the keys of the kingdom of heaven; and whatever you bind on earth shall have been bound in heaven, and whatever you loose on earth shall have been loosed in heaven." Then He warned the disciples that they should tell no one that He was the Christ.*[14]

This is the origin of the Catholic papacy. Peter was the first pope. In the earlier part of Matthew 16, Jesus basically said that the authority and teaching of the religious leaders of His time (*i.e.*, the Pharisees) was inadequate and unworthy. It was on that basis that he began to craft the new spiritual leadership out of which these Scriptural passages grew. A passage in which Jesus spoke directly to the Pharisees affirms this:

"Woe to you lawyers! For you have taken away the key of knowledge; you yourselves did not enter, and you hindered those who were entering." [15]

The priests prevented the people from acquiring the key of knowledge—the keys to the kingdom. What are these "keys to the kingdom" that Jesus passed on to Peter and His other followers? Christendom pictures Peter as standing at the gate of heaven with the keys, unlocking it for the saint and locking it against the sinner. This picture is wrong, and has caused much harm over the centuries. It implies that your individual salvation is in the hands of the church, and historically has given the church and its leaders enormous power over people, often oppressively applied.

But what Jesus gave to Peter were the keys not to the *gate* of heaven, but to the *kingdom* of heaven. The difference may seem subtle, yet it is critical. As Jesus taught it, the kingdom of heaven is a kingdom within us, here and now. It offers an ever-present opportunity to join the heavenly community. It is not the pie-in-the-sky heaven we have been led to think of.

The difference is perhaps partly explained by the passage stating that heaven is not bound by decisions made in the kingdom of heaven on earth; rather, man's decisions must be in concert with what has already been decided by God in heaven. It is for this reason very important to understand the meaning of the passage. In his *Literal Translation of the Bible*, Robert Young translated it as follows:

...and I will give to thee the keys of the reign of the heavens, and whatever thou mayest bind upon the earth shall be having been bound in the heavens, and whatever thou mayest loose upon the earth shall be having been loosed in the heavens.

Mounce's Interlinear Bible gives the same translation[16] and comments that the Messiah was telling His disciples that they must judge righteously[17]—they must know God's law and how to administer it, but they must conduct the affairs of the church with overflowing love of God and love of the brethren rather than with a bunch of legal *Do*s and *Don't*s.

Jesus did *not* tell the disciples that they could make any decision they liked, forgive any sin they wanted to forgive, or keep any sin from being forgiven; or that they could make any kind of ritual or recitation by means of which people could earn their way back to God. He told them that what God has already forbidden or allowed in heaven, as written in the Scriptures, explained in the law, and practiced in the life of Jesus and understood through the inspiration of the Holy Spirit, was the pattern for how His church, representing the kingdom of heaven on earth, should be administered.

In light of all this, the passage about conflict resolution takes on a very different meaning to that historically held. Instead of ostracizing someone who is intransigent against reconciliation, we should embrace them, as Jesus exemplified in His friendly and collegial attitude towards tax collectors:

The Son of Man came eating and drinking, and they say, 'Behold, a gluttonous man and a drunkard, a friend of tax collectors and sinners!' ...."[18]

... and towards Gentiles:

You yourselves know how unlawful it is for a man who is a Jew to associate with a foreigner or to visit him; and yet God has shown me that I should not call any man unholy or unclean.[19]

The very next passage in Matthew expounds that the principles of heaven have to be proclaimed and operationalized and used on earth. It makes the compelling argument that shunning the incorrigible is not a Godly principle. On the contrary: The incorrigible require all the love, compassion, graciousness, and forgiveness we can muster.

We tend to see reconciliation as a two-way street, with something expected of both parties. But God evidently sees it as a one-way street. He has reconciled with us through the sacrifice of His son, regardless of whether or not we reciprocate. Furthermore, reconciliation is not just a matter between us and our brothers and sisters in the community. It applies even in conflicts with our enemies. This is the way to end conflict and achieve peace:

For He Himself is our peace, who made both groups [i.e., Jews and Gentiles] *into one and broke down the barrier of the dividing wall, by abolishing in His flesh the enmity, which is the Law of commandments contained in ordinances, so that in Himself He might make the two into one new man, thus establishing peace, and might reconcile them both in one body to God through the cross, by it having put to death the enmity.*[20]

And although you were formerly alienated and hostile in mind, engaged in evil deeds, yet He has now reconciled you in His fleshly body through death, in order to present you before Him holy and blameless and beyond reproach—if indeed you continue in the faith firmly established and steadfast, and not moved away from the hope of the gospel that you have heard,...[21]

But God demonstrates His own love toward us, in that while we were yet sinners, Christ died for us. Much more then, having now been justified by His blood, we shall be saved from the wrath of God through Him. For if while we were enemies we were reconciled to God through the death of His Son, much more, having been reconciled, we shall be saved by His life. And not only this, but we also exult in God through our Lord Jesus Christ, through whom we have now received the reconciliation.[22]

Now all these things are from God, who reconciled us to Himself through Christ and gave us the ministry of reconciliation, namely, that God was in Christ reconciling the world to Himself, not counting their trespasses against them, and He has committed to us the word of reconciliation. Therefore, we are ambassadors for Christ, as though God were making an appeal through us; we beg you on behalf of Christ, be reconciled to God. He made Him who knew no sin to be sin on our behalf, so that we might become the righteousness of God in Him. [23]

But this passage also prompts the tantalizing thought that if God is so desperate to reconcile and let bygones be bygones that He was prepared to sacrifice His only begotten son for us and forgive us our every sin, surely we could touch Him up for a bit more? Why not, for instance, a Cadillac in the driveway?

Notes to Chapter 6

[1] American Bar Association (2017). "ABA National Lawyer Population Survey Historical Trend in Total National Lawyer Population 1878 - 2017." Online at https://www.americanbar.org/content/dam/aba/administrative/market_research/Total%20National%20Lawyer%20Population%201878-2017.authcheckdam.pdf

[2] Matthew 18:15-17

[3] Compare e..g. the New American Standard Bible and King James Version translations.

[4] Matthew 5:23-24

[5] 1 John 4:20

[6] Matthew 5:9

[7] Proverbs 19:11

[8] Matthew 5 and 18

[9] Note 17 above.

[10] Luke 7:36-50

[11] I regret I have lost the citations for these claims

[12] Matthew 18:17

[13] Matthew 18:18

[14] Matthew 16:13-20

[15] Luke 11:52

[16] "I will give you the keys of the kingdom of heaven, and whatever you bind on earth will have been bound in heaven, and whatever you loose on · earth will have been loosed in heaven." Mounce Reverse-Interlinear New Testament, https://www.Biblegateway.com/passage/?search=Matthew+16%3A19&version=MOUNCE

[17] *c.f.* John 7:24.

[18] Matthew 11:18-19

[19] Acts 10:28

[20] Ephesians 2:14-16

[21] Colossians 1:21-23

[22] Romans 5:8-11

[23] 2 Corinthians 5:18-21

7

Grace versus Magic

Again I say to you, that if two of you agree on earth about any-
thing that they may ask, it shall be done for them by My Father
who is in heaven.[1]

Ask, and it will be given to you; seek, and you will find; knock,
and it will be opened to you. For everyone who asks receives, and
he who seeks finds, and to him who knocks it will be opened. Or
what man is there among you who, when his son asks for a loaf,
will give him a stone? Or if he asks for a fish, he will not give him
a snake, will he? If you then, being evil, know how to give good
gifts to your children, how much more will your Father who is in
heaven give what is good to those who ask Him! "In everything,
therefore, treat people the same way you want them to treat you, for
this is the Law and the Prophets.[2]

As A BOY I used to watch a New York televangelist who called himself Reverend Ike. His slogan was:

*You can't lose
with the stuff I use!*

He told his followers they should, and could, have a Cadillac in their driveways. To get it, all they had to do was to ask God for it, and then believe that it would come. (Oh, and by the way, sending a substantial slice of their income to Rev. Ike might just speed things up a little.)

Reverend Ike was a pioneer in a long line of "prosperity gospel" preachers who included Oral Roberts, a TV preacher who once told his followers—on live TV—that if they did not send him $8 million by the end of the month, God would strike him dead.[3]

The Scriptural justification for prosperity gospel preaching was and is supplied largely by the simple, no-nonsense prayer of Jabez, as well as by passages such as those just quoted. The name Jabez signified someone whose mother "bore him with pain." This was his prayer:

"Oh that You would bless me indeed and enlarge my border [give me more land], *and that Your hand might be with me, and that You would keep me from harm that it may not pain me!" And God granted him what he requested.*[4]

In 2000, prosperity gospel preacher Bruce Wilkinson wrote *The Prayer of Jabez: Breaking Through to the Blessed Life.* The book was so popular that I received at least eight copies as gifts from well-meaning friends. It was the talk of American Christendom. It was a rallying cry for prosperity gospel preachers.

Reverend Ike and his like insist that God means what He says and does what He promises. He *will* give the things you ask for. He *will* open doors for you. But first, *you* must believe that you will get what you pray for. So if the Cadillac fails to show up in your driveway, it's not God's or Reverend Ike's fault: It's your's, for not believing strongly enough.

The belief that blessings come from God, and that if bad things happen to you then you must have done something to deserve them, is an ancient one. When they came across a blind man, the first words out of the disciples' mouths were: "Whose sin caused his blindness? The man himself or his parents?"[5]

Did Jesus mean to be taken at face value when He said "Ask and you shall receive, seek and you shall find, knock and it shall be opened"? Was He talking about health and wealth and the things that prosperity preachers like Reverend Ike say He meant?

Immediately following the "ask and receive" statement, Jesus said: "When your son asks you for bread, you don't give him a stone; when he asks you for a fish, you don't give him a serpent; if he asks for an egg, you don't give him a scorpion." Bread, fish, and eggs are qualitatively different from Cadillacs, caviar, and Rolexes. What did Jesus mean?

World War II generals Eisenhower and Patton led active prayer lives, as recounted in their diaries. Perhaps it reflects the old saw that there are no atheists in a foxhole; but more likely it reflects the simple fact that prayer is one of the most common cultural practices of humankind. It is as basic, human, and instinctual as eating and sleeping.

The notion that there is something "out there," some power bigger and stronger than us but approachable with our individual requests, is as common among people in the most advanced human societies today as it was among people in the most primitive societies of old.

One study[6] of prayer in America found that 90 percent of Americans claim to have some kind of spiritual communication with a higher power every day, be it formal prayer or informal thought or emotion. Fifty percent pray more than once every day. Of those who pray, 80 percent begin with some kind of familiar, intimate, personal greeting such as "Dear Lord," or "Father in heaven," or "Dear Jesus."

Three-quarters of the people who pray do so for themselves, their family, and their friends. One quarter pray for themselves only.

They pray for all kinds of things: From major needs such as health, work, and financial security, to things as mundane as finding a parking space or lost keys, for an airplane seat upgrade, for a pass in a school exam, or a win for the Detroit Lions football team.

Many hospitals have prayer books in which patients and visitors write down their thoughts and prayers to share with others. Most of the prayers are informal, extempore, rather than quoted from prayer books or some religious liturgy. Twenty-eight percent of such prayers, in one study, consisted both of requests and thanksgiving. Another 28 percent were requests only, and 22 percent consisted only of thanksgiving.

There is a strong interest in the link between health and prayer. There is even an emerging academic discipline called "neurotheology" led by respected scholars in schools of religion and of medicine. Their purpose is to study the effects of prayer on health and healing.

One such study found that people who attend a worship service at least once a week live three years longer, on average, than those who do not attend a worship service at all. A study of alternative medicines (a multibillion dollar industry) found that prayer is the most common form of alternative medicine in the U.S.—more common than acupuncture, chiropractic, yoga, and vitamins.

A large study in 2006 among cardiopulmonary bypass surgery patients at several major institutions, including the Mayo Clinic, set out to prove or disprove studies claiming to have found that prayer was benefiting such patients. The 1,800 study patients were divided into three groups: One that was not prayed for, one that was prayed for *and* the patients were aware of the fact, and one that was prayed for but the patients were *not* aware of the fact.

The prayers were prayed on behalf of the patients by the congregations at St. Paul's Monastery in St. Paul, Minnesota; the Community of Theresians Carmelites in Worcester, Massachusetts; and a prayer ministry near Kansas City, Missouri called Silent Unity. They used the first name and the first initial of the last name of every patient (*e.g.*, "Donald W.," "Sarah S.") and they were instructed to pray specifically "for successful surgery with a quick, healthy recovery and no complications."

At the end of 30 days, the study concluded that prayer offered by strangers had no effect on recovery and that patients who knew they were being prayed for had a higher rate of post-operative complications, perhaps because of the expectations the prayers created. In other words, the people who were told they were being prayed for might have assumed their condition to be hopeless, absent a miracle.

But that is just an hypothesis, and it should be noted that the attempt to subject prayer to scientific study was criticized by some as both bad religion and bad science; that the laws of physics do not apply in the realm of metaphysics.

Prayer has been a pillar of religion since the beginning of time, yet Scripture says we still don't know how to pray or what to pray for. Nevertheless, it tells us to pray without ceasing[7] and that "The effective prayer of a righteous man can accomplish much."[8] Jesus categorically stated that God will do anything that two or three people agree to ask of him.[9] Jesus Himself prayed often, and responded to the disciples' question asking how to pray by giving them the Lord's Prayer:[10, 11]

Some prayer is ritualized. Many denominations have their own book of common prayer. Catholics say their Rosary. One list of the "Top Ten Prayers of All Time"[12] includes the Lord's Prayer, the Twenty-Third Psalm, Make Me an Instrument of Your Peace, and others, which are taught and used in homes, schools, and of course churches, and which serve as a guide to how to compose prayer. But the 10th top prayer of all time—and perhaps the most common form of prayer—is simple silence.

Might silent prayer reflect our ignorance of how to pray? Paul said:

...we do not know how to pray as we should, but the Spirit Himself intercedes for us with groanings too deep for words....[13]

If we do not know how to pray, have not learned how to pray, or for whatever reason are unable to pray, then it seems the Holy Spirit will pray on our behalf. The "groanings" are not of the spirit; they are of a supplicant unable to find the words to express himself or herself. Paul went on to suggest that *the will of God* is the overarching concept within the context of prayer:

He who searches the hearts knows what the mind of the Spirit is, because He intercedes for the saints according to the will of God.[14]

Jesus made this absolutely explicit in the Lord's Prayer:

Thy will be done.

In what might be one of the most cited verses in Christian prayer, particularly in times of grief when people are too overwhelmed to pray, Paul made the reassuring statement:

And we know that God causes all things to work together for good to those who love God, to those who are called according to His purpose.[15]

But it too begs the question: Why do we need to pray? If we don't know how to pray, if we pray ineffectively, if the spirit will pray on our behalf when we can't find the words, and if God is working behind the scenes for the good of those who love him, then why do we need to pray at all? Paul implied that indeed we don't, because God will give us what we need anyway:

He who did not spare His own Son, but delivered Him over for us all, how will He not also with Him freely give us all things?[16]

He went on to imply that it's not just the Holy Spirit at work in prayer, but also that Jesus Himself will intercede on our behalf:

Christ Jesus is He who died, yes, rather who was raised, who is at the right hand of God, who also intercedes for us.[17]

So on the one hand, if we want to pray we must learn how; but, on the other, it seems we don't *need* to pray at all, since the Holy Spirit and Jesus pray for us anyway. The disciples opted to learn how to pray, and were given the Lord's Prayer.

Perhaps the Lord's Prayer is a pithy summation, a declaration, a mini constitution of the kingdom of heaven. It encompasses all the pillars of community. All nine of its personal pronouns are plural: It's "*our* father," not "*my* father"; "Give *us*," not "Give *me*." It's a communal prayer.

The opening line—"Our Father who is in heaven"—juxtaposes the two extremes of God: God as "daddy" (*abba*, a very personal and endearing term) and God as the mighty and hallowed ruler of the universe ("who is in heaven; hallowed be Your name.") Perhaps Jesus intended this juxtaposition to deter us from treating God too much as one or the other; to tell us that God is neither an indulgent celestial Santa Claus who will give us whatever we want, nor an entity so remote as to be unapproachable and so mighty that He has no interest in us.

The Lord's Prayer brings out the grace that we must repay by sharing it with others. It is a community prayer and a tool for conflict resolution and kingdom government. Hence, it is a constitution, a set of bylaws showing what it means to be part of the kingdom of heaven.

It has been suggested that even *this* prayer might be too demanding, that a less arrogant translation of "Give us our daily bread" might be: "Grant us our daily bread." In any case, Isaiah said that our bread and our water were assured,[18] as it was for the Israelites during their exodus from Egypt through the desert, in the form of manna from heaven.

If our prayers are answered, how would we know? The Book of Judges gave some guidance when Gideon asked for authentication as the angel of God was communicating with him:

> *The angel of the Lord appeared to him and said to him, "The Lord is with you, O valiant warrior."*[19]

Gideon's response surely strikes a chord with all of us:

"O my lord, if the Lord is with us, why then has all this happened to us?"[20]

And where are all His miracles which our fathers told us about, saying, 'Did not the Lord bring us up from Egypt?' But now the Lord has abandoned us and given us into the hand of Midian."[21]

It is the universal cry of Man to God: "If you are with me, then why am I sick? Why did I lose my job? Why am I having trouble in my marriage?" In Gideon's case, God responded directly, but with a question:

The Lord looked at him and said, "Go in this your strength and deliver Israel from the hand of Midian. Have I not sent you?"

Even so, Gideon was suspicious that this really was God:

"If now I have found favor in Your sight, then show me a sign that it is You who speak with me. Please do not depart from here, until I come back to You, and bring out my offering and lay it before You." And He said, "I will remain until you return."[22]

When he returned with his "offering" of a wool fleece, Gideon asked God for a sign:

"If You will deliver Israel through me, as You have spoken, behold, I will put a fleece of wool on the threshing floor. If there is dew on the fleece only, and it is dry on all the ground, then I will know that You will deliver Israel through me, as You have spoken." And it was so. When he arose early the next morning and squeezed the fleece, he drained the dew from the fleece, a bowl full of water.

But this wan't enough to satisfy Gideon, who said to God:

"Do not let Your anger burn against me that I may speak once more; please let me make a test once more with the fleece, let it now be dry only on the fleece, and let there be dew on all the ground."

God did so that night; for it was dry only on the fleece, and dew was on all the ground.[23]

Is it possible for us to be reassured by God, as Gideon was?

I once had a patient, Elizabeth, a young woman with a very serious pancreatic tumor. The evangelical church to which she belonged organized special prayers for her. As a surgeon, I know that such cancers as hers usually lead quickly to death, but to my great surprise and delight, she responded very well to chemotherapy followed by surgery to excise the remaining cancer. After a few months, there was no residual tumor.

Elizabeth was of course overjoyed, and gave videotaped testimony at her church of the power of prayer. She gave me a copy of the tape. Her recovery was a pleasant surprise to me too, but I knew it was not a miracle because I know how chemotherapy works and I knew that it was working in her case. But it was a miracle to her, because she did not know how chemotherapy works and had faith in the power of her church's prayers to heal her cancer.

Elizabeth was fine for about 16 months, then a CT scan revealed she had re-developed multiple tumors. When she told her church that the cancer had returned, they asked her to confess her sins and reflect upon what she had done to deserve God's revocation of His answer to the prayers they had offered for her. Needless to say, she was utterly devastated in every way. She died six weeks later.

How was Elizabeth to know whether or not God had in fact answered her prayer and those of her church? How are any of us to know? Is it even important to know? It is intoxicating to think that we can harness God's power on our own or others' behalf. But if our prayers don't appear to be answered, does that mean that He is *not* answering? Are there tests we can administer to validate our communication with God, as Gideon did?

If we have the wrong expectations with regard to the outcome of prayer, then we risk becoming disillusioned with God and our faith. Doubt sets in. But as we have seen, God uses doubt to build our faith. Indeed, faith is tempered in the crucible of doubt. God responds to our doubt with grace and compassion, as He did in the case of Gideon.

At the other end of the spectrum, the faithful Shadrach, Meshach and Abednego were in no doubt that God *could* save them from the fiery furnace into which King Nebuchadnezzar threw them for refusing to bow down to his image, but they also acknowledged that God *might* choose not to do so. So strong was their faith in God that they would rather burn alive than bow to a false god:

> *O Nebuchadnezzar, we do not need to give you an answer concerning this matter. If it be so, our God whom we serve is able to deliver us from the furnace of blazing fire; and He will deliver us out of your hand, O king. But even if He does not, let it be known to you, O king, that we are not going to serve your Gods or worship the golden image that you have set up.*[24]

They had absolute faith in God but no expectations regarding the outcome of their prayer. In short, they were saying: "Thy will be done." They knew that what is always delivered when asked, what is always found when sought, what is always opened when knocked, is that all things will work together for good, for those who love God.[25]

The problem is that *we* want to define what is good, as we did in the garden of Eden, where our desire to be able to define good and evil was at the root of Original Sin. It takes nothing less than the perfection and the knowledge of God to define good and evil reliably. The definition is a matter for divinity, not for humanity. Our obligation is to trust the Creator and not try to impose our own perspective of what is good and what is evil.

Prayer is all about faith in God's grace. Through prayer, grace finds us—we don't have to look for it. Prayer leads us onto holy ground, as it did for Moses at the Burning Bush, where grace was manifestly displayed. The Bush was ablaze yet it was not consumed. Fire that does not consume is a metaphor for grace. It gives light, but not heat.

Prayer is to the soul what the autonomic nervous system is to the body. The autonomic nervous system regulates the function of our internal organs without our consciously having to control them. You don't need to remind your heart to beat. You don't have to tell it to beat harder when you run up stairs. Usually, the system maintains your body in a state of relative rest, but in emergencies it releases adrenalin, a stimulant, into your body.

Similarly, prayer is always working in the background, and can be invoked by the spirit in a crisis.[26] It feeds and sustains that spirit, the inner light, the eternity set in every heart. It is automatic, spontaneous, perpetual, and soul-sustaining. Like the heart, it will rise to a higher level of output if we are struggling to climb steep spiritual stairs. It is always working to maintain the health of the soul. That is the one and only predefined product or function of prayer, just as the heart has only one product or function: blood flow.

Prayer can no more supply you with a new Mercedes or save your life or the life of a loved one than the heart can oxygenate your blood or digest your food. Such things are just not its function.

Thus, the Scriptural reference to our not knowing how to pray, and the disciples' request to be taught how to pray, have to do with the output, not the method, of prayer. We need to learn (or to re-learn) that its function or product or output is the health of the soul. In that sense, prayer does indeed move mountains, it does indeed bring prosperity, and it is indeed always answered—but only in accordance with God's intended function for it, which is: To keep the inner light lit, to see that faith will never be unfulfilled, and that grace will never be misappropriated.

Such being the power and the product of prayer, its effects should be anticipated on the soul, not on the body. Soul and body are linked in the same way that the heart or the intestines are linked with the brain: If the heart or the intestines don't work, then the brain is affected. But the effect is not precisely predictable and is not the proximate result of organ dysfunction. So too with prayer: Proper prayer focuses on the health of our soul, but because the soul is linked with the body it can have secondary, collateral effects on physical and emotional health.

To believe that one can penetrate the secrets of God, and know the works of God, and have His power at one's beck and call is to believe in magic. God is not a magician in our service; we are in His service.[27]

For primitive, unsophisticated, ignorant Wo/Man, for innocent children, and perhaps also for some of the mentally ill, everything in nature has inherent meaning. Scientific concepts having to do with cause and effect, and the fact that certain events will have certain consequences, are meaningless to them. The notion that we are governed by thermodynamic, gravitational, and other laws of nature are completely inaccessible to them. If a civilized and educated person tells a primitive or innocent or mentally ill person that there is going to be an eclipse tomorrow and the eclipse indeed happens, then the primitive will believe that his informant must have caused the eclipse, otherwise the informant could not have known it was going to happen.

To the ignorant, the world appears to be the playground of divine forces whose beneficent or malevolent intentions must be discovered, and whose favors must be won. So primitives concoct omens and resort to sorcery to appease their gods. This is part and parcel of the fundamental mindset of the primitive, to whom nothing that occurs in life—including death—is without meaning. Death is the result of a curse, an evil spell. The cry of a bird, the howl of the wind, the clouds in the sky all convey meaning and messages from the divine forces operating in the world.

Even today, learning, science, laws of cause and effect, and even medicine sometimes take on an aura of magic and mysticism. The common element in such thinking is fear of that which we cannot understand and control. The inability to see the mechanisms by which things work leads to this kind of fear. Modern science understands thunder and lightning, but to the ancient Greeks, they were terrifying activities of the Gods. In thunder, Job heard the voice of God, not the sonic boom of air expanding explosively as it is heated by lightning. The solution would seem simply to eradicate the innocent's belief in magic through education and (for the mentally ill) medication.

It is also true—especially for the skeptical—that many Bible stories themselves are magical, not rational. They may be beautiful, they may have poetic value; but to the skeptic they are in no way real. But science does not liberate us from the fear that drives us to magic. Every day I tell my patients how science can treat their disease, only for them to become almost more afraid of the treatment than of their disease. In some ways, and in some cases, modern, scientific, educated

Wo/Man can be just as susceptible to fear as primitive Wo/
Man—and just as receptive to magic solutions.

The popularity of lotteries, of cosmetic elixirs of youth, of
horoscopes, and so on, all seem to attest to the susceptibility
of vast numbers of otherwise rational people to belief in
magic. Once, a colon cancer patient from India, a PhD who
counted many physicians among her relatives, asked me to
change the date set for her surgery because it was "inauspi-
cious."

We still speak of "miracles of science" as though magic
were involved. Our desire to cling to magic seems insatiable.
We hunger for the marvelous and we thirst for the magnifi-
cent, provided they require little effort to obtain.

What does all this have to do with prayer?

Uncertainty is harder to bear than error. We would rather
be certain than right. A pathologist (a member of medicine's
"supreme court" for deciding whether a tissue is diseased or
not) once told me that pathologists are not always right, but
they are never in doubt. So belief in magic—even if you include God as magic—is preferred over doubt. But the Bible
points continuously to the contrast between magic and God,
and calls continuously for us to turn away from magic and
toward the true God.

The opening words of the Ten Commandments are a good
starting point in unlocking the idea of what it is to fall under
the temptation of magic. They exhort us to put no other gods
before God and to make no graven images. The temptation is
to follow false gods—magic creations of Man—rather than
the God of Creation.

Making false gods is not a very sophisticated type of magical temptation. To make false idols out of relationships, love,
artwork, one's work, morality, money, and even science is a

very primitive kind of magic, one that Scripture warns of. Jesus said: "You can't serve God *and* mammon".[28]

A much more subtle aspect to idolatry is alluded to in the Temptation of Jesus.[29] Early in His ministry, when He knew He was the Messiah and had divine power, He tried to work out how He should use it. His contemporaries expected their Messiah to overthrow the Romans. As He prayed and meditated in the desert, He encountered not only God but the devil as well. How could He distinguish between them, especially when the devil came quoting Scripture and even giving advice to Jesus to use His powers to turn stones into bread, and to fly? *Prima facie*, the devil's advice seemed benignly aimed at advancing Jesus' mission.

This was a struggle between the true God and the false god of magic. It is the most subtle of temptations, and it is one into which we fall so easily when we pray. We are ensnared into thinking we can resort to magic to further God's own cause. The devil's suggestions to Jesus seemed to meet legitimate needs and seemed to conform with Scripture. But Jesus resisted, and retorted with His own Scripture: That the devil should not tempt God.[30]

Like the devil, we try to use God's magical gifts for our own ends. We pervert His promises, the faith and the grace He has given us, the Bible He inspired, the doctrine He has revealed, and the prayer that He taught us. The subtle temptation to harness the power of God for our own ends is the definition of magic as I am using it.

The next Commandment…

Thou shalt not take the name of God in vain[31]

…is commonly interpreted as a prohibition against swearing oaths. But it might rather be intended to put us on guard against the subtle temptation of magic. In the desert, Jesus taught us that prayer can only be uttered in the very crucible of faith. We saw the same thing in the garden of Gethsemane, when Peter hacked off the ear of a servant of the high priest, whom Jesus instantly healed, saying to Peter:

> *Or do you think that I cannot appeal to My Father, and He will at once put at My disposal more than twelve legions of angels?*[32]

When we pray, we tend to pray for those twelve legions to ride in like the Fifth Cavalry to save us. Jesus rejected this, submitting Himself instead to the will of God, even to the extent of going to the cross. It makes us very uncomfortable, but the complete surrender of our will to God is *required*.

The Israelites resorted to magic when they were losing the war with the Philistines, by taking the Ark of the Covenant into battle with them as a talisman.[33] This was crude magic. They lost the war and, with it, the Ark, but God did not abandon them. The Ark became a bad luck charm for the Philistines, so they returned it to the Israelites, along with gifts, to appease the Israelite God. Samuel then encouraged the Israelites to abandon their belief in the magical power of God in favor of a true understanding of repentance and faith.

A belief in magic results in one of two potential and contrary problems. One is a reluctance to take bold action even when God requires it of us, which perhaps explains why we don't often see the power of God displayed in our daily life. The other is that through our zeal to demonstrate the power of God and the effectiveness of our prayer, we opt for the sensational, though God does not will it. In these ways, belief in magic insinuates itself into our hearts and sometimes even trails in the wake of our most authentic and genuine spiritual experiences.

The frontier between faith and magic is also the border between pious pride and ashamed humility. A humble search for God *versus* a proud claim to possess Him highlights the contrast between truth and magic. Our quarrels about religion, about the Christian church, and even about our own community church, usually involve this division between a humble search for God and the proud claim to possess Him and the only true knowledge of Him. When we do so proudly proclaim, we show ourselves as having succumbed to the temptation—of having fallen under the spell—of magic.

The interface between magic and truth is a dangerous frontier, but it is one we must cross. The idea that we serve a God who will not send us legions of angels to fight our battles is unnerving to many. Shadrach, Meshach and Abednego knew that while God was able to do so, He was not obligated.

The *outcome* of prayer is what Jesus talked about in teaching us how to pray and what Paul meant when he said in Romans that we don't know how to pray and the spirit will pray for us anyway, accompanied by our groanings. The idea that we cannot shape our prayers to be effective suggests *not* that we don't understand the technicalities of prayer (to kneel or to stand; what to say, etc.) but, rather, that we don't understand what the real outcome of prayer looks like.

It looks, as one persistent widow found, very much like grace:

Now He was telling them a parable to show that at all times they ought to pray and not to lose heart, saying, "In a certain city there was a judge who did not fear God and did not respect man. There was a widow in that city, and she kept coming to him, saying, 'Give me legal protection from my opponent.' For a while he was unwilling; but afterward he said to himself, 'Even though I do not fear God nor respect man, yet because this widow bothers me, I will give her legal protection, otherwise by continually coming she

*will wear me out.'" And the Lord said, "Hear what the unright-
eous judge said; now, will not God bring about justice for His elect
who cry to Him day and night, and will He delay long over them?
I tell you that He will bring about justice for them quickly. However, when the Son of Man comes, will He find faith on the
earth?"*[34]

Notice, first, that the judge himself did not follow the Law to
love God with all his heart and his neighbor as himself, and
openly acknowledged his disdain for God; second, that in the
society of that time, widows were among the lowest in social
standing; third, that the widow was seeking something specific; and fourth, that the words "wear me out" implied, in
the original Greek, an almost physical pummeling. The
judge's motive in acceding to her request was to avoid being
pummeled. It was purely selfish and had nothing to do with
the justice of the widow's claim.

The parable could be mistaken as associating grace with
effort; as meaning that persistent effort will be rewarded, that
God will respond favorably to prayer even if at first He is
disinclined to do so, provided we persist. The temptation is to
think that *we* can finish something that the spirit has begun;
that the spirit inspires us to pray and even initiates prayer so
that we can step in to finish it. Jesus is both the author and
the finisher ("perfecter") of our faith[35] but this parable *seems*
to imply that *we* have a role in the finishing.

Just before He gave us the Lord's Prayer, Jesus told us to
keep our prayers short. But the parable of the Importunate
Widow seems to say "Keep them going." While it is certainly
a compelling human story about a feisty underdog in dogged
pursuit of justice, it is more about a God who, in contrast to
the unjust judge, is good and merciful and gracious. Really,
the parable is about neither the widow nor the judge: It is
about God.

In it, Jesus implicitly tells us to rely on the graciousness of God, not to revel in the triumph of the human spirit without help from God. Ben Franklin's maxim that "God helps those who help themselves" is antithetical to a grace specifically intended for those who *cannot* help themselves.

Jesus told the disciples that the parable was meant to show that "at all times they ought to pray and not to lose heart" or, as the *Good News Bible* translates it: "they should always pray and never become discouraged." The real meaning of the parable and indeed the real power of prayer is that prayer offers relief from despair and discouragement. At the time of Jesus, a lonely and destitute widow had every reason to be discouraged, but the good news was that God's justice is always close at hand. The "bad" news for people who expect God's justice in this life is that "close at hand" means the next.

God's justice parallels His righteousness and grace. Jesus said:

...now, will not God bring about justice for His elect who cry to Him day and night, and will He delay long over them? I tell you that He will bring about justice for them quickly.[36]

God told the Israelites that He would...

...let justice roll down like waters And righteousness like an ever-flowing stream....[37]

Therefore the Lord longs to be gracious to you,
And therefore He waits on high to have compassion on you.
For the Lord is a God of justice;
How blessed are all those who long for Him.[38]

These passages explicitly link God's justice, righteousness, and grace. The promise of the parable of the Importunate Widow is that God's justice will eventually come. But what exactly does "God's justice" mean? Divine and human justice surely are light years apart:

"For My thoughts are not your thoughts,
Nor are your ways My ways," declares the Lord.
"For as the heavens are higher than the earth,
So are My ways higher than your ways
And My thoughts than your thoughts."[39]

The sheer volume of Scriptural references suggests that justice is part of the very character and nature of God. Here are just a handful of them:

The Almighty is beyond our reach and exalted in power;
in his justice and great righteousness, he does not oppress.[40]

The Lord loves righteousness and justice;
the earth is full of his unfailing love.[41]

I know that the Lord secures justice for the poor
and upholds the cause of the needy.[42]

I will seek the lost, bring back the scattered, bind up the broken
and strengthen the sick; but the fat and the strong I will destroy. I
will feed them with judgment.[43]

The English concept of justice conflates the Anglo–Saxon concepts of *righteousness, rightness,* and *being right* with the Greek concepts of *justification, justice, justness,* and *judgment.* We tend to use *righteousness* in more of a divine context and *justice* in a more secular context. But in Hebrew and Greek, one word is used for both meanings. In Scripture, *justice* and *righteousness* are practically synonymous, which simplifies the understanding of Scripture. The psalmist, for example, linked them not merely as peripheral attributes of God but as foundational attributes at the very core of God:

Righteousness and justice are the foundation of your throne;...[44]

The word justice is also linked to justification, the idea that one can be made righteous through the grace of God. Paul wrote that the gospel is synonymous with justice and righteousness:

> For I am not ashamed of the gospel, for it is the power of God for salvation to everyone who believes, to the Jew first and also to the Greek. For in it the righteousness of God is revealed from faith to faith; as it is written, "But the righteous man shall live by faith."[45] [Most translations say "...for the just shall live by faith."]

The commonly held notion that God's justice metes out heavenly bliss or eternal hellfire is a perversion. This key passage reveals that the justice of God is in truth the gospel of Jesus.

Justice is the ordering of things according to divine intention—according to God's will. Hence "Thy will be done" in the Lord's Prayer. The divine order of things is violated by things which God does not condone, such as poverty and oppression. For justice to be done, these must end—judgment rests on whether the judged took care of the poor and the needy.[46]

God leaves the relief of this type of oppression to the community of faith. While He might at any time miraculously intervene to relieve oppression and institute justice, His preference, it seems, is for the community of faith to assume and accept that responsibility. So there is a sense in which the prayers of those who are in need should be answered not by God directly but by those who are close by—*i.e.*, by their community. Those of us who have a relationship with God and think that the justice of God is important have an obligation to represent God, to be God's hands and God's heart, as it were, and to respond to cries of suffering and oppression.

Recall that Jesus was asked whose sin caused a blind beggar's condition: Was it the man's own sin or was it the sin of his parents?[47] It was neither, said Jesus. It was caused so that God's glory could be made manifest. Thus, it appears that the kingdom of God, justice, and righteousness all have the same theme. Jesus put kingdom and righteousness together:

But seek first his kingdom and his righteousness,...[48]

The synonymity of the kingdom of God, justice, righteousness, mercy, and grace suggests that, together, they constitute what we should expect as the outcome of prayer: It is that which we will always receive when we ask, the door that will always be opened to our knock, the object that will always be found when we look. When Jesus said (as He often did in the parables) "The kingdom of God is like *so*," we can also read it as "The justice of God is like *so*." Understanding this perhaps confers a fresh insight into what the product of prayer is, and what the gospel is ultimately all about.

It would seem, given the inestimable value of justice, righteousness, mercy, and grace, which are the outcome of prayer, that we should never cease to pray, not even for an instant.

But we should forget about the Cadillac.

Donald W. Weaver

Notes to Chapter 7

[1] Matthew 18:19

[2] Matthew 7:7-12

[3] See, for example, the February 20, 1987, issue of *Christianity Today*, or look up Oral Roberts in Wikipedia. He actually said God would "call him home" but many in his audience would have read "strike me dead" into that, I believe.

[4] 1 Chronicles 4:9-10

[5] John 9

[6] Citations for the assertions made in this and subsequent paragraphs have regrettably been lost.

[7] 1 Thessalonians

[8] James 5:16

[9] Matthew 18:19-20

[10] Matthew 6

[11] Luke 11-1

[12] http://www.Godweb.org/toptenprayers.htm

[13] Romans 8:26

[14] Romans 8:27

[15] Romans 8:28

[16] Romans 8:32

[17] Romans 8:34

[18] Isaiah 33

[19] Judges 6:12

[20] Judges 6:13-14

[21] The Midianites were a tribe that purportedly led the Israelites to sin, so God wanted them destroyed.

[22] Judges 6:17-19

[23] Judges 6:36-40

[24] Daniel 3:16-18

[25] Romans 8

[26] *ibid.*

[27] The author wishes to acknowledge these ideas were borrowed from Paul Tournier's book *A Doctor's Casebook: In the Light of the Bible* (Harper, 1976)

[28] Luke 16:13 *Mammon* means money or wealth.

[29] Told in Matthew 4, Mark 2, and Luke.

[30] Deuteronomy 6

[31] Exodus 12:7

[32] Matthew 26:53

---

[33] 1 Samuel 4

[34] Luke 18:1-8

[35] Hebrews 12:2

[36] Luke 18:7

[37] Amos 5:24

[38] Isaiah 30:18

[39] Isaiah 55:8-9

[40] Job 37:23

[41] Psalms 33:5

[42] Psalms 140:12

[43] Ezekiel 34:15-16

[44] Psalms 89:14

[45] Romans 1:16-17

[46] In Matthew 25.

[47] John 9

[48] Matthew 6:33

8

Prayer versus Free Will

To LIVE LIFE AS A CONTINUAL PRAYER is a common call in Scripture. Jesus said we should always pray and never give up.[1] We are to pray without ceasing and to be "instant" in prayer—to be ready with a prayer at a moment's notice.[2,3]

Many people of many faiths all over the world have taken the concept of living life as a prayer in a very literal way. They cloister themselves in isolated settings, free from the travails of the world, simply in order to pray and meditate in search of spiritual enlightenment. But pragmatic Christians tend to view the concept as metaphorical.

Prayer is a way of living a life with God. It does not just mean having a conversation with Him. The prophet Micah was frustrated about this. He asked God hyperbolically—as though God were impossible to please— how much prayer is enough:

With what shall I come to the Lord
And bow myself before the God on high?
Shall I come to Him with burnt offerings,
With yearling calves?
Does the Lord take delight in thousands of rams,
In ten thousand rivers of oil?
Shall I present my firstborn for my rebellious acts,
The fruit of my body for the sin of my soul? [4]

God's response begins to shed some light on what it means to pray without ceasing:

He has told you, O man, what is good;
And what does the Lord require of you
But to do justice, to love kindness,
And to walk humbly with your God? [5]

Evidently, prayer is not as Micah perceived it—nor as *we* tend to perceive it. First and foremost, it is not about the individual supplicant. To think so is one of the most subtle ensnarements. Self-centered prayer that focuses on *me* and *my* needs, *my* health, *my* piety, *my* faith, and so on, subverts the real purpose of prayer.

In the Lord's Prayer, Jesus distinctly avoided this trap by using the plural personal pronouns "our," "us," and "we," instead of "my," "me," and "I." To live a life of prayer is to live a life in community with others, doing justice and loving mercy; not for our own benefit, but for the benefit of the community and the individuals in it. And we are told to do so humbly, because humility is an impediment to selfishness.

Self-centered prayer tends to leave us feeling like Micah: No matter how hard we pray, it's never enough to get God to answer in the way we want Him to. But a focus on others— on our neighbors—removes the element of idolatry inherent to a self-centered prayer-life. It makes us better people.

The parable of the Good Samaritan was a response to a question put to Jesus about what one must do to inherit eternal life. Love God and treat your neighbor as you would wish to be treated yourself, was His immediate answer. But the parable also answered the vital question: *Who is my neighbor?*

The road between Jerusalem and Jericho, where the parable played out, is a metaphor for the road of life. On the road of life, we too will not only meet Good Samaritans, robbers, victims of robbers, and people who are indifferent to the plight of victims, but also—and not without irony—we ourselves will play *all* of these roles at some point in our lives.

Like the Good Samaritan, each of us carries a "toolbox of opportunity." But some tools, such as time and money and emotional energy, are sometimes missing. All of these are helpful and maybe even necessary in playing the role of the Good Samaritan.

God knows this, of course. He does not expect us to do the right thing by everybody all the time. On the day of judgment,[6] when we will be asked essentially "What did you do on the road of life?" God will take into account whether we had the tools to respond in situations that demanded a response. Some people need things we just cannot give, however much we may want to or feel we ought to. So to live a life of prayer, continually and humbly dispensing justice and mercy in the community, is tempered by our ability to respond.

The great personalities of the Old Testament were in constant prayerful communion with God. And they prayed some great prayers. Abraham, Jacob, and Hannah all prayed for personal advancement; Solomon prayed a prayer for wisdom; David prayed a prayer of penitence; Job prayed a prayer for enlightenment; Jonah prayed for salvation from the belly of a great fish; and, on the day of His arrest and in full anticipation of His crucifixion, Jesus prayed that God's will be done. We will examine these prayers.

Job's prayer is often used to explain why bad things happen to good people. It was not so much a request as an acknowledgment, a confession. Job was a wealthy man with many earthly blessings. But he also had an "adversary" (the devil) who accused him of taking bribes from God. This, of course, indirectly accused God of *offering* bribes. For reasons hard for us—and certainly for Mrs. Job—to fathom, God allowed the devil to reverse Job's blessings. As a result, Job ended up losing his wealth, his children, and his health. His wife said bitterly to him:

"Do you still hold fast your integrity? Curse God and die!" [7]

He replied:

"You speak as one of the foolish women speaks. Shall we indeed accept good from God and not accept adversity?" [8]

...to which the narrator of the story commented that Job was right:

In all this Job did not sin with his lips.[9]

Job's plight elicited the sympathy of three of his friends who, finding him in bad shape, themselves became so distraught they could not speak for a week. As we shall see, it would have been better for them to have stayed silent. Instead, when they recovered their power of speech, they proceeded to lecture Job, telling him in essence: "God is punishing you because you are a sinner. Confess, and God will restore everything to you."

Job responded by protesting that he was a good man, not a sinner. Therefore, God was treating him unfairly. Therefore, he would win, in principle, if he sued God for defamation:

"Behold now, I have prepared my case; I know that I will be vindicated." 10

Though confident of his innocence, Job knew that with God as judge, jury, and executioner, in practice he could not really hope to win his case. So he had better just listen and learn:

I would present my case before Him and fill my mouth with arguments. I would learn the words which He would answer, and perceive what He would say to me. 11

On the other hand, he sensed that God was also his defense counsel:

Even now, behold, my witness is in heaven, and my advocate is on high. 12

So the court that was stacked against him was also on his side. No wonder he was confused.

God Himself weighed in on the argument between Job and his friends, with a narrative dripping with divine sarcasm as He compared Himself and His awesome might to insignificant little Job. But He ignored Job's question about why bad things had happened to a good person like him. A little bit of order in life, thought Job, would prevent bad things happening to good people. But eventually, he reached a spiritual point beyond this expectation of order in life, and that's when he prayed his great prayer:

I know that You can do all things,
And that no purpose of Yours can be thwarted.
"Who is this that hides counsel without knowledge?"
Therefore I have declared that which I did not understand,

Things too wonderful for me, which I did not know.
"Hear, now, and I will speak;
I will ask You, and You instruct me."
I have heard of You by the hearing of the ear;
But now my eye sees You;
Therefore I retract,
*And I repent in dust and ashes."*13

Like Shadrach, Meshach and Abednego, the Hebrew worthies who resigned themselves to roasting in King Nebuchadnezzar's fiery furnace, Job recognized that God's will alone would and will always be done.

But more drama was to come when God chastised Job's three friends for misrepresenting Him as a God of retributive justice:

My wrath is kindled against you ... because you have not spoken
*of Me what is right as My servant Job has.*14

In the end, God never revealed why bad things happen to good people. But He left Job enlightened, and that enlightenment shines through his prayer.

Jonah prayed two notable prayers. The first says as much about what is *not* good prayer as about what *is* good prayer.

The context for both is that God told Jonah, His prophet, to travel to the city of Nineveh and persuade its inhabitants to change their wicked ways and follow the true God. But Jonah did not want the assignment, so he started heading *down* to try to escape it: He went *down* to the port of Jaffa on the eastern Mediterranean, then *down* into the hold of a ship bound for Tarsius on the west end of the Mediterranean—practically the end of the world in those days, and fell asleep.

After the ship got under way, a storm arose. It seems Jonah was the only Jew on board, since the crew of Gentiles suspected him of being the cause of the storm. He admitted he was running away from his Hebrew God and offered to sacrifice himself so that the ship could be saved. The crew took him up on the offer, and threw him overboard. *Down* he went to the depths of the sea (like the sins of which Micah spoke, which were disposed of in the ocean so God would no longer have to look upon them.)[15]

Jonah must have expected to drown, but instead was swallowed by a great fish. He went *down* into the belly of the fish, where again he was sure he must die, and prayed his first great prayer:

I called out of my distress to the Lord, and He answered me. I cried for help from the depth of Sheol; You heard my voice. For You had cast me into the deep, Into the heart of the seas, and the current engulfed me. All Your breakers and billows passed over me.

So I said, 'I have been expelled from Your sight. Nevertheless I will look again toward Your holy temple.' Water encompassed me to the point of death. The great deep engulfed me, weeds were wrapped around my head. I descended to the roots of the mountains. The earth with its bars was around me forever, but You have brought up my life from the pit, O Lord my God.

While I was fainting away, I remembered the Lord, and my prayer came to You, into Your holy temple. Those who regard vain idols forsake their faithfulness, but I will sacrifice to You with the voice of thanksgiving. That which I have vowed I will pay. Salvation is from the Lord.[16]

Jonah had gone as far down as anyone could go. He had reached rock bottom, the place of the dead, the repository of sin, a place where even God's all-seeing eye would be absent. But he prayed anyway. The most significant verse in the prayer is:

While I was fainting away, I remembered the Lord, and my prayer came to You, into Your holy temple.[17]

It seems a perplexing example of how *not* to pray. Rather than confessing, Jonah seemed to be saying that he did the right thing by remembering the Lord, implying therefore that it was *his* action, *his* prayer, that would save him. It undermines the truth that it was God's grace that saved him. In the very next verse, alluding to the Gentile crew aboard the ship who prayed to false Gods to save them from the storm, Jonah again tried to show how pious he was:

Those who regard vain idols forsake their faithfulness, but I will sacrifice to You with the voice of thanksgiving. That which I have vowed I will pay.[18]

Again, this seems to undermine the grace that actually saved him. His prayer strongly implies that by acting piously and thereby getting God to save him, he—Jonah—was the hero. It amounted to self-worship.

He also seemed to be saying that God's grace would be wasted on idolaters such as the Gentile sailors and the Ninevites. He was hinting that he still did not want to go to Nineveh. Even if he succeeded in converting them, the Ninevites would soon revert to their old ways, he thought. It would be a waste of his time and of God's grace.

There are 24 first-person pronouns in the first prayer—almost a quarter of it! But there is not a word of confession, of repentance; merely a long description of events and of how pious Jonah became.

After this prayer, Jonah was vomited (a word redolent of violence, ugliness, and distaste) by the fish onto the shore. Perhaps the fish was nauseated by the prayer! Jonah then went to Nineveh and persuaded its citizens to repent, where-upon God did just what Jonah feared: He showed the

Ninevites mercy and grace, rather than destroying them. This...

... greatly displeased Jonah and he became angry.[19]

So angry, that he prayed again:

Please Lord, was not this what I said while I was still in my own country? Therefore in order to forestall this I fled to Tarshish, for I knew that You are a gracious and compassionate God, slow to anger and abundant in lovingkindness, and one who relents concerning calamity. Therefore now, O Lord, please take my life from me, for death is better to me than life.[20]

He was telling God that He—God!—was wrong; so wrong, that Jonah would rather die than suffer God's abundance of grace and love for himself and others.

We have noted that God often answers a prayer with a question. He did so now, asking Jonah:

"Do you have good reason to be angry?"

Jonah decided to get out of Nineveh to await developments. God caused a large plant to grow and shade him, which Jonah was very happy about. But the next morning, God caused the plant to wither, leaving Jonah unprotected from a scorching sun and wind. Jonah felt so bad he "begged with all his soul to die." God responded to his begging again with a question:

"Do you have good reason to be angry about the plant?"

Yes, I do, said Jonah. So God asked him a third and final question:

"You had compassion on the plant for which you did not work and which you did not cause to grow, which came up overnight and perished overnight. Should I not have compassion on Nineveh, the great city in which there are more than 120,000 persons who do

not know the difference between their right and left hand, as well as many animals?" [21]

There is a certain tension—perhaps even a contradiction—between the concepts of prayer and free will. If we success-fully pray for help for someone else but that person does not *want* help, have we not violated that person's free will? Yet God does it all the time, as we see in the personal prayers of Jacob, Hannah, and Solomon.

Jacob essentially prayed for protection from his twin brother Esau, whom he had wronged:

O God of my father Abraham and God of my father Isaac, O Lord, who said to me, 'Return to your country and to your rela-tives, and I will prosper you,' I am unworthy of all the lov-ingkindness and of all the faithfulness which You have shown to Your servant; for with my staff only I crossed this Jordan, and now I have become two companies. Deliver me, I pray, from the hand of my brother, from the hand of Esau; for I fear him, that he will come and attack me and the mothers with the children. For You said, 'I will surely prosper you and make your descendants as the sand of the sea, which is too great to be numbered.' [22]

God responded to Jacob's prayer by physically wrestling with him, as discussed in Chapter 1.

Hannah was a barren woman, fruitless, unable to conceive; a condition then commonly viewed as spiritually related. Her husband therefore felt justified in dumping her and taking another wife, who successfully conceived and heaped scorn on Hannah.

Being a childless widow was a fate worse than death in that society at that time. Jesus had a special compassion for widows for that very reason. Hannah prayed that if God gave her a son, she would give the child back to God after he was weaned:

O Lord of hosts, if You will indeed look on the affliction of Your maidservant and remember me, and not forget Your maidservant, but will give Your maidservant a son, then I will give him to the Lord all the days of his life, and a razor shall never come on his head.[23]

Hannah was willing to give up the thing she most desired as a condition for getting it. It makes one wonder: Is the only righteous thing we can do with our free will to give it up?

King Solomon's prayer was prayed following the tumultuous and bloody start to his reign and with the foreknowledge that God would do anything for him:

You have shown great lovingkindness to Your servant David my father, according as he walked before You in truth and right- eousness and uprightness of heart toward You; and You have re- served for him this great lovingkindness, that You have given him a son to sit on his throne, as it is this day. Now, O Lord my God, You have made Your servant king in place of my father David, yet I am but a little child; I do not know how to go out or come in. Your servant is in the midst of Your people which You have chosen, a great people who are too many to be numbered or counted. So give Your servant an understanding heart to judge Your people to discern between good and evil. For who is able to judge this great people of Yours?[24]

The prayer is humble and frank but it asks for the very thing that got Adam and Eve thrown out of the garden of Eden, namely: The ability to discern between good and evil. But this time, God granted the request, as a once-in-eternity concession:

Because you have asked this thing and have not asked for yourself long life, nor have asked riches for yourself, nor have you asked for the life of your enemies, but have asked for yourself discernment to understand justice, behold, I have done according to your words. Behold, I have given you a wise and discerning heart, so that there has been no one like you before you, nor shall one like you arise after you. I have also given you what you have not asked, both riches and honor, so that there will not be any among the kings like you all your days. If you walk in My ways, keeping My statutes and commandments, as your father David walked, then I will prolong your days.[25]

The wisdom God bestowed upon Solomon was demonstrated when Solomon ordered that a baby be cut in two to satisfy two claimants to its maternity, knowing that the real mother would abandon her claim (and, in so doing, prove her claim) so as to save her baby's life.

The personal prayers of Jacob, Hannah, and Solomon essentially represent a surrender of free will in return for freedom from fear (Jacob), freedom from want of a thing desired (Hannah), and freedom from ignorance (Solomon). Compared to prayers to "Please help me find a parking space" or "Please let my team win" they are noble enough; but, more importantly, they imply that real prayer entails some loss of free will.

Some think that God does not answer prayer precisely because it would violate our free will. But would it? Does prayer fundamentally support or undermine free will, especially if we pray for ourselves rather than for someone else?

From the Book of Genesis to the Book of Revelation, there is example after example of God's readiness to intervene in the world, but scant evidence of His *un*willingness to tamper with our free will. On the contrary: Jonah tried his best to exercise his free will, but God would not let him.

We may find ourselves sometimes personally reflected in these great prayers of Scripture. Like Jonah, we are inclined to rebellion, and driven to flee God's commands. Like Jacob, we fear that past misdeeds will catch up with us. Like Hannah, we beg for things we think we need. And like Solomon, we wish we had more wisdom, more insight.

If there is an overriding principle to be found in God's responses to these prayers, it is that God has a plan: For history, for His people of the kingdom of heaven, for Job, for Jonah, for Hannah, for Jacob, for Solomon... and for you and me. The great prayers are doubtful, bargaining, self-justifying, fearful, insecure prayers—precisely the kinds we all tend to pray. They illuminate the apostle Paul's message that neither we nor the prophets of God know or knew how to pray. The meaning God wants us to derive from them is that prayer is not about us and *our* plans but about Him and *His*.

God does not hold against us our penchant for praying the wrong sort of prayer. We reveal our doubts and fears and pleas through our prayers, and His responses show us that He puts our prayers into the context of His plan. Perhaps that is why His responses often appear to us to be unrelated to the content of our prayer.

Sometimes God's plan is clear and even becomes visibly operational, but often the plan can only be grasped by faith, and even then may not be seen clearly. Paul's conclusion that "God causes all things to work together for good to those who love God"[26] is another way of saying that God has a plan for us.

When Job asked why so many bad things were happening to him, God's response was: "It's not about you; it's about my grand plan for the universe." A man of great stature—God's own prophet, Jonah—refused to accept that message. He complained instead that God would and did mess up his own plan to punish the Ninevites, by formulating a divine plan to save them instead. And God completely ignored Jacob's prayer for protection, giving him instead a new identity and disabling him. Hannah prayed for a son to be her security in old age; God gave her a son but it was not hers—it was His: His plan, His son. When Paul prayed God to remove a thorn from his flesh, God told him to put up with it and be content with God's grace.

So while these famous prayers are not model prayers like the *Our Father*, they are nevertheless real, authentic, and instructive in showing us how we pray, how God responds, and that only God's plan matters. They help us see that prayer is a way of centering or aligning or focusing ourselves on the will of God, on His plan.

But still, there remains the apparent contradiction with the concept of free will. From beginning to end, the Bible is about God's activity in history; about His interaction with His people and with individuals. It is clear in the Bible that God tampers with man's free will. He intervened, for instance, in every aspect of the exodus out of Egypt. Nowhere in the Bible, at critical junctures in human history, does God ask Man: What do *you* want? What is *your* will? By definition, prayer is an invitation to God to intervene in the affairs of man. It is an act of surrender of the will. *Thy* kingdom come, *Thy* will be done.

If God governs history, then how can history consist of the events that arise out of the exercise of our own free will and, as Job asked, why do we see so much distress and mayhem in our lives? It is undeniable that man is also responsible for making significant choices that have significant consequences. How can these two wills be reconciled? They can't. Scripture says:

Whatever the Lord pleases, He does, in heaven and in earth, in the seas and in all deeps. [27]

Remember the former things long past, for I am God, and there is no other; I am God, and there is no one like Me, declaring the end from the beginning, and from ancient times things which have not been done, saying, "My purpose will be established, and I will accomplish all My good pleasure...." [28]

All the inhabitants of the earth are accounted as nothing, but He does according to His will in the host of heaven and among the inhabitants of earth; and no one can ward off His hand or say to Him, "What have You done?" [29]

But now, O Lord, You are our Father, we are the clay, and You our potter; and all of us are the work of Your hand. [30]

The Lord said to him, "Who has made man's mouth? Or who makes him mute or deaf, or seeing or blind? Is it not I, the Lord? [31]

"Before I formed you in the womb I knew you, and before you were born I consecrated you;... [32]

Who is there who speaks and it comes to pass, unless the Lord has commanded it? Is it not from the mouth of the Most High that both good and ill go forth? [33]

The plans of the heart belong to man, but the answer of the tongue is from the Lord. [34]

The mind of man plans his way, but the Lord directs his steps. [35]

The lot is cast into the lap, but its every decision is from the Lord.[36]

I know, O Lord, that a man's way is not in himself, nor is it in a man who walks to direct his steps.[37]

No wonder Paul asked, rhetorically: "Who can resist the will of the Lord?"[38]

Is there a difference between *freedom to make decisions* and *free will*? How do we square our moral responsibility for the consequential decisions we make with the lack of responsibility if we hand over our free will to God? How did Jesus handle it?

By far the longest prayer by Jesus recorded in the gospels is sometimes called the "High Priestly Prayer" or the "Farewell Prayer." It could in fact be called the "Lord's Prayer" in the sense that it was His own personal prayer to God the Father, whereas the prayer we call the *Lord's Prayer*, the *Our Father*, or the *Pater Noster* is what Jesus taught *us* to pray.

The High Priestly Prayer was delivered following what is generally considered to be Jesus' farewell speech to the disciples. The speech was intended to prepare them for His mortal exit and for the entry of the Holy Spirit, to tell them of the meaning of His ministry, and to provide them some guidance as to how the ministry should continue to unfold after He left. The core theme was that the disciples should love others as He had loved the disciples themselves. Two major subsidiary themes were that His work had succeeded and had brought glory to God, and a petition to God to underwrite, with His love, unity amongst the disciples and followers.

That, then, was the setting. Here is the Prayer

Father, the hour has come; glorify Your Son, that the Son may glorify You, even as You gave Him authority over all flesh, that to all whom You have given Him, He may give eternal life. This is eternal life, that they may know You, the only true God, and Jesus Christ whom You have sent. I glorified You on the earth, having accomplished the work which You have given Me to do. Now, Father, glorify Me together with Yourself, with the glory which I had with You before the world was.

I have manifested Your name to the men whom You gave Me out of the world; they were Yours and You gave them to Me, and they have kept Your word. Now they have come to know that everything You have given Me is from You; for the words which You gave Me I have given to them; and they received them and truly understood that I came forth from You, and they believed that You sent Me. I ask on their behalf; I do not ask on behalf of the world, but of those whom You have given Me; for they are Yours; and all things that are Mine are Yours, and Yours are Mine; and I have been glorified in them. I am no longer in the world; and yet they themselves are in the world, and I come to You. Holy Father, keep them in Your name, the name which You have given Me, that they may be one even as We are. While I was with them, I was keeping them in Your name which You have given Me; and I guarded them and not one of them perished but the son of perdition, so that the Scripture would be fulfilled.

But now I come to You; and these things I speak in the world so that they may have My joy made full in themselves. I have given them Your word; and the world has hated them, because they are not of the world, even as I am not of the world. I do not ask You to take them out of the world, but to keep them from the evil one. They are not of the world, even as I am not of the world. Sanctify them in the truth; Your word is truth. As You sent Me into the world, I also have sent them into the world. For their sakes I sanctify Myself, that they themselves also may be sanctified in truth.

I do not ask on behalf of these alone, but for those also who believe in Me through their word; that they may all be one; even as You, Father, are in Me and I in You, that they also may be in Us, so that the world may believe that You sent Me.

The glory which You have given Me I have given to them, that they may be one, just as We are one; I in them and You in Me, that they may be perfected in unity, so that the world may know that You sent Me, and loved them, even as You have loved Me. Father, I desire that they also, whom You have given Me, be with Me where I am, so that they may see My glory which You have given Me, for You loved Me before the foundation of the world.

O righteous Father, although the world has not known You, yet I have known You; and these have known that You sent Me; and I have made Your name known to them, and will make it known, so that the love with which You loved Me may be in them, and I in them.[39]

The utilitarian, evangelistic product of this prayer is a world united in the knowledge that God sent Jesus. The unity exists in the Godhead and is extended to the followers of God, and God is glorified as a result. It is not a prayer asking for personal things, in the manner of the prayers of Job or Jonah or Hannah. Jesus simply asked that His followers be helped to recognize and demonstrate unity.

The sufferings of Job, Jonah, and Hannah were nothing to that which Jesus knew awaited Him; and He was still human enough to pray for the suffering to end—if God the Father willed it. The short prayer Jesus prayed three times in the garden of Gethsemane in His last days on earth, and the context within which it was prayed, was as follows (the prayer itself is **bolded** for ease of reference):

Then Jesus came with them to a place called Gethsemane, and said to His disciples, "Sit here while I go over there and pray." And He took with Him Peter and the two sons of Zebedee, and began to be grieved and distressed. Then He said to them, "My soul is deeply grieved, to the point of death; remain here and keep watch with Me."

And He went a little beyond them, and fell on His face and prayed, saying, **"My Father, if it is possible, let this cup pass from Me; yet not as I will, but as You will."** *And He came to the disciples and found them sleeping, and said to Peter, "So, you men could not keep watch with Me for one hour? Keep watching and praying that you may not enter into temptation; the spirit is willing, but the flesh is weak."*

He went away again a second time and prayed, saying, **"My Father, if this cannot pass away unless I drink it, Your will be done."** *Again He came and found them sleeping, for their eyes were heavy. And He left them again, and went away and* **prayed a third time, saying the same thing once more.** *Then He came to the disciples and said to them, "Are you still sleeping and resting? Behold, the hour is at hand and the Son of Man is being betrayed into the hands of sinners. Get up, let us be going; behold, the one who betrays Me is at hand!"*[40]

There are many interpretations of this prayer. According to one, Jesus was struggling to fulfill His obligation to martyr Himself for our sins, therefore our salvation was hanging in the balance while Jesus debated within Himself whether or not to "accept the cup." But it seems clear from Scripture that the plan for the salvation of the world, for the restoration of Man from the Fall from Eden, was already well worked out between God the Father and God the Son, that the Lamb of

God had been "slain from the foundation of the world" already. The notion that God the Son would renege on this plan seems implausible, to say the least. It seems that what was really at stake here was not the acceptance of the cup, but rather the plea—the prayer—that the effects of the cup would not last forever. This augured the Resurrection.

All along, Peter did not want God to be the God represented by Jesus. When Jesus told the disciples He was going to be martyred, Peter took great exception to it, telling Jesus that such talk would ruin His reputation as King of the Jews. Jesus grew so upset as to call him Satan for saying such a thing. After the prayer, it was Peter who hacked off the ear of an official, seeking by physical means to show that Jesus was a King to be defended at all costs and not some meek Lamb fit only for sacrifice.

Don't we all tend to succumb to the same temptation of not accepting God for what He truly is but for what we want Him to be? Are there parallels between the gardens of Gethsemane and Eden? Both had their share of sorrow; and in both, the will of Man was pitted against the will of God. Adam and Eve's eating of the fruit of the tree of knowledge of good and evil resulted from the same temptation as Peter's: To not let God be God, and to believe that *we* have the power to judge what is good and what is evil. But if Eden was the starting point on the road to Gethsemane, Gethsemane was the starting point on the road back to Eden.

The fall of Man from the garden of Eden came about through the exercise of his will, whereas the restoration of Man—the way back to the garden of Eden—comes about through Jesus' relinquishment of *His* will to God, in the garden of Gethsemane.

Jesus raised the issue of will with Peter, just after the Last Supper, when He said:

The spirit is willing, but the flesh is week.[41]

He told the disciples:

"You will all fall away because of Me this night, for it is written, 'I will strike down the shepherd, and the sheep of the flock shall be scattered.' But after I have been raised, I will go ahead of you to Galilee." But Peter said to Him, "Even though all may fall away because of You, I will never fall away." Jesus said to him, "Truly I say to you that this very night, before a rooster crows, you will deny Me three times." Peter said to Him, "Even if I have to die with You, I will not deny You." All the disciples said the same thing too.[42]

Peter was confident of his ability to remain loyal and maintain his relationship with Jesus, but soon afterwards, in Gethsemane, he slept through Jesus' anguish.

The apostle Paul noted that as creatures of flesh we walk by faith and not by sight.[43] Matters of the flesh are *natural*—they are related to the senses and based upon our sensory experience in, around, and through our natural world. Matters of the spirit, on the other hand, are based on *super*natural experiences not attuned to the senses as we know them but to some kind of insight—to an ability to see the world through spiritual eyes of faith and not simply through natural vision. Paul wrote poignantly of this dual nature:

For we know that the Law is spiritual, but I am of flesh, sold into bondage to sin. For what I am doing, I do not understand; for I am not practicing what I would like to do, but I am doing the very thing I hate. But if I do the very thing I do not want to do, I agree with the Law, confessing that the Law is good. So now, no longer am I the one doing it, but sin which dwells in me. For I know that nothing good dwells in me, that is, in my flesh; for the willing is present in me, but the doing of the good is not. For the good that I want, I do not do, but I practice the very evil that I do not want. But if I am doing the very thing I do not want, I am no longer the one doing it, but sin which dwells in me. I find then the principle that evil is present in me, the one who wants to do good. For I joyfully concur with the law of God in the inner man, but I see a different law in the members of my body, waging war against the law of my mind and making me a prisoner of the law of sin which is in my members. Wretched man that I am! Who will set me free from the body of this death? Thanks be to God through Jesus Christ our Lord! So then, on the one hand I myself with my mind am serving the law of God, but on the other, with my flesh the law of sin. [44]

Therefore there is now no condemnation for those who are in Christ Jesus. For the law of the Spirit of life in Christ Jesus has set you free from the law of sin and of death. For what the Law could not do, weak as it was through the flesh, God did: sending His own Son in the likeness of sinful flesh and as an offering for sin, He condemned sin in the flesh, so that the requirement of the Law might be fulfilled in us, who do not walk according to the flesh but according to the Spirit. [45]

Paul has brought us full circle back to the point where our discussion of prayer began:

In the same way the Spirit also helps our weakness; for we do not know how to pray as we should, but the Spirit Himself intercedes for us with groanings too deep for words; and He who searches the hearts knows what the mind of the Spirit is, because He intercedes for the saints according to the will of God.

And we know that God causes all things to work together for good to those who love God, to those who are called according to His purpose....

For I am convinced that neither death, nor life, nor angels, nor principalities, nor things present, nor things to come, nor powers, nor height, nor depth, nor any other created thing, will be able to separate us from the love of God, which is in Christ Jesus our Lord. [46]

This is a categorical statement about the opportunity for those who walk in the spirit—which is to say, those who love God, those who have faith—to be bonded with God, to be in His presence and to experience His love and grace; and it is pretty hard to be excluded.

Paul said that spirit is a part of the law as it is given by God. That is to say: The law is spiritual, but the keeping of it is hindered by the flesh. While spirit sets us free, flesh binds us. A spiritual mindset confers life and peace, but a flesh-driven mindset is hostile to God and leads to spiritual death. The spirit dwells within us and helps us overcome weaknesses of the flesh. It also intercedes for us in prayer. In contrast, the fleshly mindset cannot keep the law and cannot please God.

Paul talked about *being* and about *walking* in the spirit or the flesh. Walking in the spirit relies on faith rather than on the senses, yet it provides an experience that makes one see things one would not otherwise be able to see. Maybe that's what Paul meant when he said "All things work together for good." It's like analyzing the same data using different methodologies: On the one hand, it is devastating to learn that one has cancer or is suffering from some other tragedy; but on the other hand, to be able to see beyond that, to reach a new understanding, to feel a different experience, to see that somehow all things do work together for good, is intensely enlightening.

As the culture, the language, and the lens of the spirit, prayer is the means by which to see nature in a new light, shorn of the shadows of our physical senses. It is the means, literally, to enlightenment. Perhaps this was what Jesus meant when He said we don't know how to pray, and what the disciples meant when they asked to be taught how to pray: Teach us how to pray for enlightenment, so see the world differently from the often unpalatable view of it that is presented to our senses.

Many great Biblical characters seemed to *be* in the spirit in the sense of having God's interests at heart, yet did not *walk* in the spirit; rather, they used the physical and sensory realm to try to understand and resolve their problems. Abraham, for instance, was promised by God that he would be the foundation of a great nation, yet he took things into his own hands to make this promise come about (he took the child of his handmaiden, Hagar, to correct what he saw as a deficiency in the fulfillment of the promise). Though he was in the spirit, Abraham walked in the flesh: He relied upon himself, not upon God.

The fact that prayer has been ubiquitous throughout all cultures and all times hints rather strongly of its universality and its fundamental importance in life. Scripture tells us that we don't know how to pray and that we had to ask Jesus to teach us how. So on the one hand, prayer is ubiquitous, fundamental, and important; but on the other, we did not know how to do it until Jesus taught us the Lord's Prayer. Through its use of the plural personal pronouns, the Lord's Prayer is a communal prayer. Unity—*comm*unity—is therefore a central aspect or theme of prayer.

So, too, is the need for prayer to be in alignment with the will of God. We tend to approach prayer as a magic incantation that can miraculously get God to give us things we want if we pray in the "right" way. But God is not in our service; it is the other way round. And God's ways and our ways—and His plan for us and our plans for ourselves—are light-years apart. The cause and effect we observe in the natural world is not how God sees things. His ways and His plan are supernatural, not natural, yet it is the natural—not the supernatural—that tends to drive our prayer, particularly our petitional prayer, when we ask for something.

The prayers of Job, Jonah, Gideon, Hannah, and Jesus highlight the relationship between prayer and free will. On the face of it, to pray is to acknowledge that our human will is not enough to meet our needs. In the garden of Eden the exercise of Man's will led to his Fall, whereas in the garden of Gethsemane the relinquishment of it led to his redemption.

It seems that the only righteous thing to do is to relinquish the exercise of our free will and accept the will and the grace *and the plan* of God. God's grace is the assurance of the plan's success, yet it seems to be the ultimate assault on our free will. Is that why we tend to doubt it?

Notes to Chapter 8

[1] In the preamble to the parable of the Importunate Widow.

[2] 2 Thessalonians

[3] Romans 12:2 and Colossians 4:2-6

[4] Micah 6:6-7

[5] Micah 6:8

[6] Matthew 25

[7] Job 2:9

[8] Job 2:10

[9] *Ibid.*

[10] Job 19:28-29

[11] Job 23:4-5

[12] Job 16:19

[13] Job 42:2-6

[14] Job 42:7

[15] Micah 7:19

[16] Jonah 2:2-9

[17] Jonah 2:7

[18] Jonah 2:8

[19] Jonah 4:1

[20] Jonah 4:2-3

[21] Jonah 4:4-11

[22] Genesis 32:9-12

[23] 1 Samuel 1:11

[24] 1 Kings 3:6-9

[25] 1 Kings 3:10-14

[26] Romans 8:26-28

[27] Psalms 135:6

[28] Isaiah 46:9-10

[29] Daniel 4:35

[30] Isaiah 64:8

[31] Exodus 4:11

[32] Jeremiah 1:4

[33] Lamentations 3:37-38

[34] Proverbs 16:1

[35] Proverbs 16:9

[36] Proverbs 16:33

---

[37] Jeremiah 10:23

[38] Paraphrasing Romans 9:19.

[39] John 17

[40] The version quoted is from Matthew (26:36-46). Mark (14:32-42) is almost identical.

[41] Matthew 26:41

[42] Matthew 26:31-35

[43] 2 Corinthians 5:7

[44] Romans 7:14-25

[45] Romans 8:1-4

[46] Romans 8:26-28; 38

9

Forgiveness versus Justice

AT THE TIME OF JESUS, Jews were taught to forgive up to three times. But knowing that Jesus was strong on forgiveness, the disciple Peter asked:

"Lord, how often shall my brother sin against me and I forgive him? Up to seven times?"

Jesus replied, in essence, that there was no limit:

"I do not say to you, up to seven times, but up to seventy times seven."

He explained (as so often) by means of a parable, in which a servant who owed his master money begged and received forgiveness for the debt, but then refused to forgive a fellow servant who owed *him* money. This so angered the master that he "handed him over to the torturers until he should repay all that was owed him." Jesus told the disciples that God would "do the same to you, if each of you does not forgive his brother from your heart."[1]

Forgiveness is an important principle in all religions and communities. Jesus made over three dozen references to it. In the Lord's Prayer, He taught that we should pray: "… forgive us this day our debts, as we forgive our debtors," adding, as a postscript:

> *For if you forgive others for their transgressions, your heavenly Father will also forgive you. But if you do not forgive others, then your Father will not forgive your transgressions.*[2]

Furthermore, He said:

> *Do not judge, and you will not be judged; and do not condemn, and you will not be condemned; pardon, and you will be pardoned.*[3]

When God forgives our sins, He immediately forgets them:

> *I, even I, am the one who wipes out your transgressions for My own sake, And I will not remember your sins.*[4]

> *I have wiped out your transgressions like a thick cloud And your sins like a heavy mist. Return to Me, for I have redeemed you.*[5]

> *"They will not teach again, each man his neighbor and each man his brother, saying, 'Know the Lord,' for they will all know Me, from the least of them to the greatest of them," declares the Lord, "for I will forgive their iniquity, and their sin I will remember no more."*[6]

> *For I will be merciful to their iniquities, And I will remember their sins no more.*[7]

> *And their sins and their lawless deeds I will remember no more.*

> *Now where there is forgiveness of these things, there is no longer any offering for sin.*[8]

So God forgets our sins if *we* forgive *others*, but we have difficulty forgetting when people sin against *us*, even when we forgive them.

Scripture links forgiveness with confession:

If we confess our sins, He is faithful and righteous to forgive us our sins and to cleanse us from all unrighteousness....[9]

But to confess, in that context, means agreeing with what God thinks about us. We need to consider this carefully if we are to understand the power and the process of forgiveness. To be forgiven, must a wrongdoer confess? The Prodigal Son, whose story is a parable of forgiveness, thought he should:

I will get up and go to my father, and will say to him, "Father, I have sinned against heaven, and in your sight; I am no longer worthy to be called your son; make me as one of your hired men."[10]

But in the event, his father interrupted his son's confession before he could finish it:

And the son said to him, 'Father, I have sinned against heaven and in your sight; I am no longer worthy to be called your son.' But the father said to his slaves, 'Quickly bring out the best robe and put it on him, and put a ring on his hand and sandals on his feet....'[11]

So did he or did he not confess? Is half a confession better than none? Or did the father, in neither acknowledging his son's confession nor in not letting him finish it, imply that confession was neither needed nor wanted?

The New Testament word "confession" derives from Greek words meaning "the same, together" and "speak to a conclusion, lay to rest."[12] The verb form means "to say the same thing about." So the following sentence:

If we confess our sins, He is faithful and righteous to forgive us our sins and to cleanse us from all unrighteousness. [13]

could be translated: "If we agree with God that we are sinners in need of His grace—if we say the same thing about ourselves that God would say about us—then He will forgive us and cleanse us." This is reminiscent of the struggle between Jacob and God, when Jacob admitted (confessed) to being Jacob, and also of the parable contrasting the prayers of a pious Pharisee with those of a humble tax collector:

Two men went up into the temple to pray, one a Pharisee and the other a tax collector. The Pharisee stood and was praying this to himself: "God, I thank You that I am not like other people: swindlers, unjust, adulterers, or even like this tax collector. I fast twice a week; I pay tithes of all that I get." But the tax collector, standing some distance away, was even unwilling to lift up his eyes to heaven, but was beating his breast, saying, "God, be merciful to me, the sinner!" I tell you, this man went to his house justified rather than the other; for everyone who exalts himself will be humbled, but he who humbles himself will be exalted. [14]

The tax collector agreed with God—he confessed—that he was a sinner; but the Pharisee would not dream of doing so.

In telling Peter that forgiveness was to be repeated "seventy times seven" Jesus was really saying that forgiveness is eternal, which means, in our case, that it is a lifelong obligation. As we should pray without ceasing, so should we forgive without ceasing.

Forgiveness is a manifestation of God's eternal love, as is grace. But while God's love seems ethereal, His grace and forgiveness are tangible, palpable. When forgiving someone or being forgiven by someone, many of us, I suspect, have felt the powerful relief that accompanies forgiveness. It is an almost tangible warmth, whereas God's love seems more like a mystical construct we sense but don't feel. God leaves us in no doubt that He has already forgiven our sins:

> *When you were dead in your transgressions and the uncircumcision of your flesh, He made you alive together with Him, having forgiven us all our transgressions, having canceled out the certificate of debt consisting of decrees against us, which was hostile to us; and He has taken it out of the way, having nailed it to the cross.*[15]

> *I will remember their sins no more.*[16]

> *Their sins and their lawless deeds I will remember no more.*[17]

But human nature tends to forget, or not to acknowledge, acts of forgiveness and the wonderful benefits forgiveness bestows. Peter talked about the peril of forgetting that we have been forgiven, saying that those who fail to strive through faith for morality, self-discipline, perseverance, Godliness, and love have forgotten that God has forgiven them and have become "blind or short-sighted."[18] To think that we are unforgiven or cannot be fully forgiven is a great impediment to being a fruitful, productive, and responsible believer.

Our tendency to view forgiveness as unjust is another impediment. The notion that there might be no consequences for a person who hurts us goes against the grain of our notion of justice. In such circumstances, we tend to see forgiveness as a loss to ourselves, as "giving in" to injustice, and this causes our discontent and grievances to fester and grow into hatred. We become a slave to the person we hate.

If God can get over the injustice of forgiving our sins against Him, and can even forget they ever occurred, why can't we? He said:

> *I, even I, am the one who wipes out your transgressions for My own sake, and I will not remember your sins.*[19]

Why does He forgive us for His *own* sake? Does His memory of our sins cause Him pain? The notion that God can suffer in any way seems to deny His omnipotence, but at least it serves to highlight that forgiving others must be important for *our* own sakes if it is important for God's. Scripture often talks about God forgiving, leading, calling people, creating, and judging for His own sake. It is common in both the Old and the New Testaments, and particularly in the Book of Psalms:

He leads me through the paths of righteousness for his name's sake.[20]

Do not remember the sins of my youth or my transgressions;
According to Your lovingkindness remember me,
For Your goodness' sake, O Lord.[21]

For Your name's sake, O Lord,
Pardon my iniquity, for it is great.[22]

For You are my rock and my fortress;
For Your name's sake You will lead me and guide me.[23]

Help us, O God of our salvation, for the glory of Your name;
And deliver us and forgive our sins for Your name's sake.[24]

Nevertheless He saved them for the sake of His name,
That He might make His power known.[25]

But You, O God, the Lord, deal kindly with me for Your name's sake; Because Your lovingkindness is good, deliver me.[26]

For the sake of Your name, O Lord, revive me.
In Your righteousness bring my soul out of trouble.[27]

For the sake of My name I delay My wrath, and for My praise I restrain it for you, in order not to cut you off. Behold, I have refined you, but not as silver; I have tested you in the furnace of affliction. For My own sake, for My own sake, I will act; for how can My name be profaned? And My glory I will not give to another. "[28]

I am writing to you, little children, because your sins have been forgiven you for His name's sake. [29]

There is evidently some benefit to God in forgiving us. What if we combine the concept that God forgives us for His own sake with the concept that He cannot forgive us if we do not forgive others? Some of the passages refer to God acting for the sake of righteousness, of truth, of love, and so on. These are all synonyms for, or at least attributes of, God Himself.

Hundreds of studies have tried to explain the spiritual, psychological, and physiological effects of forgiveness. The Mayo Clinic devotes a web page to it.[30] A study by Stanford psychologist Frederic Luskin found a 27 percent reduction in stress symptoms such as headaches, backache, sleeplessness, and upset stomach among those who had been able to forgive grievous wrongs committed against them. There was also a 42 percent decrease in depression, a 35 percent increase in self-confidence, a 62 percent decrease in feelings of loneliness, and a 15 percent reduction in long-term feelings of anger.[31]

Physicians understand the pathology of forgiveness—or, perhaps more accurately, they understand the pathology of unforgiveness. Guilt, bitterness, anger, and resentment all tend to have disabling effects because they result in the release of adrenergic hormones (such as adrenalin, epinephrine, norepinephrine, and corticosteroids) associated with hypertension, coronaries, spasm, ulcer disease, headaches, disturbances of bowel function, psychological problems, and more.[32]

Scripture proclaims forthrightly that the act of forgiveness promotes physical healing. Jesus developed the relationship between healing and forgiveness extensively in His ministry. In one story, Jesus forgave and healed a paralyzed man. Some scribes and Pharisees who witnessed the event objected that only God could forgive sins; to which Jesus replied:

> *"Why are you reasoning in your hearts? Which is easier, to say, 'Your sins have been forgiven you,' or to say, 'Get up and walk'? But, so that you may know that the Son of Man has authority on earth to forgive sins,"—He said to the paralytic—"I say to you, get up, and pick up your stretcher and go home." Immediately he got up before them, and picked up what he had been lying on, and went home glorifying God. They were all struck with astonishment and began glorifying God; and they were filled with fear, saying, "We have seen remarkable things today."* 33

In another story, Jesus healed a man who, for many years, had not had the strength to walk to a healing pool, and had no friends to help him. Jesus said to him:

> *"Get up, pick up your pallet and walk." Immediately the man became well, and picked up his pallet and began to walk.... Afterward Jesus found him in the temple and said to him, "Behold, you have become well; do not sin anymore, so that nothing worse happens to you." The man went away, and told the Jews that it was Jesus who had made him well. For this reason the Jews were persecuting Jesus, because He was doing these things on the Sabbath.*34

Again on a Sabbath, and again to pious protests, Jesus healed...

> *...a woman who for eighteen years had had a sickness caused by a spirit; and she was bent double, and could not straighten up at all. When Jesus saw her, He called her over and said to her, "Woman,*

you are freed from your sickness." And He laid His hands on her; and immediately she was made erect again and began glorifying God.[35]

Clearly, Jesus viewed illness as being linked with an evil spirit, with Satan. But in healing a man born blind at birth, He pointedly de-linked it from any sin of the sufferer:

As he went along, he saw a man blind from birth. His disciples asked him, "Rabbi, who sinned, this man or his parents, that he was born blind?"

"Neither this man nor his parents sinned," said Jesus, "but this happened so that the works of God might be displayed in him.[36]

The contrary hypothesis—that illness is the result of sinful behavior—is somewhat prevalent even today, despite the weight of Scripture to the contrary. People still tend to see unforgiveness as righteous, and therefore sanctioned by our notion of justice. No wonder patients diagnosed with cancer often remark to their doctor that they have led relatively blameless lives and wonder what they could have done to deserve the disease.

In linking forgiveness (a thing of the spirit) with healing (a thing of the body), Jesus was simply trying to operate His ministry within the contemporary worldview that illness was associated with sin, with separation from God. Forgiveness can have a real therapeutic effect on both forgiver and forgiven. The links that Jesus made between sin and disease or deformity, and forgiveness and physical healing, troubles some as having been refuted, by and large, by science.

Have they?

Notes to Chapter 9

[1] Matthew 18:21-35

[2] Matthew 6:14-15

[3] Luke 6:37

[4] Isaiah 43:25

[5] Isaiah 44:22

[6] Jeremiah 31:34

[7] Hebrews 8:12

[8] Hebrews 10:17-18

[9] 1 John 1:9

[10] Luke 15:18-19

[11] Luke 15:21-22

[12] The word "confession" translates from the Greek homologia (ὁμολογία) of the New Testament. Homologia itself was derived from words meaning "the same, together" and "speak to a conclusion, lay to rest." *Source*: Wikipedia.

[13] 1 John 1:9

[14] Luke 18:9-14

[15] Colossians 2:13-14

[16] Isaiah 43 and Hebrews 8

[17] Jeremiah 31 and Hebrews 10

[18] 2 Peter 1:2-9

[19] Isaiah 43:25

[20] Psalm 23

[21] Psalms 25:7

[22] Psalms 25:11

[23] Psalms 31:3

[24] Psalms 79:9

[25] Psalms 106:8

[26] Psalms 109:21

[27] Psalms 143:11

[28] Isaiah 48:9-11

[29] 1 John 2:12

[30] http://www.mayoclinic.org/healthy-lifestyle/adult-health/in-depth/forgiveness/art-20047692?pg=1

[31] Luskin, Frederic. 2002. *Forgive for Good: A Proven Prescription for Health and Happiness.* New York: HarperCollins.

[32] A compendium of research findings linking unforgiveness with sickness can be found at https://nuggets4u.wordpress.com/2012/08/27/major-universities-findings-regarding-unforgiveness-and-disease/

---

[33] Luke 5:17-26
[34] John 5:1-17
[35] Luke 13:10-17
[36] John 9:1-3

10

Science versus Religion

FOR PRIMITIVE MAN, GOD WAS THE SOURCE of all observed phenomena, present in every element of the physical world.[1] He was in every star, and in every blade of grass. God explained the world. At the time of Jesus, God was the cause of, and a participant in, anything inexplicable. But Jesus presented a radically different paradigm of a world He called "the kingdom of heaven."

In our 21st century worldview, staunch believers still insist that with enough faith it is possible to heal the sick with just a word, walk on water, and love one's bitterest enemies. But the paucity of evidence of such miracles has contributed to much disillusionment and outright rejection of things of the spirit. Science makes more sense to people than God does.

The separation of things of the spirit from things of the physical world originated with the Greek Gnostics, who thought the body was controlled by physical phenomena and the spirit by spiritual phenomena, and that phenomena of some lower world were responsible for knowledge and understanding. Gnosticism promoted the authority of religious hierarchy, and led to mysticism, self-denial, and renunciation of the physical world.

A dilute form of gnosticism survives in the Christian church today, as belief in *cause and effect*: Man sins, therefore God punishes; the woman is pious, therefore the woman will go to heaven. But Jesus taught something diametrically opposite to this. He taught noble but seemingly irrational and certainly hard-to-practice concepts such as, for example, that in this radical new kingdom of His one does not get what one deserves—one gets *undeserved* grace; that to be first is to be last; and that one should turn the other cheek to an assailant.

The physical world appears to our senses as rational and Newtonian. In contrast, the spiritual world seems spooky, like aspects of quantum mechanics. Physical objects and phenomena are measurable and therefore scientifically explicable; things of the spirit are not.

Today, we live in a world in which the wind and the waves and the song of a bird are no longer the mysterious workings of God. They are physical phenomena, explicable by barometers and oscilloscopes and anemometers and spectroscopes.

As science demystifies the universe, there seems to be less and less need for God—witness the decline in church membership, especially in Europe but also in the United States.[2] The decline has led to a theory called the "God of the Gaps" which posits that God fills in the gaps in understanding that science is unable to explain. As science closes more and more gaps, there is less and less room for God, according to the logic of this theory. Indeed, in some modern cultures, one can see it happening, and on a significant scale. At Sunday services, the pews at Westminster Abbey seem to seat more voyeuristic tourists than true worshipers.

Can science and religion continue to co-exist? If, as has been said, nature is God's second book,[3] then why would He have written a book that seems to be at odds with the Bible?

The late biologist and popular science writer Stephen J. Gould proposed that science and religion occupy totally different *magisteria* or "domains of teaching authority," each made up of totally different phenomena that can never meet.[4] His theory has been challenged by people in *both* science *and* religion who believe that there *is* significant overlap between the magisteria, and that there exist dissonant areas which can coexist within the human heart and the human mind—the spirit and the intellect. The coexistence of these dissonant areas, they believe, enriches our understanding of the universe. The argument is that there are good tools of science to probe physical questions about *how* things happen and good tools of religion to probe metaphysical questions about *why* things happen.

In the absence of science, ancient Wo/Man thought God caused everything. We now have a scientific basis to understand and even control much of the natural world, and we can see that we are bound to control more and more of it as our science advances. Logically, a God of the Gaps must eventually be squeezed out of having anything to do with the universe, since science will explain and control everything—there will be no gaps left for God to inhabit.

Science measures and validates data in order to test hypotheses about how some aspect of the world works. If the tests succeed, the hypothesis becomes a theory. Over time, with advances in scientific data collection and measuring capability, theories once considered "proven" no longer hold, and new hypotheses and theories take their place. On the other hand, new data and analysis might re-confirm an established theory and lead to its upgrading from theoretical status to become a new law of nature. Valid science anticipates a continuous *modification* of view and understanding.

The spiritual truths resulting from faith, on the other hand, are not testable via data and analysis. They cannot, therefore, be proven scientifically to be true. The believer responds that spiritual truth can only be "felt" as something indefinable yet real. The Apostle Paul said law derived from jurisprudence or science cannot regulate the spirit-based attributes (of which there can be no modification) of people of faith:

> ... *the fruit of the Spirit is love, joy, peace, patience, kindness, goodness, faithfulness, gentleness, self-control; against such things there is no law.*[5]

Do we do science and religion a disservice when we seek to interface them, when we try to overlap the magisteria? Perhaps the churchgoer of faith stage 2 tries to link the two, the doubter of stage 3 separates them completely, and the all-embracing sage of stage 4 seeks to reconcile them in some way.

What will things be like a thousand years from now? A further thousand years of scientific advance will presumably leave us with a much richer understanding of our world and our universe, and correspondingly fewer gaps in knowledge. What will be the role of God, of faith, of spirit, to people then?

For much of the history of man, things of the spirit and things of the flesh were combined. They were fully over-lapping magisteria—they were not separate domains—until science came along to challenge that view. The term *science* did not even exist until the 19th century; before then, the term used was *natural philosophy*.[6] There were no scientists, only natural philosophers whose interest it was to reduce the appeal to the supernatural as a way to explain the world.

The leading natural philosopher of the 17th century (some might say, of all time) was Sir Isaac Newton. It is less well known that he was also a serious Biblical scholar, who wrote a noteworthy commentary on the Book of Daniel.[7] Newton said that the goal of natural philosophy was to understand God. But that goal began slowly and informally to change as the scientific revolution explained more and more natural phenomena without recourse to supernatural sources, even for those who believed that God was still somehow responsible overall.

Natural philosophers who espoused the changing role of natural philosophy as it became "science" were by no means necessarily atheist. On the contrary. Like Newton, they tended to be God-fearing, Bible-reading people who believed that the things of the spirit and the things of nature could not be commingled. Recognition of the laws and orderliness of nature might lead one to deduce the hand of God; but in the practice of science one may not invoke the deity, one may not apply that deduction.

By the time natural philosophy became known as science, the attribution of natural phenomena to either God or Satan was expressly rejected. In the early 1980s, the evangelist Paul de Vries proposed "methodological naturalism" as a model that would allow Christianity to explore scientific questions without attributing natural phenomena to supernatural causes.[8] A decade later, proponents of Intelligent Design insisted on just the opposite: That only God and the supernatural could explain what science has not been able to explain. Science viewed this as an attack on science.

Can a legitimate scientist be a legitimate believer, and *vice versa*? Or are the two magisteria so far apart that no accommodation is possible? Science outlaws all allusion to the supernatural, whereas religion interprets the word of God, as recorded in the Bible, as explaining everything we see in the world around us.

Could Paul be paraphrased to say: "The fruits of science are gravity, Newtonian and quantum physics, genetic certainty, the biologic and cellular basis of the cycle of life and death, and cellular mechanics; and against this there is nothing supernatural"? It seems that science and religion can only be reconciled if we accept that God wrote both the Bible and the Book of Nature, as the psalmist implied:

The heavens are telling of the glory of God;
And their expanse is declaring the work of His hands.[9]

The notion that science and religion either form an integrated whole or are mutually exclusive is generally held to be bad science, bad religion, or both. As a woodworker, Jesus was a low-level scientist of sorts. Even though He could walk on water, He would have relied on scientific and material principles to build boats. In other words, in His own life and ministry, Jesus rendered unto Caesar and God that which was theirs respectively, all the while insisting that His kingdom was not of this world and telling us to seek it inside ourselves. Thus, Jesus was able to reconcile the natural and the supernatural, science and religion.

Scripture suggests that science was a gift from God. At the conclusion of the creation, God gave Man the opportunity to "name the animals."[10] The naming and classification of the natural world is called taxonomy, and taxonomy is fundamental to science. God then established a second principle of science: That nature was provided to feed us.[11] The subjugation of the natural world in our service and to our profit, through the applied sciences of agriculture and animal husbandry and through the harnessing of electricity and oil to enable jet travel, is a gift from God.

The irony and the paradox of science is that although man can control nature, he cannot control his tongue:

So also the tongue is a small part of the body, and yet it boasts of great things. See how great a forest is set aflame by such a small fire! And the tongue is a fire, the very world of iniquity; the tongue is set among our members as that which defiles the entire body, and sets on fire the course of our life, and is set on fire by hell. For every species of beasts and birds, of reptiles and creatures of the sea, is tamed and has been tamed by the human race. But no one can tame the tongue; it is a restless evil and full of deadly poison.[12]

This can be observed in the kinds of science that end up becoming operational: The atomic bomb is harmless in its silo but deadly when activated by man's willfulness. Thus arises the notion, held by some, that science is evil because man sometimes abuses the gift through his willfulness and pride.

The Bible considers science to be a gift of God and under the control of God or of men dependent on God. The tree of knowledge of good and evil is not "the tree of knowledge" as some tend to shorten it; therefore it might reasonably be concluded that God was not against our having knowledge (or even wisdom, which he gave in answer to Solomon's prayer) —He was only against our having knowledge *of good and evil.*

For as long as Man lived under the governance of the garden of Eden then the acquisition of knowledge through the study and application of science seems not to have been a problem. But in Genesis 3, Wo/Man's goal changed. S/he wanted to become like God, knowing good and evil, and it is this that seems to have started the division between science and faith.

Science and faith both lay unique claim to honesty, integrity, and "the truth." Science bases its claim on the self-correction mechanism inherent to the scientific method: New data automatically correct erroneous theory based on old data and may lead to the abandonment of the old and the adoption of a revolutionary new theory, which in turn may lead to the betterment of civilization. Being wrong in science is not considered bad, because it is bound to be corrected in time.

The exponential increase in the volume, velocity, and variety of data (hence, "Big Data") over the past few years is resulting in qualitative improvements in our ability to understand and analyze the world and its contents, including ourselves. For instance, the human genome is now more than just a massive dataset: It is rapidly replacing the magisterium of anatomy; and the epigenome (the genome as it is subjected to environmental influences) will eventually supplant the magisterium of physiology. The gaps are closing at an exponentially accelerating rate.

Religion's claim to possess unique honesty, integrity, and truth is premised primarily or substantially on the rejection of the deliberate and purposeful skepticism and doubt that underlie scientific method. To religion, doubt and skepticism are subversive, dangerous, deceptive, and disruptive, but it offers no equivalent to the scientific method for incorporating new data, for revising and changing its thinking. Even to hint at a need for change may be viewed as heretical.

Religion adamantly refuses to accept that its Scriptures may contain error or be outdated. There is not much sign of ongoing religious evolution. Why is religion so adamant in denying the possibility of error and the possible need for changed thinking regarding its truths? The crux of the matter may be that to religion, salvation depends critically on an understanding of a truth which is unrelated to science. Jesus said:

"I am the way, and the truth, and the life; no one comes to the Father but through Me." [13]

and

"Sanctify them in the truth; Your [God's] word is truth."[14]

His truth is not related to scientific truth:

"If you had faith like a mustard seed [i.e., if you had the merest smidgeon of real faith in the truth that is me], *you would say to this mulberry tree, 'Be uprooted and be planted in the sea'; and it would obey you."* [15]

Paul said that tongues, knowledge, and prophecy—by which he may be taken to mean the ephemeral findings of scientific analysis and prediction—may serve as earthly, small-t truths for us human children but cannot serve as the capital-T Truth of Faith, Hope, and above all Love which is operational in the kingdom of heaven.[16] Just before He was condemned, Jesus had a conversation about His kingdom and His truth with Judaea's governor, Roman prefect Pontius Pilate:

"My kingdom is not of this world. If My kingdom were of this world, then My servants would be fighting so that I would not be handed over to the Jews; but as it is, My kingdom is not of this realm." Therefore Pilate said to Him, "So You are a king?" Jesus answered, "You say correctly that I am a king. For this I have been born, and for this I have come into the world, to testify to the truth. Everyone who is of the truth hears My voice." Pilate said to Him, "What is truth?"[17]

Good question.

Notes to Chapter 10

[1] Or gods. I am using "God" here simply to represent some form of supernatural power.

[2] The Pew Research Center study found that between 2008 and 2014 the Christian share of the U.S. population declined significantly, while the number of U.S. adults who do not identify with any organized religion increased. growinghttp://www.pewforum.org/2015/05/12/americas-changing-religious-landscape/

[3] See the Wikipedia entry at https://en.wikipedia.org/wiki/Book_of_Nature.

[4] Gould, Stephen J. (2002). *Rocks of Ages: Science and Religion in the Fullness of Life.* New York: Ballantyne.

[5] Galatians 5:22-23

[6] According to Wikipedia's entry for *scientist*: "English philosopher and historian of science William Whewell coined the term scientist in 1833, and it was first published in Whewell's anonymous 1834 review of Mary Somerville's 'On the Connexion of the Physical Sciences' published in the *Quarterly Review*."

[7] Sir Isaac Newton's *Daniel and the Apocalypse* with an introductory study of the nature and the cause of unbelief, of miracles and prophecy, by Sir William Whitla; 1922; Murray, London. Available in the public domain online at http://publicdomainreview.org/collections/sir-isaac-newtons-daniel-and-the-apocalypse-1733/

[8] *cf.* Poe, Harry Lee and Chelsea Rose Mytyk (2007). "From Scientific Method to Methodological Naturalism: The Evolution of an Idea." *Communication* 59:39, 213-218, September.

[9] Psalms 19:1

[10] Genesis 2:19

[11] Genesis 1:28-30

[12] James 3:5-8

[13] John 14:6

[14] John 17:17

[15] Luke 17:6

[16] 1 Corinthians 13:8-13

[17] John 18:36-38

11

Truth versus Truth

Beloved, do not believe every spirit, but test the spirits to see whether they are from God, because many false prophets have gone out into the world. By this you know the Spirit of God: every spirit that confesses that Jesus Christ has come in the flesh is from God; and every spirit that does not confess Jesus is not from God; this is the spirit of the antichrist, of which you have heard that it is coming, and now it is already in the world. You are from God, little children, and have overcome them; because greater is He who is in you than he who is in the world. They are from the world; therefore they speak as from the world, and the world listens to them. We are from God; he who knows God listens to us; he who is not from God does not listen to us. By this we know the spirit of truth and the spirit of error.

Beloved, let us love one another, for love is from God; and everyone who loves is born of God and knows God. The one who does not love does not know God, for God is love.[1]

There is no fear in love; but perfect love casts out fear, because fear involves punishment, and the one who fears is not perfected in love. We love, because He first loved us. If someone says, "I love God," and hates his brother, he is a liar; for the one who does not love his brother whom he has seen, cannot love God whom he has not seen. And this commandment we have from Him, that the one who loves God should love his brother also.[2]

JESUS TOLD PONTIUS PILATE that everyone who is "of the truth" hears God's voice. To the believer of any of the major religions, the truth about the existence and the power of God is expressed in the voice of God, as that voice is represented, in words, in their chief works of Scripture.

To the unbeliever, the truth is that there is no God; that He is a figment of human imagination and a mere opiate for the masses. Even amongst believers are those who claim *their* truth, voiced by *their* God, to be more refined, more accurate, more insightful, and more verifiable than the truth claimed by others. Thus, denominations proliferate and are more or less strong depending on how many people they can persuade or coerce to believe their version of truth.

It sounds silly to ask whether truth springs primarily from things that are true, yet the Bible *contrasts* secular knowledge —the small-t truths of scientific findings, theories, and laws of nature—with spiritual truth, the big-T Truth of existence.

The Apostle Paul wrote:

If anyone supposes that he knows anything, he has not yet known as he ought to know....[3]

Paul contrasted the transient nature of disembodied secular knowledge against the eternal truth embodied in Jesus (who, in stating that He was "the way, the truth and the life,"[4] linked truth to the living entity of His personhood, not to some inanimate, abstract, data-driven theory):

Love never fails; but if there are gifts of prophecy, they will be done away; if there are tongues, they will cease; if there is knowledge, it will be done away. For we know in part and we prophesy in part; but when the perfect comes, the partial will be done away.[5]

If one looks to knowledge for truth, one must either arrogantly assume perfect knowledge, or admit that knowledge is imperfect. But if one looks to a living model of love as the embodiment of truth, then knowledge and its advances and new theories are irrelevant.

Many see the Bible as the literal word and voice of God. I see it as a dynamic book about the drama of life. As a surgeon, I deal with that drama on a daily basis, and I find the Bible addresses much of what I see. More than just a window on the divine, it is an intimately human book full of love, tenderness, compassion, concern, hope, and all of the good things of life, as well as the bad things—hatred, violence, revenge, and corruption. It is a book of stark realism, showing us as we are, at our best and at our worst. It catalogs the afflictions, as well as the greatness, of humankind. It reveals our certainties and doubts, our aspirations, and our vileness.

This degree of realism explains, at least to me, many of the Bible's contradictions, which disturb and perplex some of us to the point of destabilizing our faith. The Bible seems to me to mirror the human heart, itself a mass of contradictions that prevent us from ever grasping but a portion of the truth, which we then expand, embroider, extrapolate from, or otherwise find ways to subvert.

We do so at our peril. God's ways are not our ways and His thoughts are not our thoughts.[6] The difference between us and God is not small: It is immeasurably big. So one ought not to look to the Bible expecting to find logic. One should look to it for life. And like life itself, the Bible offers far more questions than answers.

The Bible is not written as a book of systematic scientific thought. There is *some* deep and vital spiritual truth in even the most contradictory and scientifically nonsensical Bible stories. The Bible affirms that contradictory thoughts and ideas and inconsistencies are present in the hearts and minds of all of us. It reflects the existence, the life, of Humanity.

We long for an easy religion and easy answers, without mystery and without unsolvable problems; a religion that lets us escape our miserable human condition; a religion whose God protects us from strife and suffering and doubt and fear. We would prefer a religion free from the suffering depicted in the image of the Cross.

In the Bible, God does not exempt us from life's drama; rather, He promises to live it alongside us. The Bible evades nothing. It enters realistically into life as it is. It expresses all of our feelings, aspirations, fears, contradictions, and intuitions. On every page we see the crisis of human suffering. It provides a deep analysis of the human condition and is worth studying for that reason alone.

But it is precisely in *seeking knowledge* from the Bible that we run astray. Jesus Himself noted our tendency to rely on Scriptural knowledge rather than on the *living* truth He embodied:

You search the Scriptures because you think that in them you have eternal life; it is these that testify about Me; and you are unwilling to come to Me so that you may have life.[7]

If we study the Bible for knowledge, rather than for the mission and message in the embodiment of Jesus, then we will find the truth to be elusive. It is to be found in a person rather than in knowledge and ideas. The Word of God is the Truth:

Sanctify them in the truth; Your word is truth.[8]

...and Jesus is the living Word:

In the beginning was the Word, and the Word was with God, and the Word was God. He was in the beginning with God. All things came into being through Him, and apart from Him nothing came into being that has come into being. In Him was life, and the life was the Light of men. The Light shines in the darkness, and the darkness did not comprehend it. ... There was the true Light which, coming into the world, enlightens every man.[9]

What was from the beginning, what we have heard, what we have seen with our eyes, what we have looked at and touched with our hands, concerning the Word of Life—and the life was manifested, and we have seen and testify and proclaim to you the eternal life, which was with the Father and was manifested to us—what we have seen and heard we proclaim to you also, so that you too may have fellowship with us; and indeed our fellowship is with the Father, and with His Son Jesus Christ. These things we write, so that our joy may be made complete.[10]

Are we misguided in mixing up scientific knowledge about nature with Scriptural truth about God and things of the spirit? Is it necessary to have to constantly update Scriptural truths in the light of new scientific knowledge? Could it be that the word of God is not meant to be understood simply as the words of the Bible but rather as the life of Christ? That the truth is simply the message and the mission of Jesus? Might Marshall McLuhan's dictum, "The medium is the message," be apt here? Does the essential canon of truth consist of the Beatitudes, the Sermon on the Mount, and the other few simple precepts that formed the core (as He Himself avowed) of Jesus' teaching, and by which He lived? In our efforts to establish a correct dataset—the truth—for religious understanding, are we missing the real, simple, truth?

The quest for truth is universal, unbound by culture or time. What is so compelling about truth that we seek it so ardently? Why does it matter whether or not we know that something is true? Is it at heart a search for God, or for ourselves? Jesus said the truth sets us free.[11] Free from what?

We are so insistent about truth that we will often lie or guess rather than confess to not knowing it. Somewhat like...

The Blind Men and the Elephant

It was six men of Indostan
To learning much inclined,
Who went to see the Elephant
(Though all of them were blind),
That each by observation
Might satisfy his mind.

The First approached the Elephant,
And happening to fall
Against his broad and sturdy side,
At once began to bawl:
"God bless me! but the Elephant
Is very like a WALL!"

The Second, feeling of the tusk,
Cried, "Ho, what have we here,
So very round and smooth and sharp?
To me 'tis mighty clear
This wonder of an Elephant
Is very like a SPEAR!"

The Third approached the animal,
And happening to take

The squirming trunk within his hands,
Thus boldly up and spake:
"I see," quoth he, "the Elephant
Is very like a SNAKE!"

The Fourth reached out an eager hand,
And felt about the knee
"What most this wondrous beast is like
Is mighty plain," quoth he:
"'Tis clear enough the Elephant
Is very like a TREE!"

The Fifth, who chanced to touch the ear,
Said: "E'en the blindest man
Can tell what this resembles most;
Deny the fact who can,
This marvel of an Elephant
Is very like a FAN!"

The Sixth no sooner had begun
About the beast to grope,
Than seizing on the swinging tail
That fell within his scope,
"I see," quoth he, "the Elephant
Is very like a ROPE!"

And so these men of Indostan
Disputed loud and long,
Each in his own opinion
Exceeding stiff and strong,
Though each was partly in the right,
and all were in the wrong!

—John Godfrey Saxe (1816-1887)

The need to know the truth seems to be encoded in our DNA, even if knowing it confers no obvious benefit or is even painful. As well, we want our truth to be perfect; but we cannot have perfect truth without perfect data, information, and knowledge, which perfection is beyond the reach of science. Since ultimate truth *must*, by definition, be based upon something that is perfect, then data, information, and knowledge cannot be its source.

Are we morally obliged to seek ultimate truth? What drives men to defend, even past the threshold of violence, their concept of truth? Is truth subjective or objective? What is the relation between truth and reality? And (to echo the words of Pontius Pilate) just what is truth, anyway?

Geisler and Turek said it was:[12]

1. *Discovered, not invented.* It exists independently of anyone's knowledge of it. (Gravity existed prior to Newton's discovery of the law.)

2. *Transcultural.* If something is true, it is true for all people, in all places, at all times. (2+2=4.)

3. *Unchanging*, even though our beliefs about truth change. (When we began to believe the earth was round instead of flat, the truth about the earth didn't change, only our belief about the earth changed.)

4. *Impervious to belief.* Beliefs cannot change a fact, no matter how sincerely they are held. (Someone can sincerely believe the world is flat but that only makes the person sincerely mistaken.)

5. *Not affected by the attitude of the one professing it.* (An arrogant person does not make the truth he professes false. A humble person does not make the falsehood he professes true.)

6. *Absolute*. Even truths that appear to be relative are absolute. (For example, "I Frank Turek feel warm on November 20th, 2003" may appear relative truth, but it is actually absolutely true for everyone, everywhere that Frank Turek had the sensation of warmth on that day.)

Ever since the Enlightenment and the industrial revolution and the development of the scientific method, the acquisition of data and the integration of that data to provide new understanding of the "truth" of the material world has accelerated. This truth is inherently self-correcting.

Today, we know much more about the universe, scientifically, than we knew 100 years ago. But do we know more about God? Do we—should we—know things about God that our ancestors did not? Will our descendants know more about God than we do? Or is the truth about God a revealed truth, an unchanging one-time revelation good for all ages and all cultures and all civilizations?

Historically, what were thought to be truths were passed by word of mouth within a culture, a society, a civilization, a tribe, a people. They were then transmitted in the form of stories that came to constitute *tradition*. Later, writing and printing enabled stories and traditions to be recorded in a more formal way.

That record—that history—tells us how science and discovery have driven our understanding about God. Science and technologies in the forms of Skype, the Web, email, and a recording program called *Audionote* enabled a group of us to assemble to talk about things of the spirit and record and transcribe our conversation.

Technology enabled this book, just as Scripture was enabled by a communication technology: Writing.[13] Scripture is considered by most people of faith to be authoritative. But even though they may share common themes, people of faith tend to speak in a variety of voices. There are different Scriptures from different cultures, traditions, times, places, and religions. They all seek to proclaim the truth about God. But despite their common themes they offer very different interpretations of it, sometimes even within the same Scripture. Our religions are like the six blind men of Indostan, each jumping to erroneous conclusions about the whole after feeling different parts of the elephant.

There is for everyone an unique and personal pathway to truth, depending on one's personality, background, culture, birthplace, lineage, life experiences, and so on. As new experiences and study add to one's knowledge, something continues to evolve that leads one on a path toward the truth.

If there is just one big, overarching, all-encompassing truth, what is it? What would it be if you wanted to pass it on to your children, your students, the next generation of people seeking the truth about God? Something that would be true for all people, in all places, at all times?

That the one big truth cannot be captured in data alone can be illustrated by the temptation of Jesus, in which (you will recall) the devil used truth—quoting from Scripture—to argue with Jesus:

> *Then the devil took Him into the holy city and had Him stand on the pinnacle of the temple, and said to Him, "If You are the Son of God, throw Yourself down; for it is written,*
>
>> *'He will command His angels concerning You'; and 'On their hands they will bear You up, so that You will not strike Your foot against a stone.'"*[14]

Jesus' response showed that He held a different concept of truth; one that treats Scriptural data points with some circumspection:

Jesus said to him, "On the other hand, it is written, 'You shall not put the Lord your God to the test.'"[15]

Whereas these passages suggest that a small truth can hide a bigger truth, another shows that an untruth can reveal it; that something that is not true may still be instrumental in showing a bigger picture of truth. God used this when he told Samuel to use a ruse (a sacrifice, in this case) to hide the small truth that he was coming to anoint David as the new king of Israel, instead of Saul.[16] In hiding the small truth, God was demonstrating the bigger truth that He has a plan for His people.

And in a third example in Scripture, the prophet Hosea received this apparently preposterous instruction from God:

"Go, take to yourself a wife of harlotry and have children of harlotry; for the land commits flagrant harlotry, forsaking the Lord."[17]

Imagine the reaction in church if the pastor were to announce from the pulpit that on God's instructions he was off to the red light district to find a wife!

All these examples from Scripture suggest that the small data points—the small truths and even the untruths of Scripture, the apparently simple cause and effect—are not the big truth. Paul made a similar distinction. The small truth that one ought not to set a bad example by eating food that has been sacrificed to idols is overridden by the larger truth that there are no idols, that there is only one God:

Therefore concerning the eating of things sacrificed to idols, we know that there is no such thing as an idol in the world, and that there is no God but one. ... However not all men have this knowledge; but some, being accustomed to the idol until now, eat food as if it were sacrificed to an idol; and their conscience being weak is defiled. But food will not commend us to God; we are neither the worse if we do not eat, nor the better if we do eat. But take care that this liberty of yours does not somehow become a stumbling block to the weak.[18]

The story of Job emphasizes that sin and punishment—cause and effect—which Job and his friends attributed to God, is far from the whole truth about God. Job finally realized this and came to understand that there exists a greater truth, even though he could not grasp it. About that greater truth, Jesus said:

But he who practices the truth comes to the Light, so that his deeds may be manifested as having been wrought in God.[19]

So the greater truth endows us with something more than understanding, and that something is Enlightenment. It is, for example, enlightening that...

... that which is known about God is evident within [even ungodly and unrighteous men]*; for God made it evident to them. For since the creation of the world His invisible attributes, His eternal power and divine nature, have been clearly seen, being understood through what has been made, so that they are without excuse.*[20]

It tells us that we *can* know the truth of God's divine nature and eternal power through the things He has created. However, we often fail to acknowledge it:

For even though they knew God, they did not honor Him as God or give thanks, but they became futile in their speculations, and their foolish heart was darkened. Professing to be wise, they became fools, and exchanged the glory of the incorruptible God for an image in the form of corruptible man and of birds and four-footed animals and crawling creatures.

Therefore God gave them over in the lusts of their hearts to impurity, so that their bodies would be dishonored among them.

Here's the crux:

For they exchanged the truth of God for a lie, and worshiped and served the creature rather than the Creator, who is blessed forever.

Is the truth about God, then, revealed in this context of a Creator and His creatures? The creation theme permeates Scripture, starting with the very first words of the Bible...

In the beginning God created the heavens and the earth. The earth was formless and void, and darkness was over the surface of the deep, and the Spirit of God was moving over the surface of the waters. Then God said, "Let there be light"; and there was light. God saw that the light was good; and God separated the light from the darkness.[21]

...and ending with the very last words of the Bible, in the Book of Revelation, describing the creative power of God going back to work to create a new heaven and a new earth—a new beginning.

Adam and Eve's eating of the fruit of the tree of knowledge of good and evil undid the relationship between the Creator and His creation. God said "Behold, the man has become like one of Us, knowing good and evil." The knowledge of good and evil may or may not reveal the truth about God, but it is at least a partial enlightenment.

Paul seemed to suggest a sensory source for such enlightenment when he said God's attributes, power, and nature could be "clearly seen" through his creation of the natural world.[22] In other words, humanity has had a sensory experience of something that reveals *something* about—some part of—the truth about God, and that revelatory *something* is His creation, which we see all around us.

The 2nd Commandment forbids images of God, including (it seems reasonable to suppose) not just physical idols of stone and precious metals but also imaginary mental constructs. Yet we anthropomorphize God, making Him just like us only bigger, faster, smarter, and so on. We make Him enough like us that we suppose Him to share our point of view.

The commandment warns us against this, but we do it anyway and we often use our imperfect knowledge, our partial enlightenment, not only to build imaginary Gods that make sense to us but also (and worse) we use it to impose our image of God on others. Worst of all, we often do so with violent force.

To know good from evil appears to be God's prerogative, and His alone. Humanity can discriminate somewhat between the two, but good or evil cannot be adjudicated from any human moral code: It requires omniscience and perfect understanding of the truth about the universe from the beginning to the end of time, from *alpha* to *omega*. Lacking those divine attributes, we risk making grave errors in our judgment of good and evil.

Yet this knowledge, this partial enlightenment, does seem to have some value:

> *But now ask the beasts, and let them teach you;*
> *And the birds of the heavens, and let them tell you.*
> *Or speak to the earth, and let it teach you;*
> *And let the fish of the sea declare to you.*
> *Who among all these does not know*
> *That the hand of the Lord has done this,*
> *In whose hand is the life of every living thing,*
> *And the breath of all mankind?*
> *Does not the ear test words,*
> *As the palate tastes its food?*

Wisdom is with aged men,
With long life is understanding.[23]

And:

The heavens are telling of the glory of God;
And their expanse is declaring the work of His hands.
Day to day pours forth speech,
And night to night reveals knowledge.
There is no speech, nor are there words;
Their voice is not heard.
Their line has gone out through all the earth,
And their utterances to the end of the world.
In them He has placed a tent for the sun,...[24]

The truth about God has elements both of knowledge and of faith. If the truth about God is a timeless truth, it cannot be bound by culture or age. The elements of knowledge are manifested in everything that has been created; therefore, what we know of that timeless truth about God must increase in line with growing scientific observation and understanding of nature and how the world works.

That is not to suggest that the truth about God is trivial; that it is merely a matter of time before we discover it. Mortality limits our ability to apprehend something which, being divine and indestructible, is beyond the realm of our physical experience and beyond the realm of observation and data and knowledge. It is not, however, beyond the realm of spiritual experience:

God is spirit, and those who worship Him must worship in spirit
and truth.   [25]

Spiritual experience does not depend on knowledge, but truth can be approached at least in part through it. If God wanted the knowledge of Him to be data-driven alone, would He not have established a dataset pointing unambiguously to the truth about Him that would have been accessible in all ages and all cultures?

The natural world is a reflection of the creative and re-creative nature of God; this is the clear and unambiguous picture that is referred to. But mankind adds myriad data points beyond that, to construct a picture of God, to make God in Man's image. It is that dataset to which we so blindly cling, without adequate cause. It is that dataset I meant when I wrote that if God wanted us to know more about Him than what nature reveals, He would have given us the data.

The big picture seen in God's creative work is sufficient for faith and trust in Him. But mankind has been unsatisfied with that since the Fall. The desire is always for more discernment, more definition, and more detail. If God doesn't supply it, we make it up; and He doesn't supply it because, firstly, we wouldn't understand it since His thoughts are not our thoughts and His ways are not our ways; and, secondly, the details—the data—change, depending on time, place, culture, age, era, background, education, and so on. What do not change—what are timeless, immutable, and everlasting— are the existential questions.

The Bible notwithstanding, the observable fact that a contemporary dataset does not exist leaves us with the dichotomous dilemma of discerning how much can be known spiritually and how much can be known scientifically. The whole of the Book of Job deals essentially with this dichotomy, and it ends with God passing judgment on human views of the truth about Him. Although God said Job's view was correct, it seems far from being a full view, far from a complete understanding. In essence, the difference between the views of Job and Job's friends was that Job acknowledged the transcendent, omnipotent nature of God while his friends held

God to be a God of cause and effect who could therefore be understood through observation of causes and effects—scientifically, through data.

Job's dilemma was that the data often seemed to be at odds with this preconceived notion. His friends insisted that the data just needed adjusting so that God would fit their preconceived image of Him. Job's insight was that it was impossible for humans to conceive an image, a model, or even an hypothesis of God; that God was not bound by our notions of cause and effect and could do whatever He wanted to do; that in the end God is Goodness but because His ways are not our ways He is at strong risk of being misunderstood.

Job said that even though he could not understand God and even felt oppressed by him, yet he still believed in Him. God gave him the important concept that the greatest obstacle to discovery of the truth about Him is not ignorance but the illusion of knowledge.[26] God answered Job's questions with questions of His own that were intended not to be answered but, rather, to give him insight and enlightenment. The problem with Job's friends was that they sought to counsel Job but their knowledge of the truth about God was illusory:

Who is this that darkens counsel by words without knowledge? [27]

God went on to ask Job a series of specific questions:

Now gird up your loins like a man,
And I will ask you, and you instruct Me!
Where were you when I laid the foundation of the earth?
Tell Me, if you have understanding,
Who set its measurements? Since you know.
Or who stretched the line on it?
On what were its bases sunk?
Or who laid its cornerstone,

When the morning stars sang together
And all the sons of God shouted for joy?

Or who enclosed the sea with doors
When, bursting forth, it went out from the womb;
When I made a cloud its garment
And thick darkness its swaddling band,... [28]

This went on until Job finally got it, and surrendered to the will of God.

We are influenced heavily by the scientific method. We seek data-based truth that will enable us to draw valid, reliable, and replicable conclusions. We especially value data we can see, hear, smell, taste, and touch. Could it be that the truth about God is only accessible through a sixth sense, not necessarily independent of sensory and other data but cognizant of the limitations of such data?

Religions try to establish data points and then, through logic and reasoning and argument, to get others to see the same data points and to draw from them the same conclusions, the same understanding, that they have derived from the same small truths.

Job showed us that the truth about God is a paradox that we can never fully understand. As Paul wrote, it is a truth too wonderful to be fully known, yet not so wonderful that it cannot be known in part:

For we know in part and we prophesy in part; but when the perfect comes, the partial will be done away. When I was a child, I used to speak like a child, think like a child, reason like a child; when I became a man, I did away with childish things. For now we see in a mirror dimly, but then face to face; now I know in part, but then I will know fully just as I also have been fully known. [29]

We cannot know the whole truth, but we can have a working knowledge of it. Upon his surrender, Job said to God:

I know that You can do all things,
And that no purpose of Yours can be thwarted.
"Who is this that hides counsel without knowledge?"
Therefore I have declared that which I did not understand,
Things too wonderful for me, which I did not know.
"Hear, now, and I will speak;
I will ask You, and You instruct me."
I have heard of You by the hearing of the ear;
But now my eye sees You;
Therefore I retract,
And I repent in dust and ashes.[30]

He seemed to be saying that the truth about God requires repentance and the retraction of preconceived notions. Repentance "in dust and ashes" evokes the scene where his friends found Job sitting in ashes, a sign of silent humiliation. Indeed, he and his friends sat there for a week in silence.

Thus, the Book of Job reveals three elements necessary for understanding the truth about God:

1. Retraction of preconceived notions,
2. Repentance—turning in a new direction, and
3. Humble silence before God, allowing instruction to be heard.

Let's say you acquire these elements and now have some understanding of the truth about God. Can you—should you—share that enlightenment with others? If they won't listen, can you—should you—make them listen?

Notes to Chapter 11

[1] 1 John 4:1-8

[2] 1 John 18-21

[3] 1 Corinthians 8:2

[4] John 14:6

[5] 1 Corinthians 13:8-10

[6] Isaiah 55

[7] John 5:39-40

[8] John 17:17

[9] John 1:1-5, 9

[10] 1 John 1:1-9

[11] John 8:32

[12] These six "truths about truth" are described in Geisler, Norman L. and Frank Turek. 2004. *I Don't Have Enough Faith to Be an Atheist.* Wheaton, IL: Crossway Books, pp. 37-8.

[13] The late communications scholar Everett M. Rogers identified four main technological eras in human communication: writing, printing, telecommunication, and interactive communication, in Rogers, E.M., *Communication Technology: The New Media in Society.* New York: The Free Press, 1986.

[14] Matthew 4:5

[15] Matthew 4:6

[16] 1 Samuel 16:1-5

[17] 1 Hosea 1:2

[18] 1 Corinthians 8:1-9

[19] John 3:2

[20] This and the following passages from Romans 1:18-25.

[21] Genesis 1:1-4

[22] Romans 1:20

[23] Job 12:7-12

[24] Psalms 19:1-4

[25] John 4:24

[26] Job 42

[27] Job 38:2

[28] Job 38:3-9

[29] 1 Corinthians 13:9-12

[30] Job 42:2-6

12

Seed versus Soil

Lt. Kaffee: Colonel Jessep, did you order the Code Red?
Judge Randolph (to Col. Jessep): You don't have to answer
that question.
Col. Jessep: [contemptuously, to Judge] I'll answer the ques-
tion. *[To Kaffee:]* You want answers?
Lt. Kaffee: I think I'm entitled to…
Col. Jessep: **You want answers?**
Lt. Kaffee: *I want the truth!*
Col. Jessep: **YOU CAN'T HANDLE THE TRUTH!**

JACK NICHOLSON'S CHARACTER Colonel Jessep had
that heated exchange with defense attorney Lt. Kaffee (Tom
Cruise) in the *dénouement* of the 1992 movie *A Few Good
Men*. The colonel asserted that Kaffee's civilized, untroubled,

sheltered life left him blind to the truth, as seen from the perspective of someone (*i.e.*, himself) fighting hand-to-hand with the enemy in the trenches. Are we all like Lt. Kaffee, hearing the truth (in our case, about God) at second hand?

In the parable of the Seed,[1] seed represents the truth about God ("the word," in the parable) and soil represents the recipients of the truth—the hearers of the word. The sower, of course, represents God:

Behold, the sower went out to sow; and as he sowed, some seeds fell beside the road, and the birds came and ate them up. Others fell on the rocky places, where they did not have much soil; and immediately they sprang up, because they had no depth of soil. But when the sun had risen, they were scorched; and because they had no root, they withered away. Others fell among the thorns, and the thorns came up and choked them out. And others fell on the good soil and yielded a crop, some a hundredfold, some sixty, and some thirty. He who has ears, let him hear.

.... When anyone hears the word of the kingdom and does not understand it, the evil one comes and snatches away what has been sown in his heart. This is the one on whom seed was sown beside the road. The one on whom seed was sown on the rocky places, this is the man who hears the word and immediately receives it with joy; yet he has no firm root in himself, but is only temporary, and when affliction or persecution arises because of the word, immediately he falls away. And the one on whom seed was sown among the thorns, this is the man who hears the word, and the worry of the world and the deceitfulness of wealth choke the word, and it becomes unfruitful. And the one on whom seed was sown on the good soil, this is the man who hears the word and understands it; who indeed bears fruit and brings forth, some a hundredfold, some sixty, and some thirty.

So many questions arise from this parable! One would expect a responsible sower to try to ensure that his valuable seeds would fall only in good, receptive soil. Yet this one made no apparent effort to see that it did. He sowed randomly and took no responsibility for the outcome. Why? Could the soil help being the type of soil that it was? And why was the yield from even the good soil not uniformly bountiful?

Does it mean that the truth about God is expected to be uniformly believed? What are we to make of differences in our beliefs about the truth of God? Does the seed—the truth —see itself as eternally immutable and uniform? Must belief in the truth about God necessarily bear fruit?

Was the soil itself responsible for receiving (or not) the seed? Are *we* responsible for hearing (or not) the word—for accepting (or not) the truth? We may think our hearts are open to God and His word, His truth; but are they?

Must the sown seeds—the word, the truth about God—always bear fruit? Why does "persecution" cause the human equivalent of rocky soil to "fall away" from God, especially in light of Jesus' statement in the Sermon on the Mount that:

Blessed are those who have been persecuted for the sake of right-eousness, for theirs is the kingdom of heaven. [2]

It seems that persecution because of belief in the word can distance people from their belief; yet, despite that, the kingdom of heaven remains accessible to them.

Birds soon ate the seed sown in the soil at the side of the road. But some of these seeds could be expected to emerge not only unscathed after passing through the bird's alimentary tract and being excreted, but fertilized to boot!

Jesus told this parable to a crowd that had assembled on the beach to hear Him preach. Afterwards, He explained its meaning privately to His disciples. He said the disciples were capable of receiving the truth, yet they still needed to have it explained to them. Jesus knew that the crowd, and even some "prophets and righteous men," would not or could not have understood the parable in particular and the truth of God in general. That was not an indictment; it was a matter of fact, brought out in the parable itself. The different types of soil with their differing abilities to absorb and nurture the sown seed represent people and their varying levels of ability to absorb—to understand—and hold on to enough truth to bear fruit.

Jesus explained that the people represented as "hard soil" do not even get a chance to understand the truth—it is snatched from them by "evil ones." People represented by rocky soil are happy to receive the truth but it cannot take deep root, so if times get hard or if they are persecuted for believing it, then they will quickly relinquish it. Yet (as we just saw[3]) Jesus also said in the Beatitudes that the kingdom of heaven belongs to them. People represented as "thorny soil" also begin with the truth but are led astray by the illusory need for material things to protect them from a harsh world. And finally the person represent by "good" soil, who understands and holds on to the truth, is going to be fruitful, though to different degrees—some more, some less.

It is clear from this parable that knowledge of the mysteries of heaven—of the truth about God—has nothing to do with salvation or judgment. Jesus does not condemn the soils that do not fare well with the truth. He simply describes them matter-of-factly. They are what they are. In the Beatitudes, He even blesses them.

Furthermore, nowhere does the parable suggest that the soil has a responsibility to till itself so as to be more receptive to the seed. We have no more responsibility to cultivate ourselves so as to be more receptive to the word of God than soil is responsible for tilling and fertilizing itself. Yet many hold that we do have that responsibility.

Different types of soil all have a role to play in the economy of agriculture. Hard, packed soil is needed for roads to transport seed and harvest to and from the fields. Rocky soil supplies rocks to build walls between farms and fields. Thin, weedy soil supports thorn hedges that keep animals from eating the crops. And of course good soil is needed for a good crop. It seems inconceivable that God would expect people to play roles for which they are not suited and hold them responsible for things they do not understand and over which they have no control. While the circumstances of one's birth do matter in some way...

The Lord will count when He registers the peoples, this one was born there.[4]

...God surely did not mean to condemn people for not understanding His word. Soil is passive, in the parable as in life. But it is transformed by seeds, by His word, by life:

For as the rain and the snow come down from heaven, and do not return there without watering the earth and making it bear and sprout, and furnishing seed to the sower and bread to the eater; so will My word be which goes forth from My mouth; it will not return to Me empty, without accomplishing what I desire, and without succeeding in the matter for which I sent it. For you will go out with joy and be led forth with peace; the mountains and the hills will break forth into shouts of joy before you, and all the trees of the field will clap their hands. Instead of the thorn bush the cypress will come up, and instead of the nettle the myrtle will come up, and it will be a memorial to the Lord, for an everlasting sign which will not be cut off.[5]

This solves the mystery of why the sower was indiscriminate in sowing the seed, distributing it everywhere. But the seed's *transformational power* remains a mystery:

> *The kingdom of God is like a man who casts seed upon the soil; and he goes to bed at night and gets up by day, and the seed sprouts and grows—how, he himself does not know. The soil produces crops by itself; first the blade, then the head, then the mature grain in the head. But when the crop permits, he immediately puts in the sickle, because the harvest has come.*[6]

Seed represents the word that was in the beginning, and was with God, and was God.[7] The seed, the word, the truth, is the fount of life. It has DNA, it gives life to whatever it comes into contact with. Seed is active; soil is passive. We may at various times in our lives be different types of soil or indeed be a mixture of soil types, but we have no control over the process; we are the type of soil, the type of people, that we are. We are passive in the face of the active processes of the seed.

The metaphor of seed stretches all the way from the beginning to the end of the Bible, from Genesis to Revelation, where the tree of life straddles the River of Life and produces fruit in its season; fruit which of course contains the seed of the tree of life.

The apostle Paul used seed as a very rich concept when discussing our spiritual nature—our being in Christ and Christ's being in us. But the first use of seed as a metaphor was when...

> *... God said, Let the earth bring forth grass, the herb yielding seed, and the fruit tree yielding fruit after his kind, whose seed is in itself, upon the earth: and it was so.*[8]

The notion of "seed in itself" is key to understanding what Jesus was trying to teach. A seed propagates only its own kind, its own species. An apple seed never produces an orange. Seed begets more seed. Under optimal conditions, given good soil, more seed will be harvested than was sown. For a seed to grow, it must undergo a process of transformation. Jesus said the seed needs to die *as a seed* but not in its potential to produce more seed, if it is to progress and be transformed.

The second of the seed parables, that of the Wheat and the Tares, looks at seed from a different perspective and introduces the concept of bad seed. We can assume the soil in this parable was good, arable soil where seed would tend to grow, because it was tended. But there was some lack of attention that allowed the field to become contaminated with bad seed:

> The kingdom of heaven may be compared to a man who sowed good seed in his field. But while his men were sleeping, his enemy came and sowed tares among the wheat, and went away. But when the wheat sprouted and bore grain, then the tares became evident also.[9]

The bad tares can be taken to mean weed such as Darnel weed, which looks very similar to, and is therefore easily mistaken for, wheat. The distinction is only discovered after some time, when the tares and the wheat sprout differently. The farmworkers spotted it, and told the farmer:

> Sir, did you not sow good seed in your field? How then does it have tares?

The passage does not say so explicitly, but it seems reasonable to assume that these farmworkers were the same ones who slept while the field was being contaminated. They felt a sense of responsibility for their negligence, but the farmer immediately recognized that the contamination came from outside, telling them:

An enemy has done this!

Nevertheless, the farmworkers sought to atone for their lack of vigilance by restoring the field to its former state, and asked the farmer:

Do you want us, then, to go and gather them up?

The farmer answered:

No; for while you are gathering up the tares, you may uproot the wheat with them. Allow both to grow together until the harvest; and in the time of the harvest I will say to the reapers, "First gather up the tares and bind them in bundles to burn them up; but gather the wheat into my barn."

Jesus explained the parable as follows:

The one who sows the good seed is the Son of Man, and the field is the world; and as for the good seed, these are the sons of the kingdom; and the tares are the sons of the evil one; and the enemy who sowed them is the devil, and the harvest is the end of the age; and the reapers are angels. So just as the tares are gathered up and burned with fire, so shall it be at the end of the age. The Son of Man will send forth His angels, and they will gather out of His kingdom all stumbling blocks, and those who commit lawlessness, and will throw them into the furnace of fire; in that place there will be weeping and gnashing of teeth. Then the righteous will shine forth as the sun in the kingdom of their Father. He who has ears, let him hear.[10]

The enterprise of separating tares from wheat—in other words, the discrimination between good and evil—is not to be left to mortals. It is a divine enterprise.

The third of the three seed parables is that of the Mustard Seed. This is the one parable of the three which Jesus did *not* explain to the disciples, leaving us with less direction and more ways to (mis)interpret it. It helps that it was recorded separately in three gospels:

1. Matthew[11]

The kingdom of heaven is like a mustard seed, which a man took and sowed in his field; and this is smaller than all other seeds, but when it is full grown, it is larger than the garden plants and becomes a tree, so that the birds of the air come and nest in its branches.

2. Mark[12]

How shall we picture the kingdom of God, or by what parable shall we present it? It is like a mustard seed, which, when sown upon the soil, though it is smaller than all the seeds that are upon the soil, yet when it is sown, it grows up and becomes larger than all the garden plants and forms large branches; so that the birds of the air can nest under its shade.

3. Luke[13]

What is the kingdom of God like, and to what shall I compare it? It is like a mustard seed, which a man took and threw into his own garden; and it grew and became a tree, and the birds of the air nested in its branches.

Each version contrasts the diminutive size of the seed with the substantial size of the plant that grows from it. Though it is an annual, the mustard plant grows large enough to sustain birds' nests within one year. It is not typically grown in a garden, but is mostly cultivated in fields.[14] There are seeds smaller even than the mustard, such as dandelion and thistle, but the point might be that mustard is the smallest *cultivated* plant seed. The parable shows a yield far greater than the 100-fold harvest of the richest soil of the Sower and the Seed parable. And although Scripture prohibits the sowing of mixed seeds in one field...

> *...you shall not sow your field with two kinds of seed, nor wear a garment upon you of two kinds of material mixed together.*[15]

...nevertheless, the field in this parable was purposefully sown with mixed species of plant.

In the parable of the Seed, seed was distributed everywhere, indiscriminately. In the parable of the Wheat and Tares, the field sown with good seed was contaminated with bad seed. In the parable of the Mustard Seed, the seed had supernatural growth. Together, the three parables help reveal truths about God.

The parable of the Seed is about the transformative, life-giving power of seed. How the seed grows is a mystery; it is a supernatural process, beyond Man's ken. That God's ways are mysterious is thus a principle we can deduce regarding the truth about God.

A second, nearly identical principle is that since...

> *"My thoughts are not your thoughts, nor are your ways My ways," declares the Lord. "For as the heavens are higher than the earth, so are My ways higher than your ways and My thoughts than your thoughts."*

...then what God sees as growth and as a harvest is different from what we see:

> *"For as the rain and the snow come down from heaven, and do not return there without watering the earth And making it bear and sprout, and furnishing seed to the sower and bread to the eater; so*

will My word be which goes forth from My mouth; it will not return to Me empty, without accomplishing what I desire, and without succeeding in the matter for which I sent it. "[16]

The preceding and the following passages highlight a third principle of the truth about God: That His word has the power to transform. Seed, as Jesus said when He unlocked the parable for the disciples, is the word of God. The transformative nature of the word—the seed—of God follows:

For you will go out with joy and be led forth with peace; the mountains and the hills will break forth into shouts of joy before you, and all the trees of the field will clap their hands. Instead of the thorn bush the cypress will come up, and instead of the nettle the myrtle will come up, and it will be a memorial to the Lord, for an everlasting sign which will not be cut off. [17]

The seed has a purpose, God's purpose. It is not responsible for where it lands. In the parable of the Seed, seed lands on bad soil as well as on good soil; therefore, either the sower was reckless, or he did it on purpose. It seems that he did it on purpose; that it was not by accident that some seed fell on hard, stony ground by the side of the road. It was not by accident that birds ate that seed: It still had a function—it either fed the birds or passed through them and eventually germinated somewhere. As Isaiah said in the passage just quoted, the word does not return empty, without being fulfilled as the will of God.

So whether the soil nurtures the seed or rejects it, the soil is not blamed. God's purpose is to ensure that His seed—his word—is sown everywhere and transforms all it touches. The thorn becomes a cypress, the nettle a myrtle. As well, the transformation is everlasting, eternal. It is a memorial that reminds the future of the past—it is a cause for us to remember the word of God. For the fourth principle of truth is that it is timeless and has existed, albeit hidden, ...

... since the foundation of the world.[18]

A fifth immutable principle of the truth about God is that God was, is, and always will be the God of all mankind, not just the God of the Jews (as Scripture maintained up to that point). Paul revealed this eternal and transformational truth in saying that:

... the Gentiles are fellow heirs and fellow members of the body, and fellow partakers of the promise in Christ Jesus through the gospel,...[19]

In talking about this everlasting truth, Paul again resorted to seed-planting and seed-watering imagery:

I planted, Apollos watered, but God was causing the growth. So then neither the one who plants nor the one who waters is anything, but God who causes the growth.[20]

To summarize the eternal principles of truth that can be deduced from the metaphor of seed as the Word of God:

1. The growth of seed is a mysterious mixture of natural and supernatural.

2. God looks at His harvest differently from the way we look at harvests.

3. The indiscriminate broadcasting of seed is purposeful, to ensure it reaches everywhere where it can be transformational.

4. God is timeless.

5. God's plan rules all mankind.

God is unbounded by time, religion, culture, or theology. His seed—his Word, the Truth, God Himself—is planted in all of us, whether we are receptive to it or not. But these and other truths about God are also enveloped in a mystery we seem driven to examine, even though we know that God's ways are not our ways and that we cannot fathom Him.

So why do we keep trying? Why is our need to know so powerful? Is it possible to lead a satisfying spiritual life in the face of mystery? Can we understand what we need to understand about God and still be able to embrace the mystery? Given our overwhelming desire to know, how can a church exist on the foundation of mystery?

The need to clear up the mystery of the truth about God seems to be part of human nature. What is it that we really wish to know? What is that we should know, that we can know, and that we must know? To put it another way: What matters most?

Notes to Chapter 12

[1] Matthew 13:1-23

[2] Matthew 5:10

[3] *ibid.*

[4] Psalm 87:6

[5] Isaiah 55:10-13

[6] Mark 4:26-9

[7] John 1:1-5

[8] Genesis 1:11

[9] This and following quotes are from Matthew 13:24-30.

[10] Matthew 13:36-43

[11] Matthew 13:31-32

[12] Mark (4:30-32

[13] Luke 13:18-19

[14] There are many species of mustard, but based on its size, that referred to in the parable was probably a black or white mustard seed, the kind we use today.

[15] Leviticus 19:19

[16] Isaiah 55:8-11

[17] Isaiah 55:12-13

[18] Matthew 13:36

[19] Ephesians 3:6

[20] 1 Corinthians 3:2-7

13

Knowledge versus Mystery

So oft in theologic wars,
The disputants, I ween,
Rail on in utter ignorance
Of what each other mean,
And prate about an Elephant
Not one of them has seen! [1]

ADAM AND EVE'S TRANSGRESSION in eating the forbidden fruit of the tree of knowledge of good and evil was the quintessence of humanity's burning desire for knowledge —the desire that caused the Fall. It might therefore be argued that the root of all evil is the desire for knowledge.

It seems we so dislike *not* being "in the know" that we would rather make things up than admit to ignorance. Religions and churches throughout the ages have been more than willing to satisfy our desire, with purported knowledge presented as immutable truth supported by their Scriptures. It is puzzling, then, to see so many different truths, so many different answers, offered by so many different sects; as was pointed out by the wag who added the stanza, quoted in the epigraph to this chapter, to *The Blind Men and the Elephant* (see p. 186).

The mystery of an elephantine God is seen throughout Judaeo–Christian Scripture. The Bible's suffusion with mystery makes it more a book of questions than of answers. The Greek word *mysterion* (μυστήριον) appears 28 times in the New Testament. Although it sounds like (and is translated as) *mystery,* it denotes, rather, *truth revealed*—something previously unknown or not comprehended.[2] Jesus referred repeatedly to a truth revealed and talked about it in the context of spiritual maturity:

> *I praise You, Father, Lord of heaven and earth, that You have hidden these things from the wise and intelligent and have revealed them to infants.* [3]

In short, the truth—the mystery revealed—is something that can be understood by innocent babies, but not by the supposedly wise and intelligent. The apostle Paul emphasized that the revelation of mystery was linked to the preaching, the message, and the ministry of Jesus:

> *Now to Him who is able to establish you according to my gospel and the preaching of Jesus Christ, according to the revelation of the mystery which has been kept secret for long ages past, but now is manifested, and by the Scriptures of the prophets, according to the commandment of the eternal God, has been made known to all the nations, leading to obedience of faith;...*[4]

Paul also emphasized our inability to fathom the mystery of God Himself—the inaccessibility of God's hidden wisdom:

But we speak God's wisdom in a mystery, the hidden wisdom which God predestined before the ages to our glory; the wisdom which none of the rulers of this age has understood; for if they had understood it they would not have crucified the Lord of glory; but just as it is written, "Things which eye has not seen and ear has not heard, and which have not entered the heart of man, all that God has prepared for those who love Him."[5]

Paul referred often to mysteries hidden since the foundation of the earth. Some of them had been revealed to him, but others could only be perceived "in a mirror dimly" (or "through a glass, darkly" as the King James version of the Bible rather more poetically put it):

Behold, I tell you a mystery; we will not all sleep, but we will all be changed, in a moment, in the twinkling of an eye, at the last trumpet; for the trumpet will sound, and the dead will be raised imperishable, and we will be changed.[6]

Love never fails; but if there are gifts of prophecy, they will be done away; if there are tongues, they will cease; if there is knowledge, it will be done away. For we know in part and we prophesy in part; but when the perfect comes, the partial will be done away. When I was a child, I used to speak like a child, think like a child, reason like a child; when I became a man, I did away with childish things. For now we see in a mirror dimly, but then face to face; now I know in part, but then I will know fully just as I also have been fully known.[7]

Mystery, then, matters. It matters a great deal.

Altogether, four great mysteries were revealed by Jesus and others through Scripture. They are mysteries whose meaning all people on earth have sought to understand since time immemorial. They are:

1. *The Mystery of Godliness*—What is the origin and purpose of good?

2. *The Mystery of Iniquity*—What is the origin and purpose of evil?

3. *The Mystery of the Ubiquity of God's Grace*—Whose God is He?

4. *The Mystery of the Transforming Power of Grace*—What does grace do to us?

The mystery of Godliness was not understood before Jesus revealed it. It is essentially a mystery about the source of *goodness*:

> *By common confession, great is the mystery of Godliness: He who was revealed in the flesh, was vindicated in the Spirit, seen by angels, proclaimed among the nations, believed on in the world, taken up in glory.*[8]

The concept that God is *good* spans the Bible, from Genesis to Revelation. In the first chapter of Genesis, the goodness inherent to the creative power of God is manifested again and again:

> *God saw that the light was good.*[9]

> *God called the dry land earth, and the gathering of the waters He called seas; and God saw that it was good.*[10]

> *The earth brought forth vegetation, plants yielding seed after their kind, and trees bearing fruit with seed in them, after their kind; and God saw that it was good.*[11]

God placed [the sun, the moon, and the stars] in the expanse of the heavens to give light on the earth, and to govern the day and the night, and to separate the light from the darkness; and God saw that it was good. 12

God created the great sea monsters and every living creature that moves, with which the waters swarmed after their kind, and every winged bird after its kind; and God saw that it was good. 13

God made the beasts of the earth after their kind, and the cattle after their kind, and everything that creeps on the ground after its kind; and God saw that it was good. 14

God saw all that He had made, and behold, it was very good. 15

The final Biblical reference to God's creative power, given in the Book of Revelation, says:

Then I saw a new heaven and a new earth; for the first heaven and the first earth passed away, and there is no longer any sea. And I saw the holy city, new Jerusalem, coming down out of heaven from God, made ready as a bride adorned for her husband. And I heard a loud voice from the throne, saying, "Behold, the tabernacle of God is among men, and He will dwell among them, and they shall be His people, and God Himself will be among them, and He will wipe away every tear from their eyes; and there will no longer be any death; there will no longer be any mourning, or crying, or pain; the first things have passed away."

And He who sits on the throne said, "Behold, I am making all things new." And He said, "Write, for these words are faithful and true." Then He said to me, "It is done. I am the Alpha and the Omega, the beginning and the end. I will give to the one who thirsts from the spring of the water of life without cost." 16

The act of creation—of making something new—seems central to godliness, to the goodness of God. So, too, does the act of healing—of re*new*ing, which was at the heart of the ministry of Jesus:

You know of Jesus of Nazareth, how God anointed Him with the Holy Spirit and with power, and how He went about doing good and healing all who were oppressed by the devil, for God was with Him.[17]

Jesus used the metaphor of fruit to reveal that goodness is also synonymous with truth:

Beware of the false prophets, who come to you in sheep's clothing, but inwardly are ravenous wolves. You will know them by their fruits. Grapes are not gathered from thorn bushes nor figs from thistles, are they? So every good tree bears good fruit, but the bad tree bears bad fruit. A good tree cannot produce bad fruit, nor can a bad tree produce good fruit. Every tree that does not bear good fruit is cut down and thrown into the fire. So then, you will know them by their fruits.[18]

But the most important parameter of goodness was established when the rich young aristocrat asked Jesus:

"Teacher, what good thing shall I do that I may obtain eternal life?"[19]

Jesus replied:

"Why are you asking Me about what is good? There is only One who is good; but if you wish to enter into life, keep the commandments." ... The young man said to Him, "All these things [i.e., the commandments] *I have kept; what am I still lacking?" Jesus said to him, "If you wish to be complete, go and sell your possessions and give to the poor, and you will have treasure in heaven; and come, follow Me." But when the young man heard this statement, he went away grieving; for he was one who owned much property.*[20]

It's a tall order for a young man (or any of us) used to wealth and power to give it all up, but Jesus never compromised on this principle. In the Sermon on the Mount He emphasized that...

> ...*unless your righteousness surpasses that of the scribes and Pharisees, you will not enter the kingdom of heaven.*[21]

He was alluding to the accepted definition of righteousness as "the keeping of the law." He gave the essential meaning, the true definition, of the equivalent concepts of *goodness*, *godliness*, and *righteousness*, to the rich young aristocrat: "Give up all worldly things and follow Jesus."

Keeping to the letter of the law may or may not be a necessary condition for righteousness but is certainly not sufficient on its own. This may be the revealed truth about the mystery of godliness, of the goodness of God. It reinforces the necessity for mystery itself, as distinct from laws and commandments.

In a long series of illustrations, Jesus contrasted law-keeping with the mystery of goodness. For example:

> *"You have heard that the ancients were told, 'You shall not commit murder' and 'Whoever commits murder shall be liable to the court.' But I say to you that everyone who is angry with his brother shall be guilty before the court...."*[22]

He made similar statements concerning adultery, the making of vows, and the retributive justice of the Old Testament. He sought to replace the prevalent views of the time with diametrically opposed concepts, such as loving one's enemy and turning the other cheek rather than demanding an eye for an eye. In case all this wasn't clear enough, He nailed it by adding:

Therefore you are to be perfect, as your heavenly Father is perfect.[23]

In other words: Goodness is divine; Goodness is God. Yet to people of all faiths, goodness is usually defined in terms of personal piety: How much one gives in alms, how often one prays, attends church/synagogue/mosque/temple, and so on. Jesus said that not only should you *not* judge the goodness of others on this flimsy basis but also you should not judge yourself on it either. It's the wrong measure. He did not dismiss personal piety entirely, but as a measure of goodness, He clearly relegated it:

> *Beware of practicing your righteousness before men to be noticed by them; otherwise you have no reward with your Father who is in heaven.*
>
> *So when you give to the poor, do not sound a trumpet before you, as the hypocrites do in the synagogues and in the streets, so that they may be honored by men. Truly I say to you, they have their reward in full. But when you give to the poor, do not let your left hand know what your right hand is doing, so that your giving will be in secret; and your Father who sees what is done in secret will reward you.*
>
> *When you pray, you are not to be like the hypocrites; for they love to stand and pray in the synagogues and on the street corners so that they may be seen by men. Truly I say to you, they have their reward in full. But you, when you pray, go into your inner room, close your door and pray to your Father who is in secret, and your Father who sees what is done in secret will reward you.*
>
> *And when you are praying, do not use meaningless repetition as the Gentiles do, for they suppose that they will be heard for their many words. So do not be like them; for your Father knows what you need before you ask Him.*[24]

... and ...

Whenever you fast, do not put on a gloomy face as the hypocrites do, for they neglect their appearance so that they will be noticed by men when they are fasting. Truly I say to you, they have their reward in full. [25]

Like Isaiah, Jesus placed the fast in a completely different context from that which persists in being commonly supposed, even today. Instead of a show of personal privation and its traditional trappings of sackcloth and ashes, one's focus should rather be on reaching out to those who are oppressed:

Is it a fast like this which I choose, a day for a man to humble himself? Is it for bowing one's head like a reed and for spreading out sackcloth and ashes as a bed? Will you call this a fast, even an acceptable day to the Lord?

Is this not the fast which I choose, to loosen the bonds of wickedness, to undo the bands of the yoke, and to let the oppressed go free and break every yoke? [26]

Again it is clear: The definition of goodness that emerges from this and the parable of the rich young aristocrat has more to do with following Jesus by practicing the "fruit of the spirit", that is to say,...

...love, joy, peace, patience, kindness, goodness, faithfulness, gentleness, self-control; against such things there is no law. [27]

Practicing the "fruit of the spirit" means caring for others...

For I was hungry, and you gave Me something to eat; I was thirsty, and you gave Me something to drink; I was a stranger, and you invited Me in; naked, and you clothed Me; I was sick, and you visited Me; I was in prison, and you came to Me. [28]

...and it has nothing to do with personal piety or staying within the law. Judgment and goodness are centered upon community, not upon the individual. Thus, the mystery of Godliness, truth, and righteousness matters far more than the comforting certainty of the law and the commandments. Even Moses, the lawgiver who handed the law and the commandments down from God, could not help asking God to reveal some of His mystery. He asked the question we all want to ask:

... let me know Your ways that I may know You, ...[29]

God did not deny Moses' request directly. Instead, He said He would make His ways available to Moses by accompanying him:

My presence shall go with you, and I will give you rest.[30]

Moses then asked the favor we all want of God: "Make me and my kind your favorites":

If Your presence does not go with us, do not lead us up from here. For how then can it be known that I have found favor in Your sight, I and Your people? Is it not by Your going with us, so that we, I and Your people, may be distinguished from all the other people who are upon the face of the earth? [31]

He then asked another common request of small-minded Man: "Show me how powerful you are!":

I pray You, show me Your glory! [32]

God replied:

"I Myself will make all My goodness pass before you, and will proclaim the name of the Lord before you; and I will be gracious to whom I will be gracious, and will show compassion on whom I will show compassion." But He said, "You cannot see My face, for no man can see Me and live!" Then the Lord said, "Behold,

there is a place by Me, and you shall stand there on the rock; and it will come about, while My glory is passing by, that I will put you in the cleft of the rock and cover you with My hand until I have passed by. Then I will take My hand away and you shall see My back, but My face shall not be seen."[33]

There are many interesting things in this response, starting with the anthropomorphism of a God with hands, a face, and a back. There is the metaphor of being cradled in the hands of God for protection. Most interesting of all is that God allowed Moses to see His goodness. It is interesting because Jesus revealed that what we *can* know about God—the mystery that can be revealed—comes from knowing and seeing goodness.

At almost every tragedy and every disaster, some people will put their lives in danger to help strangers. Is this a revelation of goodness? Is this a revelation of God? Can *you* really represent the hands and the heart of God? Is the only way most people can ever get to see God through our acts of love and compassion for one another? It seems that although sometimes God does intervene in the world in a direct and supernatural way, His primary *modus operandi* seems to be to operate and to reveal Himself through us.

To see the mystery that matters most, look around you.

Godliness may seem mysterious and hard enough to understand but nothing challenges faith more than *the mystery and the problem of evil*. The argument goes: "If God exists and is pure Goodness and all-powerful, then why did He allow evil into the world to begin with? And since evil is here, why does He not eradicate it? Either: God is not pure Goodness and/or not all-powerful; or, if neither, then there is no God." Thus, the fact of the existence of evil deters belief in God. It enables the atheist or agnostic to dismiss the very notion of God, and it forces believers to confront the mystery of evil.

Through the ages, many have done just that, and have ended up wrestling with it. The 13th Century Catholic theologian Thomas Aquinas was one. He distinguished between natural and moral evil.[34] *Natural evil* includes things such as hurricanes, which deal death and destruction. *Moral evil* is perpetrated by humans. It comes about through making bad choices—through the volitional, free-willed, *selection* of evil. Aquinas absolved God of any responsibility for this moral evil. God cannot be responsible for the choices of a being that has free will.

To Aquinas, moral evil was not an entity in and of itself; rather, it was the absence of goodness. Thus, the only way to eliminate evil is to leave no room for it, to fill space with goodness. The more goodness, the less evil. He might have drawn the inspiration for this conclusion from the apostle Paul:

Do not be overcome by evil, but overcome evil with good.[35]

Since the beginning of time, mankind has inhabited a world of cause and effect, where if people were good (cause) God would reward them (effect) and if people were bad (cause) God would punish them (effect). Many people still believe in this today. Job showed us that it was wrong, and Jesus declared it wrong also when He absolved the blind man and his parents of responsibility for God's presumed "punishment" of blindness.[36] He said, in essence, that the effect—blindness—was unrelated to the supposed cause—sin.

In God's plan, distinguishing good from evil has always been His prerogative. It was not Adam's, nor was it Eve's, and neither is it ours. The parable of the Wheat and the Tares confirmed it: The laborers were told not to weed the field because they would be unable to distinguish wheat from the weeds; only the divine labor of angels could be trusted to make the distinction unerringly.

In November 2014 the parents of a young aid worker brutally beheaded by the so-called Islamic State publicly forgave their son's murderers and expressed their belief that something good would emerge from all the evil of the Islamic State. Is it possible that without evil, neither the power of goodness nor of forgiveness can be seen? That evil is necessary for the appreciation of good? That without evil, grace is meaningless? Have grace and goodness no anchor but evil?

Perhaps part of the mystery of evil and suffering is the ability, like that of the parents of the beheaded man, to see *some* goodness in them. There is Scriptural support for the notion that evil begets God's grace and that there is more righteousness where there is sinfulness:

The Law came in so that the transgression would increase; but where sin increased, grace abounded all the more,...[37]

The proportion is logarithmic: A little bit of sin evokes a lot of God's grace. Might the concept that "all things will work out for good in God's time"[38] be an answer to the mystery of evil?

Whatever the answer to these questions, there can be absolutely no doubt that when it comes to the mystery of evil, mystery matters, very much. It matters in part because of the pain it causes. Evil seems to be manifested in pain and suffering; even more so, perhaps, than in death. And not just physical pain but also emotional, psychological, economic, and conceivably spiritual pain.

Doctors deal with pain every day. Diagnosis is based to a large extent on defining a patient's pain—determining its location, type, severity, and onset. When blood flow to an organ or limb is impeded, certain patterns of pain can help surgeons to determine what might be wrong.

No normal person seeks or likes pain. Yet in serving as a warning system, pain actually does you good. In that case, is the link between pain and evil a valid link? The story of the garden of Eden seems strongly to imply that God intended His creatures to live free from pain. Such a condition is specifically stated to obtain after the restoration of paradise:

> *...and He will wipe away every tear from their eyes; and there will no longer be any death; there will no longer be any mourning, or crying, or pain; the first things have passed away.*[39]

Apparently the elimination of evil is accompanied by the elimination of pain, darkness, death, and sorrow. According to this passage, pain seems to be a common ingredient of evil and is something that requires healing. So does the absence of pain imply the absence of evil? Is pain good or bad?

Leprosy was a common disease in Biblical times, and tragically is not uncommon today in India. When mentioned in Scripture it is associated with evil: Lepers were banned from camp, and if they came near the community they were required to shout "Unclean!" to warn people to stay clear of them. And yet, a leper colony is a world without physical pain. Lepers literally feel no pain in their diseased flesh and limbs, but the consequences are horrifying. Neurosurgeon Paul Brand's work among lepers convinced him that pain is one of God's greatest gifts, because it alerts us when something goes wrong and needs our attention.[40]

So in healing lepers, Jesus was taking people who were free from pain and making them capable of feeling pain! Can responsibility for pain then be placed in God's hands? It is one thing if God *administered* a potion of pain to cure an evil, fallen world, but it is another thing altogether if He was the apothecary who *crafted* the potion. Look at the pain He caused the Egyptians before the Exodus: He turned all the water to blood so the fish died, the rivers stank, and there was no drinkable water; He caused plagues of frogs, gnats and lice, flies, and locusts; He killed all their livestock; He caused boils to break out on them; He killed their slaves and animals and destroyed all the vegetation in a hailstorm; He switched off the sun for three days; and He killed the firstborn of the people and cattle.[41] No wonder Pharaoh finally let the Israelites go!

It is apparent from this that God uses pain for rebuke. Paul agreed there is a purpose in God's administration of pain and sorrow:

What shall we say then? There is no injustice with God, is there? May it never be! For He says to Moses, "I will have mercy on whom I have mercy, and I will have compassion on whom I have compassion." So then it does not depend on the man who wills or the man who runs, but on God who has mercy. For the Scripture says to Pharaoh, "For this very purpose I raised you up, to demonstrate My power in you, and that My name might be proclaimed throughout the whole earth." So then He has mercy on whom He desires, and He hardens whom He desires.

You will say to me then, "Why does He still find fault? For who resists His will?" On the contrary, who are you, O man, who answers back to God? The thing molded will not say to the molder, "Why did you make me like this," will it? Or does not the potter have a right over the clay, to make from the same lump one vessel for honorable use and another for common use? What if God, although willing to demonstrate His wrath and to make His power known, endured with much patience vessels of wrath prepared for destruction? And He did so to make known the riches of His glory upon vessels of mercy, which He prepared beforehand for glory, even us, whom He also called, not from among Jews only, but also from among Gentiles.[42]

If time heals all wounds, then pain is time-limited. Even if it becomes chronic, people adapt, to some extent. Goodness, on the other hand, seems to be unlimited. Evil and pain are time bound, but goodness is eternal.

Pain is also a consequence of acting up our free will. It may not be God's direct action as much as it is in the nature of the universe that it is not possible to have free will and be free of pain. Which raises the question: Was it God's idea that we have free will? In the garden of Eden, everything seemed to be in good shape and there was no pain and suffering as long as Wo/Man's and God's wills were in harmony. But as soon as free will—choice—was acted upon, pain ensued.

The third mystery, which had been "hidden since the foundation of the world" until Jesus came to reveal it, was that God is the God of all mankind:

...Gentiles [non-Jews] *are fellow heirs and fellow members of the body, and fellow partakers of the promise in Christ Jesus through the gospel,...*[43]

Jesus and Paul were not the first to talk about this mystery. It had been mentioned several times in the Old Testament. God told Jeremiah that He was "the God of all flesh."[44] It is evident too in the Book of Malachi: "Do we not all have one father? Has not one God created us?"[45] That truth seems, however, to have been deliberately hidden by those who wished to keep God and His grace to themselves.

The mystery revealed was emphasized by Paul when he wrote to Timothy:

...the living God...is the Savior of all men, especially of believers.[46]

While on a missionary journey to spread Christianity, Paul developed the concept in some depth, in a sermon given to a non-Christian Greek audience on Mars Hill in Athens. Reminding them that they already had an altar devoted to "an unknown God," he proceeded to reveal the mystery:

Men of Athens, I observe that you are very religious in all respects. For while I was passing through and examining the objects of your worship, I also found an altar with this inscription, "TO AN UNKNOWN GOD." Therefore what you worship in ignorance, this I proclaim to you. The God who made the world and all things in it, since He is Lord of heaven and earth, does not dwell in temples made with hands; nor is He served by human hands, as though He needed anything, since He Himself gives to all people life and breath and all things; and He made from one man every nation of mankind to live on all the face of the earth, having determined their appointed times and the boundaries of their habitation, that they would seek God, if perhaps they might grope for Him and find Him, though He is not far from each one of us; for in Him we live and move and exist, as even some of your own poets have said, 'For we also are His children.' Being then the children of God, we ought not to think that the Divine Nature is like gold or silver or stone, an image formed by the art and thought of man. Therefore having overlooked the times of ignorance, God is now declaring to men that all people everywhere should repent, because He has fixed a day in which He will judge the world in righteousness through a Man whom He has appointed, having furnished proof to all men by raising Him from the dead.[47]

On the other hand, the Old Testament also has many seemingly contrary references to a special covenant between God and the Israelites.

The concept of a "chosen people" of God grew out of passages such as the following, in which God told Moses to tell the Israelites:

> "'You yourselves have seen what I did to the Egyptians, and how I bore you on eagles' wings, and brought you to Myself. Now then, if you will indeed obey My voice and keep My covenant, then you shall be My own possession among all the peoples, for all the earth is Mine; and you shall be to Me a kingdom of priests and a holy nation.' These are the words that you shall speak to the sons of Israel."[48]

But this passage simply allows for a chosen group of priests to serve as ministers and missionaries to all mankind. It does not in any way refute the New Testament statements that God is the God of all mankind.

The concept of possessing God is by no means unique to Judaism. All western churches think He is theirs. All creeds, statements of belief, and evangelism lay claim to exclusive knowledge of the real God. This tends, directly and indirectly, to prevent them from embracing others who also have faith in the one God of all mankind.

I once chatted with a Mormon concerned for the welfare of my soul because I did not embrace the Mormon concept of God. Being an Adventist myself, of course I thought *he* was the one at risk! I've had similar exchanges with Catholic friends, who lamented with genuine anguish that since I was not a member of the Universal Church I had no hope of redemption.

The belief in exclusive knowledge of God has serious real-world consequences, which began well before the medieval horrors of the Crusades and will probably not end with the present horrors of the Islamic State.

Why has the revelation that God is the God of all mankind not dispelled these notions of exclusivity? The reason is that it is a shocking revelation. It was shocking to the Jews at the time of Jesus, and is still shocking to Jews, Catholics, Protestants, Mormons, Shias, Sunnis, and so on today. The tragic but typical reaction to the shock of this revelation is violence and injustice perpetrated in the name of the "one true" (and usually "just and merciful") God. Wrestling with the mystery of the God of all mankind is acceptable, but denial of it has serious and tragic consequences.

Jesus broke down the separateness of our social and religious groupings and tried to make vivid the idea that He is the God of all mankind. It is a notion that might seem intuitive and self-evident, rather than mysterious. If so, and since most major religions and their sects claim that there is only one God, why is there so much strife among them?

We have noted that humans have a natural and pervasive tendency to separate into pseudo communities of like-minded or kindred individuals. We call them affiliations, alliances, and associations; clans, cliques, and clubs; factions, families, and fraternities. We have so many names to denote the simple concept of separateness and isolation.

No matter what they are called, all groups express self-identity. Identity is rooted in a way of life—in how we live, how we eat, how we dress, how we build and decorate our houses. It is embedded in our individual habits, rituals, language, and especially in the way we express things of the spirit. These become communal, ingrained in the group, and comprise its identity. We then develop the viewpoint that *our* attributes and *our* perspective and *our* identity are so unique and special that they belong only to us and cannot be shared by those who do not identify with us.

Paul talked passionately about breaking down this barrier:

...remember that formerly you who are Gentiles by birth and called "uncircumcised" by those who call themselves "the circumcision" (which is done in the body by human hands)—remember that at that time you were separate from Christ, excluded from citizenship in Israel and foreigners to the covenants of the promise, without hope and without God in the world.

But now in Christ Jesus you who once were far away have been brought near by the blood of Christ.

For he himself is our peace, who has made the two groups one and has destroyed the barrier, the dividing wall of hostility, by setting aside in his flesh the law with its commands and regulations. His purpose was to create in himself one new humanity out of the two, thus making peace, and in one body to reconcile both of them to God through the cross, by which he put to death their hostility.[49]

Surely it was good that Jesus broke down the walls that had so long divided groups, and unified them. His sacrifice made them—and *all* of us—sisters and brothers. But how come most of us still feel more secure and comfortable behind the shield of our own group, sect, tribe, class, etc.; excluding from it those not like us?

The story of the Tower of Babel might have some bearing on this question. Most remarkably, given that Jesus was all about removing barriers between people, it shows God *erecting* barriers to divide a unified people! The story is set in the time shortly after the Flood had receded and Noah's descendants had started to repopulate the earth:

Now the whole earth used the same language and the same words. It came about as they journeyed east, that they [the survivors of the Flood] *found a plain in the land of Shinar and settled there. They said to one another, "Come, let us make bricks and burn them thoroughly." And they used brick for stone, and they used tar for mortar.*[50]

The first thing to note is that technology was used in the search for God—the making of bricks and the use of tar as mortar. They would use this technology to...

...build for ourselves a city, and a tower whose top will reach into heaven, ..."[51]

The building of a tower to reach heaven is a metaphor for seeking God. It is a picture of man's attempt to reach heaven, using technology.

God could hardly have failed to notice, so He...

... came down to see the city and the tower which the sons of men had built.[52]

The Babelonians thought they had succeeded in reaching up into heaven, but the fact that God had to come down to see the tower meant that they were, in fact, not there at all. Nevertheless, when He saw it, God concluded:

Behold, they are one people, and they all have the same language. And this is what they began to do, and now nothing which they purpose to do will be impossible for them.[53]

The statement that nothing was impossible for them is reminiscent of God's statement in the garden of Eden that we would become like Gods as a result of eating the forbidden fruit. To thwart the Babelonians' Godlike ambition, God decided to...

...go down and there confuse their language, so that they will not understand one another's speech.

So the Lord scattered them abroad from there over the face of the whole earth; and they stopped building the city. Therefore its name was called Babel, because there the Lord confused the language of the whole earth; and from there the Lord scattered them abroad over the face of the whole earth. [54]

To stop them from becoming immortal and omnipotent, God divided them up by destroying their social and linguistic unity.

The undercurrent of the story is that the mystery of God and His power is impenetrable, even with technology's help. He is inscrutable. He will remain a mystery forever, therefore it must be the mystery that matters above all.

It seems God does not want people to have a unified view of Him. Why might that be? Is it better to have multiple differing views about God, including erroneous views, than to have a single, wrong, universal view? The Babelonian diaspora, which (in Biblical metaphor) brought about the development of nations and languages, was bound to lead to multiple views of God and therefore to multiple religions, diverse and often contradictory in concept, practice, and beliefs.

Theistic religions emphasize that God must be taken on faith rather than evidence. They include Christianity, Islam, Judaism, and perhaps parts of Hinduism. To Buddhists, on the other hand, God does not exist as a personal being. They believe we ascend to an other-worldly place of peace and Zen —to their version of heaven, called Nirvana—through a series of transformations that do not involve the intervention of the divine.

Despite their differences, all religions address the same existential issues of creation, revelation, and salvation. In other words, they all ask: Where did we come from, what are we doing here, and where are we going? To Christianity, Islam, and Judaism the answers are linear in time: History starts with a Creation, passes through an End Time, and ends with a New Beginning. One God oversees this historical process. But to eastern religions (primarily Buddhism and Hinduism but also many smaller ones) the process is spatial, ascending through a circular or spiral path, and there is either no God overseeing it or there is a pantheon of specialist gods.

Given such contradictions among the world's religions, logically we must conclude either that not all of them are true, or all are false, or parts of all or parts of some of them are true. The most direct contradiction relates to the very concept of God: To Christians and (in a different sense[55]) to Hindus, God is a trinity. To Moslems, He is a singularity ("There is no god but God" is the fundamental statement of faith for Muslims). To Buddhists, there is no God.

Why would the God of all mankind want to be represented in this mysteriously contradictory manner? Has He misrepresented Himself, or have we misrepresented Him? Would it not be in God's interest to use a single, easily discernible, unambiguous, timeless, demonstrably true, and completely forthright revelation of Himself, rather than the confusing and contradictory variety of revelations claimed by diverse religions? Above all, how can we reconcile the religious diversity that God the Father apparently wants with the spiritual unity that God the Son clearly wants? Which (if either) matters most?

Of the three existential issues of Creation (Where did we come from?), Revelation (Where are we?), and Salvation or Re-creation (Where are we going?) only one—Revelation—takes place before our very mortal eyes, and can therefore be examined and known directly (as, for example, knowing the state and progress of the universe). But the moment of Creation was before our time, and Salvation and Re-creation will be after our time, therefore what we can know about them can only be known through faith.

It is true that secular science has enabled us to see quite far back into the past history of the universe; to about 380,000 years after that moment (assuming—probably rashly—that the Big Bang was the moment of Creation),[56] and science may yet take us even closer to the beginning. But it seems that *in principle* science will not be able to reach the moment itself, because during that first 380,000 years or so after the Big Bang the universe was an opaque soup so dense that not even photons—the almost massless particles of light—would have been able to move through it. In any case, it took somewhere between three seconds and three minutes after the Big Bang before photons were even formed.[57] Without them —without light to see Him with—is it possible to know God? Could we know Him through reason and intelligence alone? Or is God knowable by some other method'?

Paul addressed this question:

[M]y message and my preaching were not in persuasive words of wisdom, but in demonstration of the Spirit and of power, so that your faith would not rest on the wisdom of men, but on the power of God.

Yet we do speak wisdom among those who are mature; a wisdom, however, not of this age nor of the rulers of this age, who are passing away; but we speak God's wisdom in a mystery, the hidden wisdom which God predestined before the ages to our glory; the wisdom which none of the rulers of this age has understood; for if they had understood it they would not have crucified the Lord of glory; but just as it is written,

"Things which eye has not seen and ear has not heard,
And which have not entered the heart of man,
All that God has prepared for those who love Him."

For to us God revealed them through the Spirit; for the Spirit searches all things, even the depths of God. For who among men knows the thoughts of a man except the spirit of the man which is in him? Even so the thoughts of God no one knows except the Spirit of God. Now we have received, not the spirit of the world, but the Spirit who is from God, so that we may know the things freely given to us by God,...[58]

The history of mankind, especially its spiritual history, is filled with a myriad ways in which God has revealed part of Himself. He has appeared as a burning bush that talks, as a talking donkey, as pillars of fire, as earthquakes, as storms, as ravens that brought food to a prophet, as a giant fish that swallowed a prophet, as whirlwinds, thunder and lightning, and so on. But there is one revelation markedly different from these, when He appeared as a still, small voice:

Then he came there to a cave and lodged there; and behold, the word of the Lord came to him, and He said to him, "What are you doing here, Elijah?" [As usual when God talks directly to man, the first thing out of His mouth is a question.] *He said, "I have been very zealous for the Lord, the God of hosts; for the sons of Israel have forsaken Your covenant, torn down Your altars and killed Your prophets with the sword. And I alone am left; and they seek my life, to take it away."*

So He said, "Go forth and stand on the mountain before the Lord." And behold, the Lord was passing by! And a great and strong wind was rending the mountains and breaking in pieces the rocks before the Lord; but the Lord was not in the wind. And after the wind an earthquake, but the Lord was not in the earthquake. After the earthquake a fire, but the Lord was not in the fire; and after the fire a sound of a gentle blowing. When Elijah heard it, he wrapped his face in his mantle and went out and stood in the

*entrance of the cave. And behold, a voice came to him and said,
"What are you doing here, Elijah?"*[59]

Think of this revelation from Elijah's point of view. He had
just seen a dramatic demonstration/revelation of God's power
when God came down as fire hot enough to consume a wa-
terlogged altar.[60] No wonder he was confused when—despite
having a dramatic hurricane, earthquake, and fire convenient-
ly to hand—God next showed up as just a still, small voice.
The intention was to show Elijah, and all of us, that God is
not predictable in any way, shape, or form.

We cannot put God in a box. He is, and will forever be, a
mystery. Mystery is the fount of faith and will remain so until
the Revelation.

Notes to Chapter 13

1 https://allpoetry.com/The-Blind-Man-And-The-Elephant

2 See, for example, its entry in Strong's Concordance at http://Biblehub.com/greek/3466.htm.

3 Matthew 11:25-27

4 Romans 16:25-26

5 1 Corinthians 2:7-9

6 1 Corinthians 15:51-52

7 1 Corinthians 13:8-12

8 1 Timothy 3:16

9 Genesis 1:4

10 Genesis 1:10

11 Genesis 1:12

12 Genesis 1:17-18

13 Genesis 1:21

14 Genesis 1:25

15 Genesis 1:31

16 Revelation 21:1-6

17 Acts 10:38

18 Matthew 7:15-20

19 Matthew 19:16

20 Matthew 19:17-22

21 Matthew 5:20

22 Matthew 5:21-2

23 Matthew 5:48

24 Matthew 6:1-8

25 Matthew 6:16

26 Isaiah 58:5-6

27 Galatians 5:22-23

28 Matthew 25:35-36

29 Exodus 33:12-13

30 Exodus 33:14

31 Exodus 33:15-16

32 Exodus 33:18

33 Exodus 33:19-23

34 As explicated in his magnum opus, the *Summa Theologica*,

35 Romans 12:21

[36] John 9:1-3; see p. 163

[37] Romans 5:20

[38] ...to paraphrase Romans 8:28.

[39] Revelation 21:4

[40] Brand, Paul and Paul Yancey (1993). *The Gift of Pain.* Grand Rapids, MI: Zondervan.

[41] The plagues are recorded in Exodus chapters 7 through 11.

[42] Romans 9:14-24

[43] Ephesians 3:6

[44] Jeremiah 32:27

[45] Malachi 2:10

[46] 1 Timothy 4:9-10

[47] Acts 17:22-34

[48] Exodus 19:4-6

[49] Ephesians 2:4-16

[50] Genesis 11:1-3

[51] Genesis 11:4

[52] Genesis 11:5

[53] Genesis 11:6

[54] Genesis 11:7

[55] According to Wikipedia, the Trimūrti ("three forms") is the trinity of supreme divinity in Hinduism, in which the cosmic functions of creation, maintenance, and destruction are personified as a triad of deities, typically Brahma the creator, Vishnu the preserver, and Shiva the destroyer/regenerator, though individual denominations may vary from that particular line-up. When all three deities of the Trimurti incarnate into a single avatar, the avatar is known as Dattatreya.

[56] One theory holds that there is a "multiverse"—an infinite set of universes. Presumably, each would have its own Big Bang.

[57] Source: http://physics.stackexchange.com/questions/67412/what-is-the-theoretical-limit-for-farthest-we-can-see-back-in-time-and-distance

[58] 1 Corinthians 2:2-12

[59] 1 Kings 19:9-13

[60] See 1 Kings 18.

14

Religious-awareness versus Self-awareness

CREATION AND SALVATION are the bookends of history, according to Scripture. We cannot know their reality except through faith, and we cannot have faith without accepting the mystery of God. But there is a small-r revelation that fits between the bookends, in the here-and-now; and whether we admit it or not, we all have wrestled with it. It is a unique experience for each of us, leaving a different fingerprint on each of our souls. It might be called part of the "spiritual DNA" with which the Creator has endowed us.

The DNA that makes up our genome is made up of four components—the nucleotides A,C,G, and T[1]—in an almost, but not quite, identical order in each of us. The minor differences in our individual DNA makeup are further influenced by epigenetic (which means, essentially, environmental) factors.

Using this analogy, our spiritual DNA is eventually transcribed into spiritual proteins that form the basis of our individually unique spiritual traits and behaviors—including our individual relationship with God. Which brings us back again to the issue of multiple religions, each unique to the point of conflicting and contradicting one another.

Religions are like language, insofar as we are (usually) born into them. They color our beliefs, just as our native language or mother tongue tends to color our speech, noticeably when we speak in a foreign language, unless we were raised bilingual from birth. We are raised through our languages and our religions, taught through them, and become socialized through them. It is possible to learn another religion just as it is possible to learn another language, but (with some exceptions) most of us tend to have at least a trace of an accent when speaking a foreign tongue.

Is the same true if we decide to convert to a different religion? Can a convert see the new religion's revelation of God as clearly as a believer born into it? Is the convert's new vision uncolored—unaccented—by the revelation received from the old religion? Is there benefit in receiving the revelations of more than one religion, and if not, why (again) would God not have decreed a unified religion for all time and places? Since God clearly has not done that, surely there is some benefit to God or to humankind, even from our contradictory revelations of Him.

Perhaps the way back to God is not through discovery, revelation, or insight about God. The multiplicity of paths and revelations may be God's way of teaching us that a religion that seeks or claims to penetrate the mind and the mystery of God is misguided at best and wrong at worst. The confusion of language in the Tower of Babel, the obfuscation in God's revelation of Himself to Elijah, and the delineation of so many religions as paths to God are perhaps all part of a deliberate strategy to thwart the revelation of God to humankind in any but perhaps the most perfunctory way through the intellect, the senses, or the embodied soul.

This is a striking and unsettling proposition if it is true, but it inevitably emerges in light of our discussion and must be addressed. Is it possible that religion—the way back to God—is *not* after all to be realized by greater awareness of God? That it is *not* to be realized by a more comprehensive picture or more so-called truth about God, or by even better understanding of God's ways? Is it possible that the essence of true religion is not greater awareness of God but greater awareness of ourselves?

At first glance, this idea seems preposterous, narcissistic, misguided, unholy, even evil. But is it at least possible that the mystery of God as the God of all mankind is revealed both through God's universal love and through self-awareness?

Adam and Eve lived in a God-filled, God-conscious, God-centered garden. Though aware of one another and their surroundings, the focus of their consciousness was God, not themselves. Their self-awareness seemed peripheral to their awareness of God and each other. Adam was aware that Eve was "bone of my bones and flesh of my flesh"[2] but his self-awareness seemed to be subsumed within his awareness of God. Eating of the fruit of the tree of knowledge of good and evil changed all that.

Upon hearing God approaching them in the garden after they had eaten the forbidden fruit they hid in the bushes. When God asked why they hid, they offered their fateful first self-assessment: "Because we were naked."

God's response revealed the weakness of their new, self-aware, position: "Who told you you were naked? Did you eat the fruit of the tree that makes you feel naked?" As the implications of their self-awareness dawned on them, Adam began blaming Eve, then he blamed God for creating Eve, and Eve blamed the serpent.

The knowledge of good and evil imparted by the fruit of the tree exposed the sinful self-love, self-acceptance, self-justification, self-righteousness, self-actualization, self-pity, and all other forms of self-focus, self-centeredness, and selfishness so central to the human condition. The way back to God, then, may be through a better, more accurate, more concrete, more truthful understanding of ourselves and the sinful condition we are in rather than through a better, more accurate, more concrete, more truthful understanding of God.

But a religion based upon self-realization sounds heretical and even blasphemous, and might easily be misunderstood as a religion of self-worship. On the other hand, it might rekindle the dying embers of an almost-extinguished Inner Light. It might reactivate the spiritual genome. And it might re-actualize the reality that we were created in the image of God and that our re-creation will be in that same image. Surely, this is what Jesus meant when He said:

Come to Me, all who are weary and heavy-laden, and I will give you rest. Take My yoke upon you and learn from Me, for I am gentle and humble in heart, and you will find rest for your souls. For My yoke is easy and My burden is light.[3]

This is a call to give up one's own ways, which are ways of hard labor and heavy burdens. Perhaps this is best illustrated in the self-awareness and the turning-back to God that is at the heart of the parable of the Prodigal Son who, after squandering his father's inheritance abroad, came to realize that the self-centered path he had pursued was bankrupt. Recall that...

... when he came to his senses, he said, "How many of my father's hired men have more than enough bread, but I am dying here with hunger! "[4]

Many translators have translated "came to his senses" as "came to himself." Self-awareness is what put the Prodigal on the path home to his father. Though far from home, his father had never lost sight of him.

Paul's sermon on Mars Hill also noted the nearness of God. Paul told his audience...

...that they would seek God, if perhaps they might grope for Him and find Him, though He is not far from each one of us;...[5]

It seems at least possible that our quest for the revelation of God (a quest which we *know* to be full of contradictions and we *know* to be, ultimately, impossible) is really a misguided notion of the way back to God, and that the real way back is through a new, fresh, and humble understanding of ourselves.

Paul and the parable of the Prodigal Son both implied that God is not as far away as he seems. The Greek word for "not far" is also the word for "palpable"—something that can be felt. God is palpably close—so close that one can reach out and touch Him. He is not so far as to be unreachable, untouchable, by anyone. This means that human senses can indeed bring us back into a relationship with God.

Perhaps, from God's standpoint, all of our seeking for Him is misguided. Perhaps all the different and contradictory pictures of Him were deliberately planted by God to show us that they cannot be the way back to him; that the way back to the garden, the way back to the God-centered relationship Adam and Eve had with God before the Fall, is an honest appraisal of ourselves and our state of being absent from and in need of God.

As Isaiah said, we are light-years away from understanding God. But what was lost in the Fall was *not* our closeness to God. To expand upon Paul's remark on Mars Hill:

The God who made the world and all things in it, since He is Lord of heaven and earth, does not dwell in temples made with hands; nor is He served by human hands, as though He needed anything, since He Himself gives to all people life and breath and all things; and He made from one man every nation of mankind to live on all the face of the earth, having determined their appointed times and the boundaries of their habitation, that they would seek God, if perhaps they might grope for Him and find Him, though He is not far from each one of us;...[6]

Blind as we are in our Fallen state, by groping we might still find Him close by, within an arm's length. The thing we really lost in the Fall was our true selves. Like the Prodigal Son, we have to come to our senses—to come to ourselves, to come self-aware—if we are to find our way back to our Father's house.

This is not New Age selfish, feel-good-about-yourself self-awareness. It is just the opposite: It is to be humbly aware of our failings and to care more for others than we care for ourselves. To feel truly good about yourself is to feel God about yourself, wrestling with you as He wrestled with Jacob in his anguish.

Six Biblical passages illustrate the point that the essential element of religion is to become self-aware more than it is to become aware of God. In all six, an encounter with Jesus caused the central character to become self-aware, to come to his or her senses, to realize his or her brokenness, sinfulness, corruptibility, mortality, and need of God's grace.

In the first, Jesus met a Samaritan woman at a well and asked her for a drink of water. She pointed out that as a *woman*, a *married* woman, and a married *Samaritan* woman, no Jewish man had any business asking her for anything, period. Jesus then provoked her self-awareness by revealing His knowledge that she had led a promiscuous life with multiple "husbands." At first, she tried to resist by appealing to religion, to law; but relented when Jesus offered her the gracious gift of spiritual water which, unlike H₂0, would quench her spiritual thirst for eternity. She went and told all the villagers what had happened; especially, that He had made her self-aware:

He told me all the things that I have done.[7]

In a second illustration of self-awareness, Jesus met a long-suffering Jewish woman considered ceremonially unclean because of an unabated menstrual period. No physician had been able to help her. So when Jesus passed by one day, she snuck up behind Him and touched His cloak. He felt her touch, and...

...looked around to see the woman who had done this. But the woman fearing and trembling, aware of what had happened to her, came and fell down before Him and told Him the whole truth.

That was her moment of self-awareness.

And He said to her, "Daughter, your faith has made you well; go in peace and be healed of your affliction." [8]

In a third illustration, the Pharisee Nicodemus visited Jesus secretly in the night, ostensibly to talk about God but in fact to be "born again" which, as Jesus explained it, meant becoming self-aware.[9]

Donald W. Weaver

In a fourth illustration, Zaccheus, a wealthy Jew and the chief tax collector of Jericho, was reviled by his fellow citizens because he collected taxes from them on behalf of the Romans. His life changed when Jesus invited Himself into his home, to the great consternation of the crowd that had gathered to welcome Jesus. The graciousness of Jesus helped Zaccheus to recognize himself—to become self-aware. It stopped him in his tracks, and he promised henceforth to give half of his assets to the poor and to compensate those whom he had defrauded.[10]

In a fifth illustration, an emissary from the queen of Ethiopia met the disciple Philip on the road home from Jerusalem. His moment of self-awareness came when Philip explained a passage of Scripture he (the Ethiopian) had been reading, and used it as an opening to preach Jesus to him, following which the Ethiopian asked Philip to baptize him.[11]

The sixth and most poignant example of self-awareness is that which overcame one of the two criminals crucified alongside Jesus. While one criminal...

...was hurling abuse at Him, saying, "Are You not the Christ? Save Yourself and us!" ... the other answered, and rebuking him said, "Do you not even fear God, since you are under the same sentence of condemnation?"

He continued, in this, his moment of self-awareness:

"And we indeed are suffering justly, for we are receiving what we deserve for our deeds; but this man has done nothing wrong." And he was saying, "Jesus, remember me when You come in Your kingdom!" [12]

Surely, this enlightened criminal was not feeling *good* about himself, but was as close to feeling *God* about himself as any of us, his fellow sinners, are ever likely to get. He did not ask nor anticipate a reward for recognizing his true self; indeed, he assumed he would be forgotten, and asked humbly only to be remembered, not to be saved. But he got something totally beyond his expectation when Jesus said to him:

Truly I say to you, today you shall be with Me in Paradise.

An encounter with Jesus is transformational in making us spiritually self-aware. It transforms our relationship with ourselves. The struggle is with ourselves, not with God. God helps us in our struggle, as He did with Jacob, leading us to such a point of exhaustion that we can no longer summon the strength to deny the truth about ourselves. Ultimately the real struggle is with, and within, ourselves.

Has religion been perverted from the proper pursuit of self-awareness to the forlorn pursuit of an unfathomable God? Ought we not to find *ourselves* first, and then reconcile with God through a more complete understanding of ourselves? If so, the way back to God through a supposedly true and faithful understanding of the God of our various religions is a red herring.

At the time of the story of the Samaritan woman at the well, the cultural and religious divide between Jews and the mixed-race Samaritans was about as wide and contentious as it is between Israelis and Palestinians today. There were then, as now in some religions and sects, taboos about men interacting with women.

The woman Jesus met at the well was collecting water at the hottest part of the day, suggesting that she was not welcome at the well with her fellow villagers when they fetched water in the cool of the morning. In short, she was a social outcast, perhaps because (as the story recounts) she was promiscuous, living with men who were not her husbands. Jesus transgressed racial, religious, gender, and moral bounds just by talking to her. He did so to awaken her self-awareness, to give her a new spiritual understanding.

Today, we are so accustomed to water gushing on demand from faucets that we tend not to appreciate its vital importance in the way that Jesus and the woman would have appreciated it. In that place at that time, water and thirst were literally matters of life and death. It is important therefore to recognize in the story the great strength of the metaphor of water as a spiritual life-giving substance.

Jesus was telling the woman (and through her, He was telling us) that He had something as essential for the human spirit as water is essential for the human body. And what He had was not just a bucket of water to bring temporary relief from physical drought and thirst but rather a bottomless well bringing permanent relief from spiritual drought.

Although we are aware of the state of our bodies, we often fail to be aware of the state of our souls. We know when we are thirsty for water and will go to any lengths to get it, but we may not recognize when our spirit is dying for lack of its metaphorical counterpart. We seem less willing to fight for our souls than for water.

Philosopher David Foster Wallace, who was not particularly religious, made a now quite famous commencement speech at Kenyon College in 2005.[13] The ending of his speech summarizes, I think very effectively, what self-awareness means, and I am therefore going to quote extensively from it:

[I]n the day-to-day trenches of adult life, there is actually no such thing as atheism. There is no such thing as not worshiping. Everybody worships. The only choice we get is what to worship. And the compelling reason for maybe choosing some sort of God or spiritual-type thing to worship—be it JC or Allah, be it YHWH or the

Wiccan Mother Goddess, or the Four Noble Truths, or some inviolable set of ethical principles—is that pretty much anything else you worship will eat you alive. If you worship money and things, if they are where you tap real meaning in life, then you will never have enough, never feel you have enough. It's the truth. Worship your body and beauty and sexual allure and you will always feel ugly. And when time and age start showing, you will die a million deaths before they finally grieve you. On one level, we all know this stuff already. It's been codified as myths, proverbs, clichés, epigrams, parables; the skeleton of every great story. The whole trick is keeping the truth up front in daily consciousness.

In other words: Self-awareness.

Worship power, you will end up feeling weak and afraid, and you will need ever more power over others to numb you to your own fear. Worship your intellect, being seen as smart, you will end up feeling stupid, a fraud, always on the verge of being found out. But the insidious thing about these forms of worship is not that they're evil or sinful, it's that they're unconscious. They are default settings.

They're the kind of worship you just gradually slip into, day after day, getting more and more selective about what you see and how you measure value without ever being fully aware that that's what you're doing.

There it is again.

And the so-called real world will not discourage you from operating on your default settings, because the so-called real world of men and money and power hums merrily along in a pool of fear and anger and frustration and craving and worship of self. Our own present culture has harnessed these forces in ways that have yielded extraordinary wealth and comfort and personal freedom. The freedom all to be lords of our tiny skull-sized kingdoms, alone at the centre of all creation. This kind of freedom has much to recommend it. But of course there are all different kinds of freedom, and the kind that is most precious you will not hear much talk about much in the great outside world of wanting and achieving.... The really important kind of freedom involves attention and awareness and discipline, and being able truly to care about other people and to sacrifice for them over and over in myriad petty, unsexy ways every day.

That is real freedom. That is being educated, and understanding how to think. The alternative is unconsciousness, the default setting, the rat race, the constant gnawing sense of having had, and lost, some infinite thing.

I know that this stuff probably doesn't sound fun and breezy or grandly inspirational the way a commencement speech is supposed to sound. What it is, as far as I can see, is the capital-T Truth, with a whole lot of rhetorical niceties stripped away. You are, of course, free to think of it whatever you wish. But please don't just dismiss it as just some finger-wagging Dr. Laura sermon. None of this stuff is really about morality or religion or dogma or big fancy questions of life after death.

The capital-T Truth is about life BEFORE death.

It is about the real value of a real education, which has almost nothing to do with knowledge, and everything to do with simple awareness; awareness of what is so real and essential, so hidden in plain sight all around us, all the time, that we have to keep reminding ourselves over and over:

"This is water."

"This is water."

It is unimaginably hard to do this, to stay conscious and alive in the adult world day in and day out. Which means yet another grand cliché turns out to be true: your education really IS the job of a lifetime. And it commences: now.

I wish you way more than luck.

If that is "the capital-T Truth about life BEFORE death," one wonders: What about the capital-T Truth about life AFTER it —the life that Jesus promised, through His grace and His sacrifice, awaited the woman at the well, Nicodemus, the tax collector, the criminal on the cross, and all of us?

Notes to Chapter 14

[1] Adenine, cytosine, thymine, and guanine.

[2] Genesis 2:23

[3] Matthew 11:28-30

[4] Luke 15:17

[5] Acts 17:27

[6] Acts 17:24-27

[7] John 4:11-31 and 39

[8] Mark 5:25-34

[9] John 3:1-16

[10] Luke 19:1-10

[11] Acts 8:27-40

[12] Luke 23:33-43

[13] Transcript: http://web.ics.purdue.edu/~drkelly/DFWKenyonAddress2005.pdf

15

United against Death

*Then God said, "Let the earth bring forth living creatures after
their kind: cattle and creeping things and beasts of the earth after
their kind"; and it was so....*[1]

*...Then the Lord God formed man of dust from the ground, and
breathed into his nostrils the breath of life; and man became a
living being.*[2]

BEFORE THE FALL, Wo/Man was at one not just with
God but also with nature and with live, organic beasts. God
reinforced this unity, this oneness of Wo/Man and nature, by
putting Adam to work in nature and run it:

*Then the Lord God took the man and put him into the garden of
Eden to cultivate it and keep it. The Lord God commanded the*

man, saying, "From any tree of the garden you may eat freely; but from the tree of the knowledge of good and evil you shall not eat, for in the day that you eat from it you will surely die."[3]

Adam and Eve, husband and wife, were also one, a unity:

The man said, "This is now bone of my bones, and flesh of my flesh; she shall be called Woman, because she was taken out of Man." For this reason a man shall leave his father and his mother, and be joined to his wife; and they shall become one flesh.[4]

The concept of oneness (of God and Wo/Man, of nature and Wo/Man, and of Woman and Man) is key to understanding what happened in the garden of Eden.

The garden had two significant trees: The tree of life, and the tree of knowledge of good and evil. In contradistinction to the tree of life, the tree of knowledge might seem to be a "tree of death" because...

"...from the tree of the knowledge of good and evil you shall not eat, for in the day that you eat from it you will surely die."[5]

So the tree of life and the tree of knowledge of good and evil might also be called the tree of good and the tree of evil, respectively. And since the ability to discriminate between good and evil, between right and wrong, is really a function of law, we might also think of them as the tree of grace (which bestows life indiscriminately) and the tree of law, which is capable of bestowing death.

With the Fall, oneness died in the garden. First came the loss of oneness with God, and the introduction of fear:

They heard the sound of the Lord God walking in the garden in the cool of the day, and the man and his wife hid themselves from the presence of the Lord God among the trees of the garden.[6]

Then came the loss of oneness with nature, and the introduction of pain:

To the woman He said, "I will greatly multiply Your pain in childbirth, In pain you will bring forth children;..."

And man must now **contend with** *nature in order to bring food out of the ground.*

"... Cursed is the ground because of you; In toil you will eat of it all the days of your life. Both thorns and thistles it shall grow for you; and you will eat the plants of the field; by the sweat of your face You will eat bread, till you return to the ground, because from it you were taken; for you are dust, and to dust you shall return."[7]
[Emphasis added.]

So the statement that by eating of the tree of knowledge they "would surely die" did not only refer to mortal death. It also referred to oneness, which is something that needs to be—and can be—resurrected. In oneness, there is no struggle. Before the Fall, Adam and Eve were innocent, naïve, and in communal harmony with all around them—with God, with themselves, with nature. They were not self-aware. After the Fall, they were afraid, lived in communal disharmony and individual pain, and were very much aware of themselves.

A newborn child has no sense of difference between itself and nature, between itself and its parents. Newborns seem to be at one with nature and with their parents. They are oblivious to being naked, just like Adam and Eve before the Fall:

And the man and his wife were both naked and were not ashamed.[8]

Scientific experiments have shown that up to the age of about 18–20 months children are so un-self-aware that they cannot even distinguish themselves in a mirror. When lipstick is smeared on their noses, they seem oblivious to the disfigurement. But after they reach the age of 18–20 months, they start trying to rub the lipstick off.

The most dramatic sign of self-awareness in a child comes around the age of two years ("the Terrible Twos") when the child starts to say *"No!"* The child realizes its independence, recognizing that it is different and *separate* from the parent who is treating it as though it were an extension of the parent, and the struggle begins. Scripture seems, on the one hand, to call for a reversal to that childlike state of innocence, naïveté, and oneness; back to a place where there is no fear, no shame, and no need for self-defense. We should give up the struggle and accept the blessing. On the other hand, however, Scripture seems to contradict the necessity for self-aware-ness, while relying on exactly the same verse in Nicodemus:

Truly, truly, I say to you, unless one is born again he cannot see the kingdom of God.[9, 10]

All we can be reasonably certain about is that reversal to the newborn state is the key to a mystery that matters to us al-most as much as the mystery of God Himself: The mystery of death. In one of the most powerful and portentous passages in the Bible, the apostle Paul wrote:

Now I say this, brethren, that flesh and blood cannot inherit the kingdom of God; nor does the perishable inherit the imperishable. Behold, I tell you a mystery; we will not all sleep, but we will all be changed, in a moment, in the twinkling of an eye, at the last trumpet; for the trumpet will sound, and the dead will be raised imperishable, and we will be changed. For this perishable must put on the imperishable, and this mortal must put on immortality. But when this perishable will have put on the imperishable, and this mortal will have put on immortality, then will come about the say-ing that is written, "Death is swallowed up in victory. O death, where is your victory? O death, where is your sting?" The sting of death is sin, and the power of sin is the law; but thanks be to God, who gives us the victory through our Lord Jesus Christ.[11]

The reversal of death is rebirth. The death in the garden of Eden was both a physical death and a spiritual death—a temporary stage marking our separation from God, the destruction of oneness with God. Scripture often describes physical death as a "sleep"—a temporary stage marking the end of our separation from God awaiting our return to oneness with Him. Physical death is thus spiritual re-birth. Recall that when the Prodigal Son returned, his father said:

"...for this son of mine was dead and has come to life again; he was lost and has been found." And they began to celebrate.[12]

There was great meaning in the celebration. When the elder brother complained about how lavish it was, his father said there was no choice:

But we had to celebrate and rejoice, for this brother of yours was dead and has begun to live, and was lost and has been found.[13]

"Dead" here means to be separated from the father. "Live" means to be re-united with the father. The parable is about spiritual life and death, not physical life and death.

The return to oneness with God requires a recognition that we are separated and we need His grace. This is a humble and righteous self-awareness, in contrast to the fear- and ego-driven self-awareness associated with ritual confession, and with Adam and Eve as they hid from God after dis-uniting with Him. As awful as our disunity—our spiritual death—was, our resurrection and return to unity with God in His kingdom—*the death of death*—is correspondingly wonderful and triumphant and worthy of celebration:

And I heard a loud voice from the throne, saying, "Behold, the tabernacle of God is among men, and He will dwell among them, and they shall be His people, and God Himself will be among them, and He will wipe away every tear from their eyes; and there will no longer be any death; there will no longer be any mourning, or crying, or pain; the first things have passed away."

*And He who sits on the throne said, "Behold, I am making all things new." And He said, "Write, for these words are faithful and true."*14

Salvation, that second bookend to the history of Humankind, is a return to oneness with God. The concept of reunification with God is shared by all religions, and is the ascent to paradise. Oneness eliminates the fear and the struggle. A consequence of the Fall and our loss of oneness with God was the introduction of pain into the world. Lacking omniscience and omnipotence, and without knowing God's plan from start to finish, our prerogative to distinguish between good and evil —in other words, to judge—is extremely limited, but we have no trouble recognizing pain and its proximate causes.

We can reliably distinguish pain from joy, but it is much harder for us to judge whether a given pain is evil, or a given joy is good. In retrospect, we can see instances of great goodness arising from historical events judged to be evil by the men and women of the time.

That the notion of pain as evil may be quite wrong is illustrated in the story of the raising of Lazarus, a friend of Jesus, from the dead. When Lazarus fell ill, his sisters Mary and Martha sent a note to Jesus, saying:

"Lord, behold, he whom You love is sick." But when Jesus heard this, He said, "This sickness is not to end in death, but for the glory of God, so that the Son of God may be glorified by it."

Jesus evidently did not regard the sickness with the same gravity as Martha and Mary. Yet, He showed unusual concern in delaying His journey.

> *Now Jesus loved Martha and her sister and Lazarus. So when He heard that he was sick, He then stayed two days longer in the place where He was.*

> *Then after this He said to the disciples, "Let us go to Judea again."*

The last time Jesus had been in Judea, the Jews were going to stone him, so the disciples were understandably nervous about going back:

> *The disciples said to Him, "Rabbi, the Jews were just now seeking to stone You, and are You going there again?" Jesus answered, "Are there not twelve hours in the day? If anyone walks in the day, he does not stumble, because he sees the light of this world. But if anyone walks in the night, he stumbles, because the light is not in him." This He said, and after that He said to them, "Our friend Lazarus has fallen asleep; but I go, so that I may awaken him out of sleep." The disciples then said to Him, "Lord, if he has fallen asleep, he will recover."*

The disciples were still not convinced that the delay was necessary or wise.

> *Now Jesus had spoken of his death, but they thought that He was speaking of literal sleep.*

(This is one of the many places where Scripture talks of "death" as meaning "sleep.")

> *So Jesus then said to them plainly, "Lazarus is dead, and I am glad for your sakes that I was not there, so that you may believe; but let us go to him." Therefore Thomas, who is called Didymus,*

said to his fellow disciples, "Let us also go, so that we may die with Him."

This is the man who became known to posterity as Doubting Thomas. Evidently, he already had doubts that Jesus would survive the visit to Lazarus' tomb, but was willing to sacrifice himself alongside Jesus.

So when Jesus came, He found that [Lazarus] had already been in the tomb four days. Now Bethany was near Jerusalem, about two miles off; and many of the Jews had come to Martha and Mary, to console them concerning their brother. Martha therefore, when she heard that Jesus was coming, went to meet Him, but Mary stayed at the house. Martha then said to Jesus, "Lord, if You had been here, my brother would not have died.

Notice that Martha was passing judgment on Jesus. She was blaming Him for the pain of Lazarus' death, and implied that allowing it was evil.

"Even now I know that whatever You ask of God, God will give You." Jesus said to her, "Your brother will rise again." Martha said to Him, "I know that he will rise again in the resurrection on the last day." Jesus said to her, "I am the resurrection and the life; he who believes in Me will live even if he dies, and everyone who lives and believes in Me will never die. Do you believe this?"

Jesus was declaring the reversal of death, the end of our separation from oneness with God. The contrast between Jesus' responses to Martha and Mary is the contrast between the divinity of Jesus and the humanity of Jesus. To Martha, Jesus had just proclaimed His divinity, which she acknowledged:

She said to Him, "Yes, Lord; I have believed that You are the Christ, the Son of God, even He who comes into the world."

But now the story turns to Mary:

When she had said this, she went away and called Mary her sister, saying secretly, "The Teacher is here and is calling for you." And when she heard it, she got up quickly and was coming to Him.

Now Jesus had not yet come into the village, but was still in the place where Martha met Him. Then the Jews who were with her in the house, and consoling her, when they saw that Mary got up quickly and went out, they followed her, supposing that she was going to the tomb to weep there. Therefore, when Mary came where Jesus was, she saw Him, and fell at His feet, saying to Him, "Lord, if You had been here, my brother would not have died."

Notice again the human judgment, the human interpretation of life's events. Something bad has happened, so it must be God's fault. But instead of proclaiming His divinity, as He had with Martha, Jesus now showed His humanity:

When Jesus therefore saw her weeping, and the Jews who came with her also weeping, He was deeply moved in spirit and was troubled, and said, "Where have you laid him?" They said to Him, "Lord, come and see." Jesus wept. So the Jews were saying, "See how He loved him!" But some of them said, "Could not this man, who opened the eyes of the blind man, have kept this man also from dying?"

Again, they blame God—they blame Jesus. But now Jesus proclaims both His divinity and His humanity:

So Jesus, again being deeply moved within, came to the tomb. Now it was a cave, and a stone was lying against it. Jesus said, "Remove the stone." Martha, the sister of the deceased, said to Him, "Lord, by this time there will be a stench, for he has been dead four days." Jesus said to her, "Did I not say to you that if you believe, you will see the glory of God?" So they removed the stone.

Then Jesus raised His eyes, and said, "Father, I thank You that You have heard Me. I knew that You always hear Me; but because of the people standing around I said it, so that they may believe that You sent Me." When He had said these things, He cried out with a loud voice, "Lazarus, come forth." The man who had died came forth, bound hand and foot with wrappings, and his face was wrapped around with a cloth. Jesus said to them, "Unbind him, and let him go."[15]

The "unbinding" of Lazarus from his burial shroud is a metaphor for the release from, and the reversal of, death. Death is no longer a mystery to be afraid of. The release of Lazarus is the rebirth, the new birth about which Jesus spoke. It reverses everything that was lost in the garden. The brokenness is fixed, the disease is healed, the struggle is over.

We are One again.

Notes to Chapter 15

[1] Genesis 1:24

[2] Genesis 2:7

[3] Genesis 2:15-17

[4] Genesis 2:23-24

[5] Genesis 2:17

[6] Genesis 3:8

[7] Genesis 3:16-19

[8] Genesis 2:25

[9] John 3:3

[10] In the nanoscale world governed by quantum mechanics, sub-atomic particles are in two states at once: Both on and off, up and down, left and right, and so on. The contradiction can, at a stretch, be explained if we assume the baby at the instant of birth to be in a quantum state, existing as a potential in which it is both totally self-aware and totally un-self-aware.

[11] 1 Corinthians 15:50-57

[12] Luke 15:24

[13] Luke 15:32

[14] Revelation 21:3-5

[15] John 11:1-44

Conclusions

THE STORY OF JACOB is the story of all of us. Selfish, self-centered, and self-promoting, we not only employ those characteristics in our secular life but also, regrettably, in our spiritual life as well. Little do we comprehend how these evil traits influence our walk with God. It is easy to fall into the trap of self-centered piety, Bible study, prayer life, and interpersonal relationships—even while holding the noblest and most righteous intentions. As we become aware of how fallen we truly are, God encounters us in our darkness, in our fear, in our moments of greatest doubt.

As with Jacob, and as shown in so many stories in the Gospels, God seeks that intimate experience to point out to us our need for self-awareness. The struggle brings it out. The very things we think we need most—a clear, full frontal, light-enhanced view of God—is found in our doubt, our fear, our darkness.

Jacob spent his entire life running away from himself, until eventually in darkness he found not only God—he found himself. In finding *our*selves, we also find God. Jacob sought to know God, even asking God that most personal of questions: "What is your name?" But God never reveals His name. God is not the answer man; He is the questioner. And when God asked Jacob *his* name, a whole new insight overcame Jacob. He saw himself not only for who he really was —a supplanter and deceiver—but more importantly his newly found self-awareness led him to seek God's blessing. This is the value of humble self-awareness: It shines an exposing light on our wretched human condition and sounds the clarion call to wake up and seek the blessing.

What is that blessing if it is not the true and righteous birthright? Jacob had spent his life regretting the stolen blessing, the empty birthright. The new blessing was not a product of Jacob's own hand, it was not the result of his duplicitous efforts. This was a blessing, free and full, from the hand of God Himself. It was neither more nor less than His everlasting mercy and grace. The blessing cannot be obtained though connivance, collusion, or conspiracy. It can only be collected, apprehended, embraced, and reveled in.

The God of Jacob is the God of all people and of all religions. Many of His prophets—Elijah, Jesus, Buddha, Mohammed, even (in a Moslem interpretation of the Hindu god) Lord Krishna, and even (again, in the Moslem interpretation) Jesus—are shared by name, at least among some or all of the Abrahamic religions. They all prophesied a God (or told of a Buddha) of peace and love.

Unfortunately, too many of His followers, over the ages and still today, appear not to believe in that God nor in His prophets. Whether or not people believe in Jesus or acknowledge Him as either a prophet or the son of God, the principles established through His ministry are universal. They are valid and accessible to people of any and every religion.

They include the rightness of communal caring *versus* individual selfishness and personal piety. Caring individuals are important to the community of the kingdom of heaven, therefore God will go to any lengths to save any individual, as we saw with Jacob and other lost sheep.

But the kingdom of heaven is a scary place, unlike any that we know. It is a place where the laws of life as we know them are up-ended. It is a place where the last come first. It is a place where you turn the other cheek, you love your enemies, and you lose your life in order to find it. In it, the dead come to life, gravity no longer binds us to the earth, and the cause and effect on which we mortals so strongly depend is replaced by its nemesis, grace, which bestows upon us the mercy of God and forgiveness we do not deserve.

Grace and forgiveness are the oxygen of the kingdom of heaven. Its most fundamental principle is that the grace we are given must not be hoarded, lest it turn toxic. Jesus established this principle as a bedrock of the kingdom of heaven. To forgive, after all, is nothing but passing on to others the grace that has been freely given to us. Our failure to forgive—our hoarding of that grace—is the Unpardonable Sin,[1] the sin against God the Holy Ghost, who convicts us of our faults, covers us with His grace, and asks us to pass that consideration on to others.

Indeed, the obedience asked for from all kingdom denizens is nothing more nor less than passing on the grace given to us. It is the answer to the question: "If I am saved by grace, what need is there for obedience?" In the parables of the Prodigal Son, the Talents, the Good Samaritan, and many other stories, Jesus emphasized this important point. It is encapsulated in the commands to love God with all our hearts, to accept His grace and to pass it on by loving our neighbor as ourselves.

The difference between the metaphorical sheep and goats of the Bible is the willingness to pass on grace in its broadest, spiritual, sense—the deferential acceptance that we are sinners in need of God's mercy—and also in a material sense in the form of financial and emotional resources.[2] Obedience of the converted soul is rooted not in personal piety, as we have long believed, but in passing on the grace.

Proclaiming our Bible study, prayer, righteousness, and other props of piety exposes us to the danger of self-worship. Jesus pointed us toward the needs of others, and to the resources He has given to us to be cognizant of His love; knowing of course that in the service of others we enter into a deeper and more meaningful relationship with He who is the author and the finisher of our faith. Even if the relationship ends up as a wrestling match.

There is one type of individual God cannot save: The type who refuses to forgive his fellow Wo/Man. Churches and even entire religions may be guilty of this unpardonable sin when they excommunicate, shun, or disfellowship people. As they see it, the unpardonable sin seems to be to doubt their versions of God.

But to doubt is divine. Jesus had doubts in the desert and at the time of His crucifixion, but He showed how to conquer doubt, emptiness, and fear through faith and love; and how to emerge from the crisis stronger in both.

A person who has transitioned through doubt emerges at a higher stage of faith. Many would love to continue to enjoy the fellowship and activities they enjoyed in the community before they transitioned. They have no problem continuing in the comfortable catechism to which they have grown accustomed and fond, and they continue to appreciate the pastor's

Scriptural interpretations—but, now, with the benefit and joy of additional insight and enlightenment.

Churches would rather have their members focus on personal piety, avoid sin by following the Law of the Scriptures, and above all have no doubts about the veracity of the interpretation of Truth they are given. But Jesus would rather we focus more on forgiveness of sin in others than on the avoidance of sin in ourselves. Sin will *always* find God's grace— *except* the unpardonable sin of not forgiving others, of hoarding God's grace and so suffocating the inner light, the Holy Spirit of God set as an eternity within each of us, with an oxygen turned toxic. That light, that spirit, is the door to eternity, to God. If we willfully shut it, His grace will re-open it from the other side; but if we remove it and brick up the opening so others can't get through, oneness with God becomes unattainable.

Far from shunning sinners, doubters, and infidels, churches (and temples and mosques) should welcome them above all. After all, God does. His kingdom is not an exclusive club: It is a community open to everyone, where forgiveness and reconciliation are vital, and disputes are actively and quickly resolved. Blackballing and discrimination are the antithesis of forgiveness. They signify clubbiness and rejection, rather than community and acceptance.

Disillusionment from seemingly unanswered prayer is a cause of doubt and lost or shaken faith. The less we feel our prayers are answered, the less sure are we that God is listening, or is even there. But if we work through our doubts, then, like Job, Jonah, and Jacob, we emerge at a higher level of faith based on a deeper, more enlightened understanding of God. If God loves the opportunity to argue and wrestle with His doubters —as Job, Jonah, and Jacob discovered, to their ultimate great benefit, that He does—then why shouldn't we? Why should we shun them?

It is antithetical to Christ's teaching to (mis)represent God as a divine Santa Claus, dispensing wealth and health at the drop of a prayer and an appropriate sum into the prosperity gospel preacher's pocket. The gospel promises nothing of the sort. It says we *should* pray, and it says that prayer *will* be answered. But it does not say that prayer will be answered in the way *we* want it answered, or that we will even recognize the responses of a God of mystery, a God who is untold and untellable light years beyond us in understanding, who answers our prayers in His own way and in His own time.

In our modern world, doubt is further fueled by the growing encroachment of physics on metaphysics. The metaphysical becomes the merely mechanical. But secular science uncovers new metaphysical mysteries about the origin of the Big Bang, what goes on inside black holes, what are dark matter and dark energy, and why antimatter was produced in blessedly smaller proportion than matter. (If they had been produced in equal amounts, they would have annihilated one another and there would be no universe.) These questions are just as big, existential, fascinating, and ultimately as mysterious as the origin of good and evil, the nature of God, and life after death.

Science and religion both seek Ultimate Truth. To science, truth can emerge only through the collection of data and knowledge, and through observation, experimentation, and other tools of scientific method. To religion, truth is plainly written in the Scriptures. But what is really plain is that neither side can even *in principle* know the ultimate truth they seek, because that truth is spiritual. It is not physical and it is not metaphysical. At best, we can only get an inkling of the truth *by living life*—and here religion perhaps has an edge over science in providing questions rather than answers, which serve to guide us toward Enlightenment.

As a surgeon, I rely on science to diagnose and treat God's greatest Creation: Wo/Man. But we must be careful not to substitute scientific understanding of Nature (which is not that hard to get) with spiritual understanding of the nature of God (which is). Compared to scientific understanding, spiritual understanding is so hard we easily grow frustrated, disillusioned, doubtful, and even despairing. But so desperately did we want to know the ultimate truth, that we gave up Paradise for it.

So what did we get out of our deal with the devil? What have we learned? We may not understand God yet, but we ate of the fruit of the tree of knowledge of good and evil, so surely we understand good and evil? The rich young aristocrat showed us the limits of our understanding. We don't *want* to understand, because (as Jesus showed the rich young aristocrat) good is hard and painful, while evil is easy and, like leprosy, pain-free.

Go ahead, take the easy way out: Feel good about yourself (if necessary, here's a pill that will help you do so). Avoid pain at all costs (more pills), for pain is a product of good that serves to put evil into stark relief. It is the antidote to evil and it is always dispensed along with its *own* antidote: Grace. And who in his or her wrong mind would want *that*?

As finite mortals, we cannot hope to see and understand an eternal, infinite, divinity. The composite picture of God that may be drawn from our multiplicity of religions probably does not even remotely resemble the real thing. We must assume it does not. Since God is too supernaturally bright to be observed from the outside, we must look inwards, towards the inner light that is His spirit. But not for unequivocal answers; rather, to appreciate the glorious mystery of it.

The Bible keeps pointing us in that direction, but we don't seem to get it. When we look inwards with honesty and humility, then we start to understand ourselves, to become self-aware, without worrying about a God we can't begin to fathom directly. Enlightenment through self-awareness was the message of the Prodigal Son, and of the humbler of the two convicts crucified next to Jesus. The convict was saved not through pious efforts to seek salvation, but by acknowledging his unworthiness for salvation.

It is only through humble self-examination and self-awareness that we can find the Way to Enlightenment, know the Truth—the mystery!—about God, and be able to live the Life of Jesus. Before the Fall, when Man was one with God—when the will of Man was aligned with the will of God—awareness (whether of God or self) was not an issue. But oneness was severed during the Fall. It has to be reconnected, and it can only be achieved through humble self-awareness and acceptance of God's grace.

I wish churches and religions would do more to help us reconnect with God. I believe they can do so by helping us see Scripture as often asking questions, rather than providing simple answers. They can help us see the value of doubt as a means to spiritual progress, not regress. They can help us become spiritually self-aware.

As well: It seems to me, with respect, that it would behoove all churches and religions to examine themselves, to combat clubbiness and alienation, and to establish support structures, programs, and opportunities not only for lost sheep and people "not of this fold" but also for people seeking to transition to higher levels of faith.

This book has tried to provide a Scriptural foundation and argument for the need for personal and communal spiritual renaissance. The beginning of that renaissance comes with the realization that God loves you. It is enhanced by the acceptance of God's grace and by your willingness to pass on that grace to others.

If you have to ask what that means, then your wrestling match with God has begun, and at the dawn, the blessing will be yours.

Notes to Conclusions

[1] Matthew 6:14-15 — "For if you forgive others for their transgressions, your heavenly Father will also forgive you. But if you do not forgive others, then your Father will not forgive your transgressions."

[2] 1 Corinthians 12, Romans 12.

Made in the USA
Lexington, KY
29 November 2019